BREAKING THE ICE

BREAKING THE ICE

The Black Experience in Professional Hockey

Cecil Harris

INSOMNIAC PRESS

Copyright © 2003 by Cecil Harris

All rights reserved. No part of this publication may be reproduced, stored in a retrieval system or transmitted, in any form or by any means, without the prior written permission of the publisher or, in case of photocopying or other reprographic copying, a license from Access Copyright, 1 Yonge Street, Suite 1900, Toronto, Ontario, Canada, M5E 1E5.

All interior photographs courtesy of the Hockey Hall of Fame except for page 200, courtesy of the University of Toronto.

National Library of Canada Cataloguing in Publication Data

Harris, Cecil, 1960-
Breaking the ice: the Black experience in professional hockey / Cecil Harris.

Includes bibliographical references and index.
ISBN 1-894663-58-6

1. Hockey players, Black--Canada--Biography. 2. Hockey players--Canada--Biography. 3. National Hockey League--Biography. I. Title.

GV848.5.A1H37 2003   796.962'092'396071   C2003-904442-4

The publisher gratefully acknowledges the support of the Canada Council, the Ontario Arts Council and the Department of Canadian Heritage through the Book Publishing Industry Development Program. We acknowledge the support of the Government of Ontario through the Ontario Media Development Corporation's Ontario Book Initiative.

Printed and bound in Canada

Insomniac Press
192 Spadina Avenue, Suite 403
Toronto, Ontario, Canada, M5T 2C2
www.insomniacpress.com

For Etheline and Othniel, Andrew and Christopher.

Table of Contents

Foreword by Anson Carter 9
Introduction 13
The Big Tree 17
A Pioneer in Search of Fame 35
Wrong Place, Wrong Time 59
Unstoppable 75
A Brand New Game 91
Somebody Always Wanted Me 111
Masked Men 129
The N-Bomb 147
The Jackie Robinson of Amherst 159
Hired Hands 173
Tiger Hunting 185
Tomorrow's Game 201
Afterword by Grant Fuhr 205
Source Notes 208
Index 218

Anson Carter, shown here in an Edmonton Oilers uniform, has been a potent scorer in the National Hockey League since his debut in 1996. Edmonton traded the speedy forward to the New York Rangers in March 2003.
Dave Sandford/Hockey Hall of Fame

Foreword

When people realize that I'm entering my eighth National Hockey League season, the first question I'm usually asked is, "Where are you from?" After learning that I'm from Canada, some ask, "Why is a brotha' playing hockey?" The next question usually is, "How does it feel to be a black hockey player?" The honest answer to that is I don't know what it feels like to be a white hockey player so let's move on to the next question!

I live and train in Southern California in the off-season. I spend my mornings at the gym with my personal trainer, T.R. Goodman. Afternoons are spent working on my company, www.bigupentertainment.com, developing movies and hip-hop acts.

My parents emigrated from Barbados to Toronto in 1967. Strangely enough, that was the last time the Toronto Maple Leafs won the Stanley Cup. My Mom and Dad celebrated that victory with the rest of Toronto without really knowing what they were celebrating. I grew up in Scarborough, a suburb of Toronto. All of my friends played hockey and it didn't matter what colour or sex they were.

I was eight when I started playing hockey. I could stickhandle and I knew the game. But I couldn't skate. It became apparent that skating was an integral part of the game and if you weren't good at it, it could set back your development.

I quickly progressed through junior-league hockey but not without the odd racial slur from kids on other teams. Even more disappointing were the slurs from other parents and adults. That's where my parents really helped because they educated me earlier on that I'd face those situations in the world and the best way to handle them was to ignore them, and be proud of who I am and what I look like. I'm proud to say I still adhere to that.

It wasn't until I was 17 that I really started to think about playing in the NHL. The Quebec Nordiques selected me in the 10th round before I went to Michigan State, but I wasn't happy that I was chosen so late. I used that to motivate me to get to the NHL.

After four great years at MSU, I turned pro and played for the Washington Capitals for half a season before being included in a "blockbuster" deal with the Boston Bruins. I loved Boston and made a lot of friends there that I still cherish. Unfortunately, the business side of hockey reared its ugly head and I was traded to the Edmonton Oilers.

Playing in western Canada was a wonderful experience and, just like in Boston, many friendships were forged. When I was traded to the New York Rangers in March 2003, I was blown away. I always wanted to experience playing at Madison Square Garden. When I heard about the trade, I was excited by the prospect of plying my trade in the home of the Yankees, Times Square and the late rapper, The Notorious B.I.G.

After the Rangers missed the playoffs, I was asked to play for Team Canada in the World Championships in Finland. I was honoured by the invitation. To top it off, we brought back the gold medal. I scored the game-winner in overtime and was named the Most Valuable Player—all on Mother's Day! It was a feeling that I can't even begin to explain. After the game, I did interviews with the international media.

The beautiful thing about those interviews was there was no reference made or question asked about me being a black hockey player. Hopefully, my performance along with Jarome Iginla's two goals for Team Canada in the 2002 Olympic gold-medal game showed the world that black hockey players have arrived and we're here to stay.

Anson Carter
September 2003

The St. Catharines Orioles, an all-black team, competed in the Niagara District Hockey League in the early twentieth century (the exact year is unknown). The entire twelve-man team is shown here along with team officials and Sylvia Moore, the Orioles' mascot.
Hockey Hall of Fame

Introduction

Sports were discussed and debated constantly in the Bedford-Stuyvesant section of Brooklyn, New York, where I grew up. Just try to argue that Walt "Clyde" Frazier was a better basketball guard than Earl "The Pearl" Monroe, or that "Smokin'" Joe Frazier was a superior boxer to Muhammad Ali, or that Reggie Jackson was a more fearsome slugger than Hank Aaron, and emotions would run high for hours, if not days.

Although I weighed in on every argument, one sport that I learned to love was never discussed: hockey. In my predominantly black neighbourhood, nobody played hockey, nobody watched hockey and nobody who looked like us played hockey—or so we thought. I became a hockey fan during the 1970–71 National Hockey League season, because in those days my ten-year-old eyes watched every sport possible. In an era before twenty-four-hour sports cable networks, New York Rangers games were shown on Channel 9 every Saturday night, and I got hooked. I loved hockey's rapid pace, fierce hitting, accent on teamwork and, yes, the fighting. I also liked the way Guy Lafleur's blond hair flowed on his end-to-end dashes that often resulted in a Montreal Canadiens goal against my Rangers. I enjoyed the challenge of trying to follow the puck on my twelve-inch, black-and-white television set. I appreciated the symmetry of the constant personnel changes that make hockey resemble a crazy ballet on ice.

But my devotion to hockey was a singular pleasure. There was nowhere for me to learn to play, nowhere to skate, no one to accompany me to a game, no one with whom I could talk hockey. I remember being so enthusiastic about hockey on the morning I stayed up past 1 a.m. to listen to Marv Albert's play-by-play on WNBC Radio of the Rangers' 3–2 playoff win over the Chicago Blackhawks on Pete Stemkowski's goal in triple overtime. It happened at Madison Square Garden; blank stares from schoolmates suggested I was describing something that had happened on Pluto.

It seemed I always had to justify my affinity for hockey. Friends and family couldn't understand it, and when I became a sports journalist it was not until I left New York for a job in Raleigh, North Carolina that I had a chance to cover hockey. "Why would you want to do that?" "What if the players don't want to talk to you?" "What if you're the only black guy at the game?"

Because I kept hearing those questions, and because I occasionally was mistaken for a messenger while trying to enter an NHL arena even though I was a journalist with a press credential dangling from my neck, and because I once had a beer-carrying Rangers fan in a Brian Leetch jersey say to me the night I covered my first game back home at Madison Square Garden, "What the fuck you doin' here? The Knicks ain't playin'," I began to wonder how black hockey players felt in the same environment. I've interviewed many of them, as well as family members, teammates, opponents, coaches, general managers, journalists and numerous others who make their living in hockey.

Each black player, I found, has had to wage a personal battle for acceptance and respect. Some eventually receive it while others never do. But to every black man determined to make a way in professional hockey, self-respect has always mattered more. Facing abuse that is verbal, physical or psychological because of their colour has been an unfortunate reality for almost all of them. How black players dealt with that reality, and continue to deal with it, is what makes each one unique. But what unites them is a sheer love of the game and a desire to make the ice smoother for those who follow in their skate marks.

The term "black hockey player" may seem like an oxymoron, but since the dawn of the twentieth century black players have overcome economic, geographical, racial and cultural barriers to have a significant impact on the sport. How significant? Jarome Iginla, son of an African-born attorney, skating on ice smoothed by his progenitors, was named the NHL's Most Valuable Player in the 2001–02 season.

Breaking The Ice is the first book to tell the stories of Iginla as well as his black peers and predecessors. It is the first book in which Iginla and other black hockey players talk candidly about themselves and one another.

Of the more than six hundred players on NHL rosters at the end of the 2002–03 season, only fourteen were black. However, that number represented a high watermark for blacks in any season in hockey's premier league, which was formed in 1917. Yet because of the talent and determination of today's black players and their forebears, a career in hockey has become both realistic and lucrative. The NHL's fourteen blacks in 2002–03 played for a combined salary of $19.5 million.

The all-time list of black NHL players numbers thirty-eight and starts with Willie O'Ree, known as "the Jackie Robinson of hockey" for breaking the league's colour barrier in 1958. The list includes Grant Fuhr, a goaltender who in 2003 became the first black inducted into the Hockey Hall of Fame, and Mike Marson, a 1970s "bonus baby" whose career was derailed by racial conflicts on and off the ice. O'Ree, Fuhr and Marson are from Canada, as are nearly all the black men profiled in *Breaking The Ice*— men who overcame adversity, indifference and hostility to make an indelible mark upon hockey. Yet the list also includes Mike Grier, the

NHL's first African-American star, as well as players whose parents emigrated to Canada from the Caribbean or Africa, and players who have been adopted by white families and encouraged to partake in Canada's pastime.

Absent from the list, but certainly not from these pages, is Herb Carnegie, a star in various hockey leagues for three decades who regrettably will be remembered as the best black player *never* to appear in the NHL. His story is chronicled here, as well as the ongoing effort to have him enshrined in the Hockey Hall of Fame.

Thanks to trailblazers such as Carnegie and O'Ree, blacks today are impact players at every position on the ice: goal scorers, goal stoppers, defensemen, rugged cornermen and hard-fisted enforcers. Their accomplishments are all tangible signs that the efforts of hockey's black pioneers have not been in vain. And thanks to the pioneers who broke the ice then made it smooth, a prodigy whose roots extend all the way to Nigeria has been able to take the lead.

Calgary Flames right wing Jarome Iginla moves into scoring position against the Toronto Maple Leafs. In the 2001–02 season, Iginla led the National Hockey League in goals and points and became the first black ever to be named Most Valuable Player.
Dave Sandford/Hockey Hall of Fame

The Big Tree

While Jarome Iginla pulled himself into a custom-made tuxedo on the first night of summer in 2002, he had every reason to hum a triumphant tune. A tune from the kind of full-blown theatrical production favoured by his mother, a singer and aspiring dramatist. A tune like "If They Could See Me Now."

Yeah, Iginla thought, as he slipped into a pair of resplendent black leather shoes in his Toronto hotel suite. What if all the people in western Canada who had doubted me could see me now? What about all those parents back in Edmonton who looked on quizzically when I, the only brown-faced boy, took part in floor hockey games when I was five? How they used to pretend to be nice when asking the question I couldn't stand: "Why do you want to play hockey?" And what about those other boys who shuffled across the floor in sneakered feet just like me? They asked the same question. Or they took the inquisition a step further: "Don't you know that blacks don't play hockey?"

Even then Iginla, a budding hockey player and offspring of a failed interracial marriage, had to justify his actions. Looking back, the questioners actually prepared him well for the hordes of skeptical adults who would see him on the ice and ask, "Why?"

"I play hockey because I like the game," he would say, then and now. There were but a handful of black players in the NHL when Jarome took the ice for the first time at age seven. But it never deterred him. Instead, it inspired him. He knew the names of the few black professionals in the NHL, knew he had had his picture taken beside the great black goaltender Grant Fuhr after an Edmonton Oilers practice in the 1980s, knew he wanted to be just like the hockey stars whose action posters adorned his bedroom wall.

"I saw Grant Fuhr and he was a big idol to me," Iginla says in a soft but clear voice. "And I saw Tony McKegney scoring all those goals in the NHL. Those guys made me aware that there were black hockey players, so I never felt strange or anything. I just wanted to grow up to be like my idols."

If his old teammates could see him now. Surely those Canadian boys, now men in their mid-twenties like himself, could not have missed hearing about his star-making 2001–02 season for the NHL's Calgary Flames. It's likely they had heard about Iginla becoming the seventh player in Flames history and one of less than a hundred players in league history to score fifty goals in a season. And they must have read somewhere, perhaps in *The Hockey News*, that he had lived up to his unusual surname: Iginla [pronounced uh-GHIN-la] means "Big Tree" in the Yoruba language of his father's native Nigeria. Iginla had indeed become a "big tree" in his sport, too tall and strong to overlook. This is why he donned a tuxedo on a summer night two months after his hockey season had ended.

As family and friends looked on, Iginla wrapped a bluish-grey tie around a white shirt collar. Now he was ready to enter an arena previously foreign to him: the show business arena. On the night of June 20, 2002, Iginla would receive the Rocket Richard Trophy for most goals scored in a season and the Art Ross Trophy for most points in a season. Spacious courtesy cars with dark tinted windows were ready to take Iginla, his mother and grandfather—the pair most responsible for introducing a black boy to the overwhelmingly white sport of hockey—his father, his father's current wife and his half-siblings to the John Bassett Theatre at the Metro Toronto Convention Centre for the 2002 NHL Awards ceremony. For Iginla, a robust six-foot-one and 201 pounds, the event was a coming-out party. His season of dominance in Calgary, the smallest of the NHL's thirty media markets, tested the theory of whether a tree falling in a forest with nary an onlooker truly made a sound. But even in Calgary, a place the local media refer to as "Cowtown," Iginla proved a "big tree" that produces fifty-two goals and ninety-six points in one season cannot be ignored.

As the courtesy car carried Iginla to the show, he steeled himself for the two speeches he knew he would have to make. Public oratory doesn't come easy to a hockey player. Rarely is it required. But he had the advantage of being used to thinking on his feet and fielding impertinent questions with a politician's diplomacy. That's one fortunate by-product of being among only fourteen black players (out of more than six hundred players) in the 2001–02 season and being one of thirty-eight black players to ever perform in hockey's premier league.

If they could see him now. Not only would they see the most celebrated black hockey player ever, they would see him taking bows in a shiny black tux, and they would learn a bit more about his remarkable life.

◆ ◆ ◆

Earlier in the day, Iginla received the Lester B. Pearson Award as the players' choice for the league's Most Valuable Player—the first black player so honoured. "Hockey players really *understand* the game," Iginla said, "and it's a huge honour to be voted the MVP by them." The Pearson Award gathering was a low-key lunchtime affair at the Hockey Hall of Fame in downtown Toronto. At the Hall, Iginla could thank his peers and loved ones without worrying about a verbal misstep. The Pearson is the MVP award players respect most, because they vote for it. The Hart Trophy, however, is the far more publicized MVP award, because only hockey writers and broadcasters do the voting. And on this night, the Hart's reputation would drop several notches in the minds of Iginla and many of his peers.

Iginla took to the Bassett Theatre stage three times, to receive the Richard and Ross trophies and to join five other players selected to the league's first team of All-Stars. He was voted the league's premier player at his position: right wing.

His contingent, occupying front-row seats in the mezzanine, turned misty-eyed when he received the Richard, an honour named for Maurice "Rocket" Richard, a Montreal Canadiens icon who was the first player ever to score fifty goals in a season. Richard did it in fifty games in 1944–45, in a watered-down league while many top players were fighting in World War II. An NHL season now consists of eighty-two games. Richard died at age seventy-eight on May 27, 2000, and his funeral became a national day of mourning in Canada. Though Richard retired seventeen years before Iginla was born, the emerging right wing paid homage to the legendary right wing in a speech he had rehearsed assiduously in front of a mirror for days:

"When I was seven years old," he began, "I remember one of the first books I ever read was about a prolific goal scorer and this prolific goal scorer had a favourite stick. The stick used to talk to him and he'd talk to the stick. That struck a key with me right away because when I was younger I had a lot of favourite sticks. Anyway, the player's favourite stick broke and this goal scorer was so worried he wouldn't be able to continue without it. But the stick had just enough life in it to look up at him and say, 'It was never within me, the stick. It was always within you. Believe in yourself.' This story always meant a lot to me and it means even more now because the character in the book was Maurice "Rocket" Richard, and it's a real honour to receive this award in his name."

Beaming and awash in applause, Iginla was having an exquisite evening. There sitting among Iginla's family, pounding his hands to the point of soreness, was Willie O'Ree, the first black man ever to play in an NHL game, having debuted on January 18, 1958 with the Boston Bruins. Not even O'Ree could calculate the number of on-ice racial slurs, cheap shots and off-ice acts of indignity he endured in a three-decades long pro career to smooth the ice for the likes of Iginla.

"I always hoped to see something like this," said O'Ree, the sixty-eight-year-old director of youth development for the NHL/USA Hockey Diversity Task Force. "But it's a great thrill to actually see it happen. Now, black kids can point to Jarome as their role model."

Iginla, a young man with a sense of history and a deeper sense of gratitude, made sure O'Ree shared in an evening that was unforgettable. Unforgettable but not perfect.

◆ ◆ ◆

Perfection would have meant becoming the twelfth player in the previous thirteen years to take home the Pearson *and* Hart awards. But Iginla, who scored 27% of his team's goals in 2001–02, the third-highest percentage by a player since 1929, saw his hopes crash like the stock market because of a technicality and an outrage. Iginla and Montreal goalie Jose Theodore, whose stellar play lifted an unheralded Canadiens team into the playoffs, finished tied in overall Hart points with 434. But instead of having co-winners, the NHL gave Theodore the Hart because of a tie-breaking provision that favours the player with more first-place votes. (Theodore had twenty-six to Iginla's twenty-three.)

Each voter can put up to ten players on his ballot, ranking them from first place to tenth place. But shortly after the results were announced word came that at least one media member had inexplicably left Iginla off his ballot. True, Iginla's team had missed the Stanley Cup playoffs for the sixth straight season and a hardened cynic could ask, "How valuable a player can he be if his team didn't make the playoffs?" But to suggest that the league's leading goal scorer—the only player to reach the magical fifty-goal plateau—and leading point producer was not among the ten top players in the league was outrageous. Even if the as-yet unidentified media member had placed Iginla tenth on his ballot, in recognition of the finest individual season by any NHL player in 2001–02, Iginla would have had enough overall points to win the Hart.

Iginla reacted publicly to the Hart snub like all too many black players who have suffered indignities in hockey: he didn't make waves. "There's nothing I can do to change the voting. It was out of my hands," he said evenly. "At least I was the only guy to go on stage three times. And the players did make me *their* MVP."

Hockey players don't whine, Iginla told himself. And his mature reaction probably won him some new fans. But Iginla's mother had no desire to curry favour with the hockey press and influence fans. She spoke from the heart about the pain she felt, a deep-rooted pain her only child must have shared. Expressiveness has always come easy to Susan Schuchard. A native of Medford, Oregon, she left America with her parents during the Vietnam War for western Canada, ostensibly to secure teaching positions, but also to divorce themselves from a government that had sent too many vital young men off to die. Young Susan was encouraged to speak her mind and pursue her dreams in her new hometown of Edmonton, Alberta. She would vigorously pursue a singing career until becoming pregnant with Jarome curtailed her plans. Still, she has managed an occasional singing gig, including stints performing the Canadian and American national anthems at Jarome's NHL games in Calgary. Show tunes like "Oh, What a Beautiful Morning" from *Oklahoma*, is what she favours. But after the 2002 NHL Awards, she sang the blues.

"We're very humble people, but if you deserve something you should be acknowledged for it," she said. "Even the Edmonton papers here—and Jarome is a homeboy—had on the front page, 'Jose Theodore Cleans Up at NHL Awards.' Jarome won three awards and made first-team All-Star and he won the Pearson Award. Where was that on the front page? Theodore wasn't even voted the first-team All-Star goalie. That was Patrick Roy [of the Colorado Avalanche]. How could the press vote Theodore the MVP of the league and he wasn't even voted the first-team All-Star goalie? I wish somebody would explain that."

Now Schuchard (pronounced SHOO-hard) projected her aria of injustice to the back row of the balcony: "The Calgary papers said there was one sports writer that didn't even have Jarome on his ballot. How could you not have him on the ballot? That was an outrage! Just an outrage! But you see, Jarome as a rookie scored the most points (among rookies), but he didn't win the Calder Trophy."

The Calder is hockey's Rookie of the Year award. Iginla scored fifty points on twenty-one goals and twenty-nine assists in 1996–97. Bryan Berard of the Toronto Maple Leafs scored forty-eight points on eight goals and forty assists—a high total for a defenseman—and was awarded the Calder. Iginla finished second.

"Jarome hardly got any votes for the Calder," Schuchard said. "How could that be? This is just a mother wondering."

A white mother, with short-cropped dyed hair of the same hue, who used to urge her son to be strong enough to parry any verbal blows from those who resented a brown-skinned boy on the ice. A mother who taught her son that by being a good person he would win over enough important people to continue doing what he loved. The hard-headed ones? Well, just pay them no mind.

"The first time I ever heard somebody call Jarome a name it was a kid, and Jarome just shrugged his shoulders and said, 'So?' The kid shut up after that, because he saw that he couldn't hurt Jarome. I sometimes overheard parents saying things about him because they didn't know I was his mother. I'd hear things like, 'You know how those black people are in sports? They're so aggressive. Look at him.' But my response was to say nothing. I've seen so many of Jarome's games, more than anyone. It wasn't anything like what they wrote in that magazine [*ESPN The Magazine*], that Jarome heard racial things almost every time he went on the ice. I don't know where they got that. I witnessed a few occasions where his colour did come up, but nothing ever scarred him. I'd like to think that I and his father had a lot to do with Jarome being so strong mentally."

Jarome had to be strong the time a white boy at a peewee-league game called him "nigger" at a concession stand. He didn't know what the slur meant, but his mother affirmed it had been said to try to hurt him. And he had to be strong after another peewee game in Swift Current, Saskatchewan, when, during the post-game handshake at centre ice, a white boy studied the face of a now-helmetless Iginla and said, "Oh, you're just a nigger." And he had to be strong at age fifteen at a baseball tournament in southern Alberta when a group of local boys chanting, "We want the nigger" chased him from an arcade all the way back to his hotel. The boys then tried to break down the door to his room. His parents taught him not to be scarred by such incidents, and he would not be.

That Iginla's parents could be so different and could have taken such divergent paths to find each other as teenage freshmen at the University of Alberta likely prepared him well for life in a sport where his being different would, for a time, become Topic A.

◆ ◆ ◆

Elvis Iginla is an adventurous type with skin several shades browner than his son's. He had always expected to leave his native Nigeria in search of greater opportunity elsewhere. But not even he thought he would end up in frosty Alberta. As a teen, he followed his cousins to Toronto and tried to decide whether to become a doctor or a lawyer. But after a year, he found Toronto too big and busy. Since Canada's glacial winters didn't bother him he set out on his own, farther west.

"Edmonton offered more opportunities work-wise and school-wise," he says in a voice as soft as his son's but more African-accented. "In Nigeria you never have to wear a sweater. But I was more concerned about making it than surviving the weather. I knew it would be easier to become a lawyer in Edmonton."

Breaking the Ice

He dropped his birth name Arthur and renamed himself Elvis. He insists, however, he was not paying homage to Elvis Presley. He just likes how the name sounds.

When Elvis, the studious black pre-law student from Nigeria, met Susan, the free-spirited white drama major from America, it was infatuation at first sight.

"At the age we were when we had Jarome, I don't think either of us was thinking too deeply about anything," Elvis Iginla said with a laugh. "She was eighteen when she had him. It was July 1, 1977. She was like a child, and I was just a year older. Relationships like that tend to break up early when you get older and you just grow apart."

The marriage lasted a year and a half. Susan took custody of Jarome. Had the parents stayed together, conflict may have arisen over Jarome's participation in sports because Mom was for it and Dad was not.

"When I heard Jarome was playing hockey, I didn't take it seriously," Elvis Iginla said. "I thought he would grow out of it. My goal was for him to go to college and graduate and become a professional man like his father."

"I taught Jarome to roller skate," Schuchard said, "and when I realized he could skate circles around me I got him into a hockey program when he was five. He was voted most improved player after the first year. He was just so gifted. My father [Rick Schuchard] had been a youth hockey coach, and I made sure he would be there for Jarome when I couldn't be there for practices or games. But I seldom missed a game. Jarome started travelling when he was eight, and I went on almost all the trips.

"He was the youngest player in his level of hockey at fifteen, and he won the scoring title. Jarome started playing at the D level, the very beginners. In youth hockey in Canada, there are levels A through D. Every year, Jarome moved up to a higher level. He did so well in his early teens that the league had a meeting. He was allowed at fifteen to play with the sixteen- and seventeen-year-olds."

Every Canadian boy who wants to play hockey can play it in some form, whether it's on a frozen pond or on a street corner with sneakers for skates, a ball for a puck and homemade sticks. But if a boy plays in an indoor rink in an organized league, then hockey can be quite an expensive proposition.

"In Jarome's last year in midget hockey, it cost us $300 a month," Schuchard said. "But I didn't have any fees waived because I didn't want Jarome to feel different. It was important to let him know that he would have the same chance to play hockey as the other boys. He was already feeling different, not only because he was black but because he was being raised by a single mother. I only met one other single mother during the time I took Jarome around to the games. St. Albert, the community we lived in, was very settled. There just weren't many single parents."

Where Schuchard cut corners was on Jarome's road trips. Rather than pay for expensive team bus rides to cities hours away, she or her father drove Jarome to the games. At age ten, when Jarome was invited to play in an all-star tournament in Los Angeles, he and his mom took a days-long train ride from Edmonton rather than break the family budget for plane tickets.

"I remember being disappointed at first that I couldn't fly to L.A. because I had never been on a plane," Jarome said. "But the train trip turned out to be one of my favourite times as a kid. We got to see a lot more of the United States from that train than we ever could have from a plane. Looking back, I have to thank my mom and granddad. They made so many sacrifices just so I could play hockey and baseball."

Baseball, a game his mother taught him, was also a passion for Iginla. Action posters of Bo Jackson and Deion Sanders, who starred professionally in Major League Baseball and the National Football League, shared wall space in Iginla's bedroom with hockey stars Fuhr, McKegney, Wayne Gretzky and Mark Messier. Jarome, a pitcher and an infielder, dreamed of becoming a two-sport star like Bo and Deion. But once Iginla reached his mid-teens, he knew hockey would be the sport that would take him places.

◆ ◆ ◆

At sixteen, Iginla made a decision to which American boyhood sports stars are unaccustomed: the decision to leave home and live with a different family. To cultivate his hockey skills, he left Edmonton and spent two years with a family in the city of the junior-league team that owned his playing rights. In Canada, this is known as the billet system. Every issue of *The Hockey News* carries advertisements from leagues seeking parents that for a fee of several hundred dollars a month will house and feed a boy while he plays junior hockey and attends school in that city.

Imagine a New York City teen spending his junior and senior years of high school with an unfamiliar family in California so he could play basketball for a well-connected coach and improve his chances for a college scholarship or an early invite to the National Basketball Association. And in return, the California high school federation reimburses the family for room, board and meals. Far-fetched? In the U.S., yes. But it's a time-honoured tradition in Canada. Hence, Jarome spent two years with a billet family while playing for the Kamloops Blazers of the Western Hockey League.

"It was great for my development as a player," he said. "There were a few other black kids in that high school, but I was the only one playing hockey. But I was used to that."

"We had to go through the mountains to get to Kamloops," Schuchard said. "I went to his opening game and I went at Christmas time, through a snowstorm, because it was important to be there for him. I'd also go to the final game and all the playoff games. Jarome could complain that I went too much—I mean, I had my own life—but I just enjoyed watching him play so much. I wasn't a major hockey fan. I never saw an NHL game until Jarome played in his first one. I've always been a Jarome fan."

Elvis Iginla, meanwhile, worked his way through school and established a practice as a personal-injury lawyer in Edmonton. He had little time to attend hockey games. That, Susan Schuchard decided, was reason enough to attend more of her son's games than any other parent. If she or her father didn't go, who would? Still, Jarome understood that even if his father was not in the stands on game days, he could always be counted upon for encouragement and counsel.

Jarome grew up a black boy in a white world, without black friends because there were none in the neighbourhood and without one black hockey teammate until he was fifteen (current Washington Capitals defenseman Jason Doig). Nevertheless, Jarome liked his station in life. "When I was growing up, I never felt different," he said. "If I felt anything, I felt special."

♦ ♦ ♦

Ask Iginla when it all changed, when he became a player who inspired more questions about his status as an accomplished goal scorer (and role model) rather than his racial background, and he'll say September 2001.

As the world was being rocked by the cataclysmic terrorist attacks in New York City and at the Pentagon near Washington, D.C., more than two dozen supremely gifted hockey players convened in Calgary, to forge the team that would represent Canada in the 2002 Olympic Games. Iginla, as wide-eyed as a kid on a motion picture set, was among the players but not yet among the stars. His place on Team Canada was far from assured.

Indeed, Iginla's presence at the Olympic practices owed more to serendipity and common courtesy than to his solid hockey credentials. Practices were held at Calgary's Saddledome Arena, home rink of the Calgary Flames, a downtrodden team that has not qualified for the Stanley Cup playoffs since 1996. That Calgary is Iginla's pro team is what got his skate in the door. Wayne Gretzky, hockey icon and executive director of Team Canada, believed the best player from the host city should be invited to practice with the other Olympic hopefuls. All that kept Iginla from being considered a token invitee was an injury to Simon Gagne, the Philadelphia Flyers forward, which opened up a roster spot.

Iginla had already decided to give it his all at the practice sessions whether he made Team Canada or not. He believed Gretzky, a boyhood idol, deserved nothing less. He also believed the opportunity to match his burgeoning skills against those of Canada's established stars—Mario Lemieux, Steve Yzerman, Brendan Shanahan, Paul Kariya and Joe Sakic—would at least fine-tune his game for the 2001–02 NHL season. Never did Iginla have the chance to skate alongside such a constellation of stars in his first six seasons with Calgary.

◆ ◆ ◆

In those spirited practices with Canada's elite, Iginla learned something that pocked his arms with goosebumps: he belonged. "I kind of thought I could skate with those guys and compete with them on this kind of level, but you don't really know if you can until you do it," Iginla said. He spoke about his Team Canada experience with typical affableness, but at an unusual venue for him: the midtown Manhattan offices of the NHL. The forty-seventh floor conference room afforded Iginla a picturesque view of the famed Radio City Music Hall and the General Electric building, home of NBC television, across the street.

What brought the hockey player from Cowtown to the big city in the middle of July 2002 was a league-sponsored publicity tour. Never in the history of the NHL had the league had a black player with so much promise and worldwide marketing potential. Handsome, courteous, well-mannered, well-spoken. Smooth café au lait skin with a smile that, unlike other hockey players, does not evoke images of a jack-o'-lantern. Yet Iginla carries the unmistakable frame of a hockey man: the broad, sloping shoulders, thick neck, large hands and thunderous thighs. Iginla's New York adventure included a photo shoot for *Gentleman's Quarterly* magazine, a round of print media interviews, a sit-down with Black Entertainment Television and a pre-game visit to Shea Stadium for batting practice with the New York Mets.

As Iginla emerged from the NHL offices on Avenue of the Americas, curious onlookers suspected he was somebody important, but they didn't know his name. Nobody would thrust a piece of paper in his face for an informative autograph, or ask ungraciously, "You're somebody, aren't you?"

"Well," Iginla said with a shrug, "it's not hockey season anymore. New York has so much going on, it's hard for people to keep up with everything."

The NHL has a ways to go to raise the profile of America's fourth-most popular team sport, but it's working at it. If the marketing push succeeds, Iginla will be among the prime beneficiaries. He is the living, breathing response to a pair of questions still asked too often: *Are there black hockey players? If there are, then who's the best of the lot?*

Iginla knows the NHL needs unconventional players like him to excel to increase the sport's clout and visibility outside Canada, and he needs to see the NHL's popularity rise to draw more people into the arena to watch him perform. "The league knows I'll do everything I can to sell the game because I think it's the greatest game in the world," he says. "I've always promoted hockey in my own way. Now, I've got a chance to do it on a bigger scale."

The media blitz could have severely tested Iginla's patience, but he betrayed no annoyance. He kept a straight face while fielding the following queries:

Q: "How long have you been a black hockey player?"
A: "As long as I've been playing hockey, since I was five."
Q: "How does it feel to be a black hockey player?"
A: "That's all I've ever been, so I don't know what it feels like to be anything else."
Q: "Does it feel strange to be the only black guy on the ice?"
A: "I'm not always the only black guy out there. I've had black teammates before, even though I don't have any black teammates now. There are other black guys in the league. But the thing is, when the game is on you have to focus on the game and do your job. If you don't do that, you won't last."

Iginla, who brought his fiancée Kara along for the New York media blitz (they married in July 2003), never failed to mention that had it not been for his confidence-building practices with Team Canada in the wake of 9-11-01 he would not have scored a league-best fifty-two goals (eleven more than anybody else) in the 2001–02 season, or a league-high ninety-six points, or been the NHL Player of the Week in late October or the NHL Player of the Month in November, or been named to his first All-Star team in January 2002, or been the *best* player on the ice in the Olympic gold-medal game against the U.S.A., or become the first black man to win a gold medal in a Winter Olympiad, or been named a first-team NHL All-Star or been voted by his peers as the league's MVP.

♦ ♦ ♦

Iginla opened the eyes of Gretzky and Team Canada coach Pat Quinn with an ability to mesh with the skating styles of his linemates, even though Quinn often juggled line combinations. Quinn, once a rugged NHL defenseman, has always favoured hard-charging players who win battles for loose pucks, take the body defensively and make smart and quick passes to generate a scoring chance. In each of those vital areas, Iginla showed himself to be a player on whom Quinn could rely.

Thinking back to the physically and mentally draining practices under the intense scrutiny of the Canadian Olympic brain trust, Iginla says, "Your game goes to a higher level and your confidence level is sky-high when you step on that ice against the best players in the sport and you more than hold your own. You're just a different player when you come off the ice against those guys than you were when you went on it."

He's not the biggest player, nor is he the strongest, fastest or smoothest skater. But Iginla is a rare player, tough enough to out-battle opponents for a puck along the boards or in the corner, and skilled enough to snap a wrist shot or power a slapshot through an infinitesimal opening in the crook of a goaltender's arm. He is blessed with a fine pair of hands, soft enough to deaden the puck on his stick and maintain full control and nimble enough to quickly maneuver it from the forehand to the backhand and back again in a way that mesmerizes a defender or an opposing goalie.

In the NHL, intricate defenses and often-unpenalized acts of interference have made goal scoring exceedingly difficult. An average of 5.2 goals per game in 2001–02 was the NHL's lowest in thirty years. Nevertheless, Iginla made the most of his chances.

"He's an opportunist," New York Rangers forward Anson Carter, another of the NHL's fourteen black players in 2002–03, said with admiration not envy. "He's strong and he's got great hands. If he gets one good scoring opportunity in a game, he'll put the puck in the net."

Iginla has always had a knack for putting the puck into the net. As a fifteen-year-old, he scored eighty-seven points (thirty-four goals, fifty-three assists) in thirty-six games for the St. Albert Midget Raiders. Two years later, he scored seventy-one points (thirty-three goals, thirty-eight assists) in seventy-two games for the Kamloops Blazers. A year later, he had an astonishing sixty-three goals and seventy-three assists for 136 points in just sixty-three games for the Blazers. The Dallas Stars made him the eleventh overall pick in the 1995 draft—higher than any black skater had ever been drafted. However, the Stars saw Iginla not as a potential franchise player but as a bargaining chip to acquire veteran talent. Before he ever appeared in an NHL game, he was traded along with centre Corey Millen to Calgary on December 19, 1995 in exchange for centre Joe Nieuwendyk. The same Joe Nieuwendyk who would stand on a podium with Iginla, shiny gold medals around their necks, at the 2002 Olympics in Salt Lake City.

The trade meant Iginla would play his NHL home games in Calgary, just a three-hour drive from his boyhood home. Now Iginla, as a black hockey player, would be much more than a curiosity. He would be a professional, living out the dream of literally millions of Canadian boys, satisfying the hopes and dreams of his parents who must have expected big things from him. Why else would they have given him a name that reads like a military roll call? Their child's birth certificate reads: Jarome Arthur Leigh Adekunle Tig Junior Elvis Iginla. As Schuchard is proud to mention, she chose the name Jarome.

◆ ◆ ◆

After earning a spot on the Canadian Olympic team, Iginla rode the crest of that success and scored eighteen goals in Calgary's first twenty games of the 2001–02 season. Playing on a line with two strong defensive forwards, centre Craig Conroy and left wing Dean McAmmond, Iginla could afford to take chances at the offensive end. Possessing a strong slapshot, a crisp wrist shot, a reliable backhand, enticing fakes and a wraparound move (carrying the puck around the net and scoring from the other side) taught by his grandfather, Iginla could beat a goalie in a variety of ways. In February, a month after his first All-Star Game appearance, he headed to the Olympics in Salt Lake City.

Elvis Iginla wasn't much for hockey, but he wouldn't have missed the Olympics for anything. Elvis was in the building, along with his wife and their four children, Susan Schuchard and her father. Even if Elvis had been absent, the life lessons he taught Jarome likely would have been evident. At his father's urging, Iginla donates $1,000 for every Flames goal he scores to KidSport Calgary, a group that provides hockey equipment and funding for youth programs. The same altruistic spirit compelled Iginla to pay the hotel tab for three Canadian fans he met at the Olympics who had been sleeping in their car.

"I taught Jarome that the more you give, the better you become," Elvis Iginla said. "And what you give you should give privately to honour your father in Heaven. There are lots of things that Jarome does for people that the public doesn't know about. He doesn't do it for publicity. He does it because he should. Jarome takes his faith very seriously. He knows there are other people as talented as he is, as dedicated as he is. So when he achieves success, he understands it's not his doing. It's God's doing."

Faith notwithstanding, Iginla was a nervous wreck before the first Olympic practice. He was chosen to skate on a line with two Detroit Red Wings superstars, centre Steve Yzerman and left wing Brendan Shanahan.

"I didn't say much because my mouth was usually too dry," Iginla said, laughing. "I would shoot the puck in practice and my stick didn't feel right because of the nerves. I was even afraid to shoot the puck too hard because I was worried about injuring the goalie. And there was so much media there. So many cameras, geez!"

◆ ◆ ◆

Collective stage fright helped sink Canada in the opening game, a 5–2 loss to Sweden. The defeat conjured images of Canada's failure to medal at the 1998 Games in Nagano, Japan, the first time NHL stars participated in the Olympics. Gretzky, who played on the ill-fated '98 team, was the executive director and architect of the 2002 squad. Certainly, "The Great One" did not want to be remembered as a two-time Olympics flop. He demanded changes. So coach Quinn rearranged all the line combinations. Now, Iginla would skate with Joe Sakic, the centre and captain of the 2000–01 Stanley Cup champion Colorado Avalanche, and, ironically, with Simon Gagne, the left wing whose pre-season injury helped Iginla get an Olympics tryout in Calgary.

The Gagne-Sakic-Iginla line jelled immediately. Each man brought speed, offensive creativity and toughness to the ice. Opposing teams had a difficult time trying to contain them. Canada's other reshuffled lines also performed well, as did the defensemen and goalie Martin Brodeur. No longer was Canada an Olympic-sized underachiever. After three wins, Canada headed into a gold-medal game showdown against the U.S.A.

Players on both teams were grateful for the 12:30 p.m. start. A night game would have just meant more time to vomit because of nervousness. For the U.S. the game was important, an opportunity to win Olympic gold on home ice for the third consecutive time (after 1960 in Squaw Valley, Colorado, and the 1980 "Miracle On Ice" in Lake Placid, New York). For Canada, the game simply meant everything. Because of the humiliation in Nagano and the influx of European superstars into the NHL in the past two decades, Canada's pre-eminence in the sport it created had slipped away. The gold-medal game on February 24, 2002, the final day of Olympic competition, would give Canada a chance to reclaim its supremacy and calm the psyche of a worried nation.

Breaking the Ice

"We knew the whole country would be watching," Iginla said. "It had been fifty years since Canada won a gold medal in hockey. Fifty years! Even the NHL stars couldn't do it in Japan. I've never been more excited or more nervous before a game. The intensity in our dressing room was amazing: confident, but quiet; a lot of nervous energy. Guys who had won Stanley Cups said it was the biggest game they would ever play in. We all wanted to win it for Canada, and we didn't want to lose to the U.S. This wasn't like the Stanley Cup finals. That's a best-of-seven-game series. This was one game. And everybody back home would always remember this game. So I just kept telling myself, 'No mistakes.'"

Team USA had a twenty-four game unbeaten streak (twenty-one wins, three ties) in Olympic matches on home ice. The Americans' bid to make it twenty-five began in earnest eight minutes and forty-nine seconds into the game when a goal by Tony Amonte produced a 1–0 lead. Deafening cheers and a flurry of red-white-and-blue flags from a crowd of 8,599 filled the arena. But Canada kept its poise and drew even on Paul Kariya's goal six minutes later.

As time ticked away in the first of three twenty-minute periods, Iginla and Sakic collaborated on some on-ice magic to put Canada on top.

"We had a two-on-one break and I was driving to the net," Iginla recalled. "I went around [USA defenseman Gary] Suter and I didn't know if Sakic would pass the puck to Gagne on his left or pass it to me going to the net. I'm telling you, there was so much going on between where I was and where Sakic was that I could not see the puck. But we're taught as players to go to the net and keep your stick down. Always be ready. So I kept my stick down and I *felt* the puck hit it. I didn't see the puck hit my stick at all. I had to look around and find the puck in the net. That's when the crowd started going nuts, and that's when I started going nuts!"

Iginla later earned an assist on a Sakic power play goal that put Canada ahead 3–2 in the second period. Canada would not relinquish the lead, but neither the team nor its anxious fans could exhale until Iginla struck again with four minutes left in the game.

"I was skating behind the play and Yzerman and Sakic were on the rush," he remembered. "Yzerman veered off to the left corner and I came all the way up from our [defensive] zone. I was thinking, 'Oh, I hope he sees me.' But of course, he's Yzerman, so he saw me. He passed me the puck and I one-timed it [shot the puck in one motion without letting it settle on the stick]."

The crackling slapshot caromed off the glove of goalie Mike Richter and twisted in the air like a flipped coin.

"It felt like the puck was moving in slow motion. I couldn't wait for it to come down," Iginla said with a laugh. "I was saying, 'Come down! Come down!' Finally the puck comes down, and it's just over the goal line. I was more excited about that goal than the first one because it gave us a two-goal lead. It really took the pressure off. Now guys were on the bench saying, 'We're gonna win it! We're gonna win it! We're gonna win the gold!'"

In a jubilant Team Canada dressing room after the 5–2 win, a relieved Gretzky said, "Jarome Iginla is a real special story in that he just got better every game all year long and just earned his way onto this team. He was tremendously successful."

Added Yzerman: "Jarome was really quiet when the Olympics started. I guess he didn't want to overstep his bounds. But he got more and more comfortable as the Games went on, and his play was awesome."

Iginla's family also bathed in the Olympic afterglow. "You have no idea how many people I've met who talk to me about the gold-medal game," Susan Schuchard said. "When it comes to Canada and hockey, there's enormous national pride. I knew Jarome was involved in something big, but since the Olympics we've found out just how big."

And Iginla, at twenty-seven, is still finding out how much higher his star can rise. He knows how high he wants it to rise. That can be summed up in a song his mother would favour: "How High The Moon."

"I believe next season will be better than the last. That's my goal," he said during the New York media blitz. "You have to set high goals and not worry about raising the bar. I'm excited about what the rest of my career can be. Not making the playoffs sucks and it feels worse every year. But that just makes me hungrier and hungrier. If I can help my team get into the playoffs, then more people will be aware of me and I can be more of a role model."

Iginla's visage in an NHL-sponsored "Hockey Is For Everyone" campaign will raise his public profile somewhat. But not as much as a successful run in the Stanley Cup playoffs. For that, Iginla will have to wait, maybe for quite some time. The Flames crashed and burned in the 2002–03 season, finishing dead last in the Northwest Division with one of the league's lowest point totals. Iginla, beset by physical fatigue—the inevitable result of a whirlwind summer of public appearances and insufficient rest—a nagging right shoulder and defenses bent on stopping him, had just fifteen goals in the first four months of the season. However, he got a second wind in February. He appeared in his second straight All-Star Game and scored thirteen goals in twelve games, including his first career four-goal game in a win at Phoenix. But while Iginla rose like a phoenix, Calgary could not. The team won only two of its twelve February games.

Iginla finished 2002–03 with thirty-five goals, seventh-best in the league, and sixty-seven points. His offensive numbers were excellent, particularly on a team that was never in playoff contention, a team that fired its coach during the season and dismissed its general manager after the season. But largely because of an overwhelming lack of support, Iginla fell considerably short of matching his 2001–02 output. If he feels trapped on one of pro hockey's weakest teams, he doesn't let it show. What the public sees is a player still pushing himself to improve, still determined to excel and inspire others.

"I'd love to be a role model for black kids, whether they play hockey or not," he said. "Just like Grant Fuhr and Tony McKegney showed me it was possible to do what I'm doing, I want to be someone who shows kids that it's possible to be whatever they want to be."

Back in September 2002, Iginla ended a brief boycott of Flames' training camp and signed a two-year, $13 million contract. The distinct possibility of a league-ordered lockout of the players after the 2003–04 season undoubtedly influenced Calgary's decision to give Iginla a two-year contract. The deal pays him $5.5 million in American dollars the first year and a franchise-record $7.5 million in year two. He made $1.7 million in the 2001–02 season. The brevity of his contract helps both sides. A Canadian-based franchise such as the Flames is at a distinct economic disadvantage compared to its American counterparts since Canadian teams must pay player salaries in U.S. dollars while taking in revenues from such sources as ticket sales and broadcast rights in weaker Canadian dollars. A Canadian dollar is worth roughly 70¢ U.S. Hence, the Flames believed they could not afford to give Iginla a longer, more lucrative deal and still have enough money left to add the supporting players needed to make the team competitive. Yet the current deal could allow him to leave Calgary for a larger media market—and a better team—as a restricted free agent (the Flames would have the right to match any offer) beginning July 1, 2004.

Never could Iginla have dreamed as a boy that someday he would be paid $7.5 million a year to play hockey. But because he plays for a cash-poor, Canadian-based franchise, he is frequently the subject of trade rumours. He would love to stay in Alberta because it's home. But he knows Calgary could send him packing prior to or during the 2003–04 season in a "business move." Still, living with trade rumours is a small price to pay for the best black player ever to appear in the NHL. It is far better than being the best black player *never* to appear in the NHL.

Herb Carnegie (No. 7), along with his brother Ossie Carnegie (No. 10) and Manny McIntyre (No. 11), formed The Black Aces, a prolific line in Canadian semi-pro hockey in the 1940s.
Hockey Hall of Fame

A Pioneer in Search of Fame

What Herb Carnegie needed more than anything else during the prime years of his athletic life was a sponsor. He needed his own Branch Rickey. Rickey was the baseball visionary that, as general manager of the Brooklyn Dodgers, signed Negro League baseball star Jackie Robinson to a contract in October 1945. It was a business transaction done in an era of systemic racial oppression that changed the face of sports history.

During the same years Robinson augmented a reputation as a four-sport star at UCLA, Carnegie—also a man of a darker hue—excelled on hockey rinks, often in Canadian mining towns, usually on the periphery of the spotlight.

Some who saw Carnegie perform in person—including Jean Beliveau and Frank Mahovlich, two of the greatest centres in hockey history—marvelled at his multi-faceted skills and considered him among the finest players of his time. Unfortunately for Carnegie, he would never perform on his sport's premier stage, the NHL. And for that, the gatekeepers of the NHL must bear most of the blame—and Carnegie himself must bear at least some.

An NHL hopeful in the 1930s, '40s and '50s, Carnegie predated the widespread media coverage now devoted to hockey. Hence, his contributions to the sport received inadequate exposure then and are a source of debate now. The issue of whether his credentials are worthy of induction into the Hockey Hall of Fame has become a political football, and Carnegie's side is trailing by a considerable margin on the scoreboard.

"I wish somebody from the Hall of Fame would have the decency to phone me and sit down with me and say, 'Herb, this is the problem. This is why it hasn't happened,'" he said, struggling to mask the pain. An immensely proud man, he lives in northern Toronto, less than one hour's drive from the Hall of Fame, but perhaps light years away from hockey's shrine philosophically.

Had his pursuit of an NHL career not been derailed by a league-wide policy of exclusion that may have been given public voice in 1938 by Conn Smythe, the powerful and influential owner of the Toronto Maple Leafs, Carnegie likely would have become the NHL's first black player. The history-making ascension would have occurred more than a decade before Willie O'Ree broke the league's colour barrier in 1958. Carnegie's debut in hockey's major league also could have occurred during the 1948–49 season, or shortly thereafter, were it not for his own bold, but ultimately self-defeating, decision—a decision that may have done irreparable harm to his candidacy for the Hall of Fame.

Even today, as an octogenarian, Carnegie could use a sponsor. He would welcome the opportunity to face his detractors on the Hall of Fame's selection committee, although he can no longer see them. Robbed of his sight a dozen years ago by glaucoma, he is cared for today by Audrey Carnegie, his wife of sixty-three years. But do not pity Herb Carnegie. Pity is the one thing he neither wants nor needs.

"I feel I've been blessed," says Carnegie, who turned eighty-four on November 8, 2003. "It would be nice to be in the Hockey Hall of Fame, not only for myself but on behalf of my wife and my [four] children and all those who have helped me over the years. But it is something that is out of my hands. It has always been out of my hands. So I've never felt that I should not go on living my life just because I haven't been accepted by the Hockey Hall of Fame."

A helping hand from someone high above the ice, in a seat of power and influence, is what Carnegie truly needed to properly showcase his skills during his best years in hockey. But he chose to devote his life to a sport that at the time had no visionary. A Branch Rickey who defied the social and racial mores of his time and handed a baseball contract to a black man for the most sensible of reasons—it would make his team better—probably would have been drummed out of hockey. For hockey had no man with the courage to see past the darkness of racial discrimination and give *all* of the sport's gifted players during most of the first half of the twentieth century an opportunity to perform in the NHL.

"Let's face it, Herbie Carnegie was one helluva hockey player," wrote one sportswriter who watched him many times. "He could have been a star in the six-team NHL were it not for the colour bars that kept all black athletes out of all major sports at the time."

Had it not been so important to the fathers of hockey for so long to keep the NHL white, Carnegie almost assuredly would have become the Jackie Robinson of his sport. While he starred in semi-pro leagues from his late teens to his late twenties, he did not get a call from the Toronto

Maple Leafs, Montreal Canadiens, Detroit Red Wings, Chicago Blackhawks, Boston Bruins or New York Rangers.

Instead, Carnegie achieved a measure of popularity in lesser leagues while teaming with his older brother, Ossie, and Manny McIntyre to form a potent all-black line known from 1941 through 1949 by various nicknames, including The Black Aces. Herb wore No. 7, Ossie No. 10 and Manny No. 11.

Herb Carnegie, the centre and conductor of the trio, stood at 5-foot-8 and weighed 165 pounds. "My thrill was in setting plays," he said. "To me, the game is a beautiful thing when you can set up a winger. That's an art."

He was an unusually handsome man in his younger days, with bronze skin, thin-slit brown eyes, a pencil-thin mustache and black hair chemically straightened into the conk style made famous by bandleader Cab Calloway. His appearance might have served him well as a leading man or action hero in the "race" movies of the era, such as 1939's *The Bronze Buckaroo*.

Although Carnegie would be considered woefully undersized for his on-ice position today, smallish centres were not an unusual sight in 1940s hockey. However, smallish *black* centres were highly unusual. An all-black line was unprecedented. Ossie Carnegie, the right wing, possessed a crackling slapshot. McIntyre, the left wing, provided the muscle. If one of the trio was going to answer a racial slur from an opponent or spectator with his fists, it would likely be McIntyre.

And there was no shortage of racial slurs directed toward The Black Aces. Audrey Redmon Carnegie, the light-skinned daughter of transplanted Chicago natives, sat in the stands on many occasions and heard her husband Herb called "nigger" and sundry other words of hate by spectators seated nearby, people who did not realize she was black and married to the best player on the ice. She managed to hold her tongue while in the company of haters, because that is how blacks generally dealt with hate in that era.

The Carnegie brothers had been a popular duo in the mines league (hockey teams playing in mining towns) beginning in 1941 with the Buffalo Ankerites, a team owned by a group of Buffalo-based businessmen, and whose games were played in Canada. Hockey players, even NHL players, made so little money in that era that the brothers also worked as machine operators for the Ankerite Company. For a hockey player, a second job was necessary. If a player made $100 a week from hockey then he was doing quite well. The Carnegie brothers' financial status improved significantly when McIntyre joined the Ankerites. A native of Fredericton, New Brunswick, McIntyre correctly sensed the economic potential of an all-black line and successfully lobbied for his inclusion.

"They were good enough as a line to play in the American League, which was a level below the NHL," said Red Storey, a Hall of Fame referee who played against Herb Carnegie in junior hockey. "But Herbie was the leader. They couldn't have gone anywhere without Herb. He was good enough to play in the NHL. It was strictly colour, not talent, that kept him out."

While the all-black line racked up points and inspired applause throughout the semi-pro circuit, it inspired an assortment of colourful sobriquets from the sporting press: The Dark Destroyers, The Ink Spots, The Brown Bombers (a reference to heavyweight boxing champion Joe Louis), The Dusky Speedsters. There was even one reference to the players' varying skin tones: 8-Ball, Snowball and Haile Selassie (the former emperor of Ethiopia). But the name the trio liked best was The Black Aces. By any name, the all-black line made a profound impression on Mahovlich, a Hall of Fame forward who first saw them in 1942.

"The black line was so amazing because of their great skills—the skating, the passing, the goal scoring," he said. "I was a centreman for many years. I might have envisioned myself going down the ice like Herb Carnegie. In my mind I said, 'I guess if I ever become a hockey player, I'm going to be playing against a lot of blacks.' However, that was the only time I ever saw three blacks on the same line."

Mahovlich would never see any of The Black Aces in an NHL game. Herb Carnegie, the most gifted of the trio and the finest black player of the pre-expansion era (before 1967), would never display his considerable skills as a puckhandler and playmaker in his sport's premier league. And many who watched him perform under dimmer lights and before lesser crowds in other venues believe hockey fans themselves were cheated for having missed him.

Said one fan of Canada's pastime: "I saw a lot of hockey when I was in Quebec in the old mines league. The Carnegie brothers, Ossie and Herbie, were there. They could have played in the NHL but they [the NHL] wouldn't let them in because they were coloured, which was awful."

In September 1948, however, the NHL pried open a door just wide enough to acknowledge Herb Carnegie. But instead of doing his utmost to kick the door down, he unwittingly closed it on himself.

◆ ◆ ◆

With no advance word, a letter arrived at the Carnegie home one August morning in 1948 from the New York Rangers, inviting the twenty-eight-year-old Carnegie to report to the team's training camp in Saranac Lake, New York on September 14. Carnegie had not even been aware the NHL was paying attention to him. No NHL team had contacted him while he excelled as leader of The Black Aces line in the 1944–45 season for the oddly named Shawinigan Falls Cataracts for a salary of $75 a week in the semi-pro Quebec Provincial League (QPL), whose calibre of play was below that of the NHL and perhaps comparable to a professional minor league. Carnegie had not heard from the NHL after he scored five goals in one game against Cornwall that season. Nor had he heard from the major league after he and his black linemates moved on to the Sherbrooke Randies of the QPL for the next two seasons. Carnegie remembered The Black Aces combining for eighty-four goals and ninety-eight assists in 1945–46, and he remembered narrowly losing the scoring title to former Montreal Canadiens winger Tony Demers of the St. Hyacinthe team, 79–75. He remembered scoring a Gretzky-like 127 points in fifty-six games in the 1947–48 season with Sherbrooke. But he didn't know the NHL had taken notice.

The missive from the Rangers was a form letter sent to twenty Canadian amateur or semi-pro players inviting them to try out for berths on the NHL team's roster. The invitees would report to Saranac Lake and work out at an arena in nearby Lake Placid, under the scrutiny of coach and general manager Frank Boucher until the arrival of members of the Rangers and two of their minor-league clubs, the New Haven Ramblers of the American League and the New York Rovers of the Eastern League, for the official opening of training camp September 21.

The inclusion of Carnegie among the invitees was significant because up until 1945, each of the four major professional sports leagues in North America had excluded black talent. Various sports writers in the U.S., particularly those from the black press such as Wendell Smith of *The Pittsburgh Courier* and Sam Lacy of *The Baltimore Afro-American,* wrote forceful columns denouncing Major League Baseball's refusal to admit black players. Some players from the Negro Leagues, including Robinson, had been promised tryouts, but big-league officials and white players sometimes would not even bother to show up. Not until Robinson officially joined the Dodgers' organization on October 23, 1945 had any black baseball player signed with a big-league club. The National Basketball Association did not include blacks until 1950 when the New York Knicks signed Nat "Sweetwater" Clifton, the Boston Celtics drafted Charles "Tarzan" Cooper and the Washington Capitals played Earl Lloyd in an October 31 game. Charles Follis was the first black professional football player, in the early 1900s, in a league that predated the National Football League. The NFL, however, tacitly banned black players from 1933 until 1946 when the league admitted Woody Strode and Kenny Washington so it could secure a lease to play games at the Los Angeles Memorial Coliseum.

The signing of Robinson by Brooklyn and his extremely successful debut with the Dodgers undoubtedly emboldened a few other team executives in major pro leagues to give an opportunity to black athletes. Carnegie said he had followed Robinson's career during the 1940s and often wondered which of the two would be the first to break the colour barrier in his sport. However, the events at Rangers' camp in 1948 strongly suggest Carnegie had not followed Robinson's story closely enough.

In the first week of workouts at the Lake Placid arena, Carnegie matched his skills against players he considered inferior to those he faced regularly in the Quebec Provincial League. He had just won his second consecutive MVP award in the league and led Sherbrooke to the league championship. Carnegie remembers eagerly awaiting the September 21 arrival of Rangers stars such as Buddy O'Connor, the 1947–48 NHL MVP, and Edgar Laprade.

But as Carnegie wrote in his 1997 autobiography, *A Fly in a Pail of Milk*, he was called into an office during the first week of camp by minor-league coach Muzz Patrick and offered $2,700 a year to sign with the Rangers' organization and play for the team's lowest-level farm club in Tacoma, Washington. The $2,700 was far less than the $5,100 he had made in the 1947-48 season with Sherbrooke, so he turned the offer down. After practice the next day, Carnegie wrote, he was summoned by minor-league coach Lynn Patrick, Muzz Patrick's brother, and offered a $3,700 contract to sign with the organization and report to the Rangers' farm club in St. Paul, Minnesota. Again, he refused. The next day, he wrote, Rangers coach Phil Watson offered him $4,700 to sign and play for the team's top farm club, the New Haven Ramblers. He declined the offer while telling Watson he thought himself more than capable of earning a spot on the Rangers roster.

Carnegie's literary account contains one notable error: Frank Boucher was the Rangers coach and general manager at the time, not Phil Watson. Watson would not coach the Rangers until 1955. In 1948–49, Watson coached the New York Rovers, a team Carnegie would face that season in minor-league hockey. Boucher stepped down as Rangers coach on December 21, 1948, after the team got off to a poor start—six wins, eleven losses, six ties—and was replaced by Lynn Patrick. Boucher continued as general manager until 1955. When the 1948–49 training camp began, Lynn Patrick was the coach of New Haven. So why would Lynn Patrick be the one to offer Carnegie $3,700 to play for St. Paul? Carnegie does not recall. He said Muzz Patrick offered him $2,700 to play for Tacoma, and indeed Muzz Patrick coached Tacoma at the time. But why were the Rangers making such lowball offers to Carnegie in the first place? Surely they must have known he had made $5,100 the season before at Sherbrooke. Simply, the Rangers knew they could get away with it. The NHL had only six teams in 1948. There were only 126 jobs for hockey players in the premier league. No player had an agent, and an NHL players union would not exist until 1967. Hockey teams wielded a mighty hammer in 1948. And if Carnegie, just another nail in the board, truly wanted to fulfill what he had described as a lifelong dream to play in the NHL, then it would have behooved him to get the best deal he could, swallow hard and try to make the best of it. While he is deserving of credit for not jumping at either of the first two lowball offers, he seriously overplayed his hand by turning down the third.

Carnegie's stay at Rangers' camp lasted eleven days. After initially turning down the $4,700 offer to play for New Haven, he said he persuaded Rangers management to let him remain in camp for the second week so he could show his talent against real NHL players. He took the ice for four successive days against the Rangers, including centres O'Connor and Laprade and goalie Jim Henry. "I had proven myself beyond a shadow of a doubt," Carnegie said. "I had shown the Rangers I could play as well."

Perhaps he had. But the Rangers still had the hammer to dictate the terms of whatever relationship they would have with Carnegie, as they would with every other player in a league where only the owners had clout. The Rangers' relationship with Carnegie would be regrettably short. On his eleventh day in camp, he remembers meeting with Boucher, the coach and general manager. Again he was offered $4,700 to begin the 1948–49 season with the Rangers' top farm club in New Haven, just one notch below the NHL, just two hours away from Madison Square Garden if he needed to be promoted in a hurry. Again, he declined.

The final deal offered Carnegie by the Rangers was essentially the same deal the Brooklyn Dodgers had offered Robinson. The Rangers may well have looked to their New York baseball counterparts and used as a blueprint for their dealings with Carnegie the Dodgers' handling of Robinson. The baseball star's deal called for him to play the entire 1946 season for the Dodgers' top farm club, the Montreal Royals. He would not advance from the Negro Leagues directly to Major League Baseball. Robinson would spend a year in the minors, Rickey explained, so he could be sure Robinson could excel on the playing field *and* handle the inevitable racist slurs and various other indignities a black man would surely face as the only player of his colour in an organized league one notch below Major League Baseball. If all went well, Rickey said, Robinson would join the big leagues in 1947.

After Robinson accepted the terms of the deal and played his way into the majors, he indelibly etched his name in the annals of sports and world history. Baseball players had no agents or union representation at that time, either. There were no salary negotiations. A player took whatever money he was offered, or he left the room and looked for other work. So when Rickey told Robinson to start in Montreal—just to be sure—Robinson, already a star in black baseball, did not take offense to being asked to spend a year in the minor leagues. He took the deal, for it would benefit not only him but also the black players who would follow him. Indeed, by 1948, the year after Robinson carried the banner for blacks in Major League Baseball, three other blacks (Larry Doby, Roy Campanella and Satchel Paige) had joined him in the elite league.

While there was no black hockey league in the late 1940s, no on-ice equivalent of the Negro Leagues, there were a few other blacks who played hockey besides Herb Carnegie, such as his brother, Ossie, and Manny McIntyre, both of whom went on to play pro hockey in France. In Herb Carnegie's own words, Boucher wanted him to start in New Haven "just to be sure." The Rangers likely had a legitimate concern about how well Carnegie would play with linemates other than his brother and McIntyre who, in the opinion of Hall of Fame referee Storey, were not of NHL potential. A strong start by Carnegie in New Haven would have eliminated that concern. Boucher also said he would "make every effort" to promote Carnegie during the 1948–49 season. Had Carnegie taken the offer, he would have been on the cusp of an NHL career while making the ice somewhat more solid for other black hopefuls.

The major difference, then, between sports pioneers Robinson and Carnegie was this: Robinson took the deal and Carnegie did not.

◆ ◆ ◆

Carnegie, married and a father of three at the time (his fourth child was born in 1951), felt no need to take a $400 pay cut and play minor-league hockey in New Haven, when he could continue playing semi-pro hockey in Canada and be closer to his family. He returned to Sherbrooke, reuniting briefly with Ossie and McIntyre, then joined the Quebec Major Hockey League from 1949 to 1953, and the Ontario Senior Hockey Association for the 1953–54 season.

"He stayed in Canada because he had a better future here financially," said Storey, who lives in Montreal. "He could do better in the Quebec League financially than he could in the NHL."

Breaking the Ice

In Carnegie's view, he proved to Rangers players in four days of drills and scrimmages that his skills were at least comparable to theirs. He also said the other players were truly surprised to see him leave camp. Only a few men who attended that camp fifty-five years ago are still alive. Don "Bones" Raleigh, a spindly 150-pound centre, was there. The seventy-seven-year-old said he saw Carnegie on the ice but remembers nothing specific about him. Laprade, a Hall of Fame centre, recalls being surprised that Carnegie left. But he remembers little about Carnegie the player.

"I can't recall if he was above average in any particular thing at all," said Laprade, who is eighty-four. "But I don't know why he didn't take that New Haven offer. Two things: he would have been one step from the Rangers or one step from another NHL club if the Rangers decided to trade him, and he could have been the first coloured player. I guess he made the decision not to go. That's his. Has he ever regretted it?"

A 1973 article in *The Toronto Sun* quotes Carnegie as saying, "I missed the NHL by the stroke of a pen. Frankie Boucher was coaching the New York Rangers in 1948 and he told me he thought I was a good player, but he wanted to be sure whether I could play in the NHL. So he suggested I sign and start playing in New Haven. I was twenty-nine [actually twenty-eight] at the time and I didn't feel like playing there. For in those days there were not too many thirty-year-old players in the NHL and I knew that if I didn't make it immediately, I wouldn't get another chance."

Carnegie said on April 10, 2003 that he did not recall expressing any regret about his decision. Asked if he would have signed with the Rangers organization if he had it to do over again, he said emphatically, "No. I don't even have to think twice about that. I'm at the end of my career and it's no time for me to be going to the minors to start a new career with teenagers and twenty-year-olds. I didn't think it would have made any kind of sense."

But in the late 1940s, an NHL team's top minor-league affiliate was not quite the kiddie corps Carnegie made it out to be. Remember, there were only six NHL franchises then, only 126 major-league jobs. The top minor-league teams had many players in their late twenties and early thirties trying to play their way into the NHL. And had Carnegie been promoted to the Rangers after turning twenty-nine during the 1948–49 season, he would not have been a greybeard by any means. He would have been five years *younger* than forward/defenseman Neil Colville, three years *younger* than O'Connor and defenseman Bill Moe, the same age as Laprade, winger Alex Kaleta and defenseman Wally Stanowski and one year older than goalie Chuck Rayner.

Furthermore, Detroit Red Wings centre Jim McFadden won the NHL Rookie of the Year award in the 1947–48 season—at age twenty-eight.

Incidentally, Robinson, born January 31, 1919, was a mere forty weeks older than Carnegie when he broke baseball's colour barrier and won the National League Rookie of the Year award. Robinson clearly had not considered himself too old to spend a year in the minors to play his way into the big leagues.

"Herb wouldn't have been the first guy to start off in the minors before getting to the NHL," Laprade said. "You don't just jump into the National Hockey League. You go to the minors, get experience, then maybe after two or three months or a year, they'd call him up."

Perhaps it would have taken Carnegie less than a month after reporting to the New Haven team to become the "Jackie Robinson of hockey." On October 8, 1948, six days before the Rangers' season-opening game against the Montreal Canadiens, O'Connor and Laprade—the team's two best centres—were among four players injured in an auto accident in Lacolle, Quebec, near the U.S.-Canadian border. "Buddy was driving. We got permission to take his car to New York and an old wagon full of apples pulled up in front of us and he hit it," Laprade said.

Broken ribs sidelined O'Connor for six weeks. Laprade played the Montreal game despite a broken nose and a concussion. Had Carnegie, a centre, been with New Haven at the time he could have been called up to the Rangers as a replacement. (That is how Willie O'Ree became the NHL's first black player in 1958. The Boston Bruins called him up from the minor leagues to replace an injured player.) Instead, New York made a pair of trades to replace the injured players.

"Don't you think the Rangers would have called me back if they had been serious about wanting me?" Carnegie asked. But he effectively answered his own question as he recalled his final conversation with Rangers management at training camp: "They told me that if I signed with the Rangers and went to New Haven I would make international headlines. I told them my family couldn't eat headlines. That was probably when the Rangers decided to forget about me."

The rest of the NHL forgot about him as well. He never got another call from the major league.

The Rangers probably could have done a better job of trying to convince Carnegie that he should start the 1948–49 season in New Haven. They did not have to, but they could have. The Rangers could have pointed out, and Carnegie does not recall them doing so, that the minimum NHL salary that season was $5,000, meaning if he had been promoted to the major-league club his pay would have been at least commensurate with his Sherbrooke salary. Further, it could have been bettered, had he been offered a salary more than one hundred dollars above the league minimum. And with an opportunity to cash in on new-found fame and status as the

NHL's first and only black player, Carnegie could have generated even more money. Yes, the Rangers could have allowed Carnegie to start the season with the big club. But the Dodgers in 1946 didn't do that with Robinson, and by 1948 everybody could see how well Brooklyn's plan had worked. And yes, the Rangers could have summoned Carnegie from Sherbrooke after the injuries to O'Connor and Laprade.

But NHL teams had no obligation to satisfy Carnegie or any other player, only themselves. Carnegie, for his part, refused to be treated like just another nail in the board. If only he had had the leverage to match his intractability. He will be remembered as the best black player *never* to reach the NHL, partly because of the racism that circumscribed the lives of all blacks in North America during his athletic prime and partly because of an insistence on trying to dictate the terms under which he would sign with an NHL organization in 1948—a year in which hockey players, black or white, could not dictate *anything* to management.

"The Rangers at that time were not exactly a powerhouse; we finished in last place," said Emile Francis, a backup goalie in 1948–49. "You think Boucher was concerned about race? Heck, he was trying to win games. He would have played any player who could have helped us win games."

Francis' viewpoint is noteworthy, not merely because he's a member of the Hockey Hall of Fame after five decades as a goalie, coach and general manager, but because he sits on the Hall of Fame selection committee—a group called upon to consider Carnegie's candidacy in 2000. It certainly did not help Carnegie's chances to be elected as a player then, and will not help in the future, if he is regarded by at least one selection committee member as simply a career semi-pro. Asked if Carnegie had been a good enough player to get into the Hall of Fame, Francis said, "You'd have to play in a better category of hockey than that. That's not the NHL."

Larry Zeidel, a former NHL defenseman who played against Carnegie in the Quebec Senior League, said in a 1972 interview he believed money, not race, was a bigger factor in Carnegie's exclusion from the NHL. "Ossie and Herbie were making terrific money in the Quebec [Provincial] League and had side jobs which gave them more security," he said. "There was no reason to try for the NHL."

Herb Carnegie, whose brother Ossie died in 1991, disputed Zeidel's assertion and said it was a boyhood dream of his and Ossie's to play major-league hockey. Racism kept the Carnegie brothers out of the NHL, he said, which is precisely what their father told them would happen.

◆ ◆ ◆

The son of Jamaican immigrants, Herb Carnegie was born in Toronto and grew up playing hockey on the pond rinks in Willowdale, north of the city. Herb and Ossie Carnegie spent many hours on the pond developing a symmetry that would make them semi-pro stars years later. Herb, however, would become a master improviser. He could lift fans out of their seats with a feathery pinpoint pass, exquisite puckhandling or a brilliantly conceived play. He had the soft and quick hands required of a centre along with a penchant for creativity and keen instincts for the game.

"I was just amazed at the way he played; he was much superior to the others on the ice," said Mahovlich, a fifteen-time NHL All-Star. "I've known Herb pretty much my entire life, since the first hockey game I ever witnessed at the age of four way up in Northern Ontario ... in a little mining community called Timmins. My dad had taken me to a game in the mines league. Every mining town had a hockey team, and Herb was playing for the Buffalo Ankerites."

Carnegie's performances in the mines league have largely been lost to history. Accurate statistical records are hard to come by. Carnegie, who could have become "the Jackie Robinson of hockey," has instead become "the Josh Gibson of hockey," a kindred spirit of the often-overlooked slugging catcher who entered the Negro Leagues well before Robinson and found racism an impenetrable barrier to entering Major League Baseball.

From sun-up to sundown on many a winter's day, Herb and Ossie Carnegie cultivated their hockey skills on the pond and dreamed of displaying them in the NHL. That no black man had yet played in the major league was not lost on either boy. Ossie and Herb expected to be the first ones, in that order. But their father, George, could never envision the possibility. "You know they won't let any black boys into the National Hockey League," he said.

George Carnegie worked as a janitor and wife Adina as a homemaker and, being among the earliest Caribbean émigrés, they were determined to see that their children had a better and richer life. Since others would be sure to tell Herb Carnegie he would never play in the NHL, his father wanted to be sure Herb would not neglect his studies or stunt his personal growth in pursuit of a dream that could be denied by forces and institutions more powerful than he.

Herb Carnegie's earliest remembrance of bigotry came at age four when neighbourhood children slurred him. He remembered responding to taunts of "nigger," "coon" and "Rastas" with his fists, which he considered a fitting response from a strong-minded Scorpio.

It seemed whenever Herb was not playing hockey, he was fighting for any modicum of respect he could extract from schoolmates and neighbours.

As his confidence in being able to physically defend himself grew, so did his devotion to and proficiency in hockey. He also took a liking to baseball and golf. In the twilight of his athletic life he would win the Canadian Senior Golf championship in 1977 and '78.

In high school hockey, Carnegie earned the nickname "Swivel Hips" because of his elusiveness on the ice. He also heard other names on the ice. He recalls a game attended by several thousands in which one megaphone-voiced spectator repeatedly yelled, "Get the black bastard!" However, a stunned Carnegie heeded the advice of a coach who said the most effective response to bigotry was to score goals. Carnegie filled the net with pucks and garnered his share of laudatory clippings from Toronto-area newspapers. His father hoped he would become a doctor, but Herb had visions of an NHL residency. He excelled in the sport by day and relished Foster Hewitt's vivid radio accounts of Toronto Maple Leafs games at night. Carnegie closed his eyes and saw himself on the Leafs' bench right beside the famed "Kid Line" of Charlie Conacher, Joe Primeau and Busher Jackson. He saw himself showered with standing ovations from fans at Maple Leaf Gardens. He saw action photos of himself in the Sports pages of the Toronto dailies.

◆ ◆ ◆

Carnegie thought himself a step away from NHL stardom when he joined the Toronto Junior Rangers, also known as the Young Rangers, in 1938. He would be the lone black player on the team, but race would have no effect on his ice time. And he would respond to any racial slurs he would hear on the rink or from the stands by filling the net with pucks. The Young Rangers played in an NHL arena, Maple Leaf Gardens, and prepared teenaged players for the NHL. Under the tutelage of Ed Wildey, Young Rangers Jim Fowler, George Parsons, Jim Thomson and Jim Conacher went on to hockey's elite league. Carnegie believed he would follow, in part because of his glowing press clippings: "Herb Carnegie, the Young Rangers coloured centre player... gave one of the most brilliant displays ever seen here, scored five goals and assisted on another."

As Carnegie remembered it, he was practicing one day at Maple Leaf Gardens when Wildey alerted him to the presence of a hockey powerhouse in the arena's upper reaches. It was Conn Smythe, the man who had shrewdly built the Toronto Maple Leafs into the NHL's most glamorous franchise. Although not a large man physically, he was considered imposing, if not intimidating. The Toronto native had served as a major in two world wars. In 1927, he used $160,000 in loans and successful horse racing bets to purchase the Toronto St. Pats and change its nickname to Maple Leafs to stimulate more national interest. Since an NHL player draft did not yet exist, he stockpiled Toronto-area talent such as defenseman Red Horner and the aforementioned "Kid Line," transforming the franchise into a perennial contender for the Stanley Cup. Yet Smythe, who would manage the Leafs to seven Stanley Cups, also had his detractors.

"He was a little dictator; I never liked the guy," said Laprade, the former New York Rangers centre. "I didn't like it when he said, 'If you can't beat 'em in the alley, you can't beat 'em on the ice.'"

Yet another quote attributed to Smythe would prove traumatic to Carnegie. He said his eyes beamed when he spotted Smythe in the stands that day. Everybody in hockey knew of the formidable man called "The Major." However, nothing in Carnegie's first nineteen years had prepared him for Wildey's relaying of Smythe's comment about his chances for an NHL career: "He said he'd take you tomorrow if he could turn you white."

"That comment created such anger in me. It hurts to this day," Carnegie said in an August 17, 2002 interview. "The Toronto Maple Leafs was the team I rooted for as a boy. And to find out that was how the owner of the team I rooted for felt about me was shattering, just shattering. I felt at the time that my dream of playing in the NHL had been dashed."

Some doubt has arisen over the years as to whether Smythe had indeed uttered that remark sixty-five years ago, or the somewhat different and more widely quoted version: "I'd give any man $10,000 who could turn Herb Carnegie white." Some historians regard the quote as apocryphal. Some regard the quote as credible given Smythe's often grating personality and apparently bigoted remarks on other matters, yet they admit to having no concrete evidence.

At least one Canadian hockey fan considered Smythe a bigot, and not just against blacks. "Conn Smythe was an advocate of racism," the hockey fan wrote to *The Toronto Star*. "He not only discriminated against black athletes but would not hire young Jewish men to sell programs and refreshments at Leafs games. He traded away defenseman Alex "Mine Boy" Levinsky because Al was Jewish." Levinsky was traded by Toronto to New York in April 1934.

Smythe and Wildey, Carnegie's junior-league coach, are deceased. However, Storey, a 1967 inductee to the Hall of Fame, is alive and he believes Smythe uttered the damning quote. He believes this, although he did not hear it himself.

"It was in the newspapers. That's where I saw it, and I believe that is an accurate quote from Conn Smythe," said Storey, who turned eighty-six in May 2003. "There's a reason why Herb Carnegie did not play in the NHL. It's very simple: he's black. Don't say we don't have any rednecks in Canada. But I'm not saying Conn Smythe was bigoted, either. Basically, Conn Smythe was a good guy away from the arena. I think he said the quote, but I think he meant that with Herbie being black, he wouldn't be able to put him in the same hotels with the rest of the team and have him eat at the same restaurants and there could be problems if he took him to the States to play against the NHL teams there. The NHL games weren't sold out then, and the owners might have been worried about losing the fans they already had. Basically, you were blocked out of everything if you were black then, and I think Conn Smythe didn't want to take a chance on him. So he was saying, 'I'd take him if you could turn him white.' But I still would have taken a chance on Herb Carnegie if I were Conn Smythe."

In Carnegie's autobiography, he wrote that Storey confirmed the Smythe quote in an audiotape he sent that included his recollections on his years in hockey, football, baseball and lacrosse. Carnegie quotes Storey as saying on tape, "And I remember Conn Smythe, many years ago when Herb was in his prime, saying 'I will give $10,000 to anyone who can turn Herbert Carnegie white.'"

When told that Storey said he had *read* the quote, rather than heard it, Carnegie said, "Whatever I wrote in my book is accurate. I believe I still have that tape somewhere in the house, but I wouldn't know where it is."

Carnegie said even after Smythe's apparent dismissal of his NHL aspirations, he continued to play hockey because he loved the game and believed a major-league franchise other than the Leafs would give him a tryout. With the onset of World War II, which Canada entered in 1939, Carnegie believed both he and Ossie would have a chance to enter the major league since many white players were trading hockey uniforms for military garb. But Herb Carnegie was treated no better during wartime: no call came from the NHL. Hockey barred him from the major league just as his Negro Leagues-playing brethren were kept out of Major League Baseball during World War II. The St. Louis Browns could find room during the war years for Pete Gray, a white outfielder with one arm, but Major League Baseball refused to make room for black talent. The NHL was every bit as deficient.

Carnegie said that neither the Smythe quote nor the NHL's failure to give him a tryout during wartime had entered his mind while at Rangers camp. However, the aforementioned incidents could have made it difficult for him to trust the intentions of an NHL general manager that wanted him to report to the minor leagues. Asked if he trusted Boucher, Carnegie sighed and finally offered, "I don't think it would do me any good to put into words what I thought of him."

◆ ◆ ◆

Back in Canada for the 1948–49 season, Carnegie won his third straight MVP award with Sherbrooke. He scored four goals in a playoff series to eliminate the Quebec Aces, whose player-coach was George "Punch" Imlach. Carnegie accepted Imlach's offer to jump to the Aces of the Quebec Senior League (it became the Quebec Major Hockey League in 1950), and for two full seasons starting in 1951 he teamed with and mentored Beliveau, a future Hall of Famer. Together, they would win the league championship in 1953.

"Herbie was a super hockey player, a beautiful style, a beautiful skater, a great playmaker," Beliveau said. "In those days, the younger ones learned from the older ones. I learned from Herbie."

Beliveau, a 6-foot-3, 205-pound power centre, also remembered watching Carnegie perform on The Black Aces line in the 1940s and marvelling at their cohesion, puckhandling abilities and offensive prowess. Carnegie was thirty-two when he and Beliveau became teammates, two ships passing through a hockey port. Nothing stood in the way of Beliveau becoming hockey royalty. No racial or social mores prevented a white French-Canadian from playing hockey at the highest level and winning ten Stanley Cups in eighteen full seasons. The Quebec native actually preferred to play for the hometown Aces instead of the Montreal Canadiens, with whom he spent two games in the 1950–51 season. The Canadiens acquired the thirteen-time NHL All-Star only after buying a controlling interest in the Quebec League in 1953. Beliveau signed a five-year, $105,000 contract with the Canadiens that year—Carnegie's next-to-last year in hockey. (Carnegie had twenty goals and fifty-five points for the Owen Sound Mercuries of the Ontario Senior Hockey Association in 1953–54.)

Since Carnegie ended up playing another six seasons after his invitation to Rangers camp, his professional hockey life could well have been markedly different had he taken the New Haven deal. Six solid seasons in the NHL—presuming he got a big-league promotion in the 1948–49 season and stayed there—combined with his prolific scoring and playmaking on The Black Aces line in the '40s, might have added enough sheen to his resumé to win over an eighteen-member Hall of Fame selection committee.

But to Art Dorrington, another black hockey pioneer, Carnegie's absence from the NHL register should not matter. Carnegie, he said, belongs in the Hall, and he did not need to go to New Haven to prove it:

"With the experience Herb already had at the time, he wasn't going to play in a minor-league town. He wasn't a young kid anymore. I think Herb did the right thing."

Dorrington said that even though he, like Robinson, took the deal.

◆ ◆ ◆

A 5-foot-8, 160-pounder who played centre and left wing, Dorrington left his hometown of Truro, Nova Scotia in 1950 to join an amateur team in Connecticut. It was his first foray into the U.S., and he travelled alone. During a team practice at Madison Square Garden, he caught the eye of a Rangers scout. The scout offered him a contract to play for the New York Rovers, an Eastern League team affiliated with the NHL club. Dorrington, then twenty, took the deal and waited for the Rovers to return from a road trip. And waited. And waited.

"I was in a hotel in New York City by myself for four days and I felt homesick," he said. "I got impatient so I told the Rangers that I needed to play some hockey. They arranged for me to go to Atlantic City for a weekend tryout with a team that they had a working agreement with."

Dorrington, whose best attribute was his skating speed, impressed the Atlantic City Sea Gulls enough to earn a contract with the Eastern League club. No black had ever played professional hockey in the U.S. before. Atlantic City impressed Dorrington enough that he has lived there ever since. In 1951 he had eighteen goals and thirty-four points and led the Sea Gulls to the league championship. The year would be an extremely busy one. He signed as a centre fielder with the Boston Braves' organization and played on the major league baseball club's farm teams in Watertown and Wellsville, New York.

"I didn't have one week off in '51," he said with a throaty laugh. "I went right from a hockey uniform to a baseball uniform. I ended up missing the Braves' spring training in Myrtle Beach, South Carolina because of hockey."

Dorrington was spared the indignity of the segregated hotels and restaurants in Myrtle Beach that year, but he encountered those odiously racist restrictions in most other American cities he visited in the 1950s.

"It was a shock to me to see the racism in the United States," he said. "I went to places in the Eastern League like Washington, D.C., Baltimore, Charlotte, Greensboro and the rest of the team would go into a hotel or a restaurant and I wouldn't be allowed to go in. I had to put up with the same kind of racism that Jackie Robinson put up with in baseball. The racism and the discrimination I faced in hockey was the same. Even though I had anger about it, I couldn't act on it. I had to accept things the way they were and hope that they would eventually change."

In order to let his body recuperate from the rigours of hockey, he abandoned hopes of a Major League Baseball career and focused on his favourite sport from 1952 onward. No brown-skinned man had played in the NHL yet, and he set his sights on becoming the first. In terms of quality, the Eastern League was below the American League, which was one level below the NHL. Yet it would have been possible for him to advance from the Eastern League to the AHL to the NHL. Each of the three professional leagues had only six franchises in Dorrington's day, and the NHL kept close tabs on all the promising minor leaguers.

Because of the transient nature of minor-league sports franchises, Dorrington played for six different Eastern League teams. For each he played well. He had twenty-five goals and forty-seven points for the Johnstown Jets in 1952–53; thirty goals and forty-eight points for Johnstown the following season; thirty-three goals and sixty-eight points for the Washington Lions in 1954–55; and thirty goals and sixty-one points as an aptly named Philadelphia Rambler in 1955–56.

By this time, Dorrington had begun the process of becoming a U.S. citizen, which made him eligible for the draft. His hockey career was curtailed for two years when he entered the Army in 1956, meaning an invitation he had received to try out for an AHL club that year would have to be declined. After an honourable discharge, he rejoined the Ramblers in 1958. Eleven games later, his hockey career ended.

"I was playing in Utica, New York, and I was carrying the puck up the ice when a defenseman stuck out his leg and tripped me. I broke my left leg," he said. "I needed four operations in the next two-and-a-half years. That injury ruined my hockey. I lost my speed. I didn't consider [the injury] a racial thing. I don't. I just beat a guy on a play and he stuck his leg out. Most of the Eastern League players were Canadians. We had more in common than not."

Dorrington returned to Atlantic City, where he met his wife Dorothie, where their daughter Dorrie was born, where he worked for the Atlantic County Sheriff's Department for twenty years, where he serves on the boards of a local golf club and a baseball umpires association, where he founded a youth baseball organization named after a Negro Leagues great and Hall of Famer John Henry "Pop" Lloyd, where he serves as a goodwill ambassador for the local East Coast Hockey League team called the Boardwalk Bullies, and where he founded and operates a self-named foundation devoted to providing free hockey equipment and instruction, academic guidance and social services to inner-city youth.

Once his U.S. citizenship became official in 1958, he became the first black American to play professional hockey. His Atlantic City Sea Gulls jersey No. 16 is on display at the Hockey Hall of Fame. But his dream of playing in the NHL was dashed in a freakish injury on a rink in upstate New York. Bitterness? No. Dorrington, now seventy-three, has no use for it.

"I look at it like this: if God meant for me to get to the NHL, then it would have happened," he said. "Maybe God meant for me to work with kids and try to help them become good citizens."

◆ ◆ ◆

Carnegie also has devoted a significant part of his post-hockey life to improving the lives of others, particularly children. He still loves hockey—not the men running it and certainly not the politics of it—but the game itself. He endeavoured to create a legacy to the game, a means by which people could learn hockey through the principles he considered essential. In 1955, he founded the Future Aces school, which is believed to be the first hockey school in North America. He developed a Future Aces creed—one that is taught in Toronto-area schools to this day—based on four components: attitude, cooperation, example and sportsmanship. The school included on-ice hockey instruction, with an emphasis on learning the fundamentals (skating, shooting, passing, defense, teamwork), as well as lessons in fair play, tolerance and diversity that he hoped would create a more tolerant, compassionate and colour-blind society. His Future Aces Foundation holds a fundraising golf tournament each August and awards scholarships to help financially needy students attend college. He built the Foundation while working for thirty-two years for a financial investment company, retiring as a senior executive.

"I really was a bitter person when I left hockey and I knew that I needed to do something to redirect my energies and emotions into something positive and constructive," he said. "As far as I know, no professional hockey players have come out of the Future Aces program, but I've taught countless people the fundamentals of the game. No one can tell me the program has not produced better hockey players and better and more knowledgeable hockey fans. No one can tell me the program did not contribute to the betterment of hockey or the betterment of those who took part."

Without question, Carnegie has built an impressive foundation. Now the question becomes, has he built a resumé that a committee of eighteen men will deem worthy of the Hockey Hall of Fame? There are three categories in which a person can be inducted into the Hall: player, builder and referee/linesman. A builder of the game is defined as a person with "coaching, managerial or executive ability," one whose "sportsmanship and character" contributed to the betterment of his organization in particular or hockey in general. Those advocating the induction of Carnegie hope the selection committee will give more merit to his humanitarian efforts than it gave in 2000 to his hockey-playing credentials. They hope the committee will be as noble-minded as Marvel Comics, which saw fit to immortalize Carnegie in a Spiderman comic book in the 1990s.

The campaign to enshrine Carnegie as a player was launched by Richard Lord, the first black to play college hockey in the U.S. He captained the 1949–50 Michigan State Spartans. Now an immigration court judge in Montreal, Lord advocated Carnegie's candidacy the way any other citizen could have: he wrote letters to the Hall of Fame selection committee. A letter along with supporting materials such as newspaper clippings can be sent to any of the eighteen members. The members' names and biographies can be found on the Hockey Hall of Fame Web site (www.hhof.com). Nominations to the committee must be made by March of each year. The letter and supporting materials are shared among all committee members who then are expected to research the merits of a candidate on their own. At a closed-door meeting (the 2003 meeting took place June 11), a candidate's qualifications are discussed and debated before a vote is taken by secret ballot. For a person to be enshrined, he must receive at least fourteen of the eighteen votes from the selection committee. The new members are announced on the day of the voting and the enshrinement takes place in November.

"I can tell you Herb Carnegie's name has been up for consideration before, but I can't chat about whatever reservations have been discussed in the meetings," said Hall of Fame president William C. Hay, who does not have a vote on the selection committee. "What is said in those meetings is confidential. I would never discuss publicly what has been said about a candidate at a committee meeting. That's the one protection area that we allow our selection committee. It's all done in confidence and that's the reason we're able to get each and every member of the selection committee speaking so freely at the meeting."

Lord's campaign for Carnegie earned an advocate on the selection committee in long-time *Toronto Star* sports editor Jim Proudfoot. But Proudfoot suffered a stroke before the June 2000 meeting and was unable to argue Carnegie's merits before the full committee. Proudfoot resigned from the committee for health reasons, and died in May 2002. No other member of the selection committee has taken up the cause for Carnegie in the player category since his candidacy was defeated in 2000.

"Unfortunately, I don't have the opportunity to be in the board room to give a reasonable response to whatever is being said about me," Carnegie said. "I wish I could be a fly on the wall and hear what they are saying about me."

In all likelihood, it would burn his ears. For starters, there is the aforementioned comment from Francis, the former NHL goalie, coach and general manager, about Carnegie needing to have played "in a better category of hockey" than semi-pro leagues and the Quebec Senior League because "that's not the NHL." Francis added, "I don't think there was any part of him not being able to play in the NHL because of his colour." Then there is a comment from a March 2001 *Toronto Star* column quoting selection committee chairman Jim Gregory on how racism did not keep Carnegie out of the NHL: "I did some investigation when I was younger and what I found out was that it [racism] didn't exist." Has the selection committee concluded Carnegie must have left the Rangers camp in 1948 rather than report to the New Haven team because he himself had doubts as to whether he could have played his way into the NHL? Only the fly on the wall Carnegie wished himself to be on voting day could know for sure. But what about the NHL's failure to give Carnegie a tryout prior to 1948, especially during the war years when jobs were available? Is the committee suggesting racism did not exist then?

"The Hall of Fame committee people are without heart," Carnegie said. "They knew of the comments that were made by "The Major" [Smythe] and they fell in line. The Smythe comments strongly indicate that I was good enough to play in the NHL. He said he'd give any man $10,000 if he could turn me white. His comment just cut me off at the knee."

Perhaps Carnegie would stand a better chance for induction if more people who actually saw him play could vote. "If I had a Hall of Fame vote, Herb Carnegie would get my vote tomorrow," said Storey, the Hall of Fame referee. Storey is not on the selection committee, which includes a mix of former players and coaches, team executives, media members and one former referee.

◆ ◆ ◆

Hall of Famers Mahovlich and Beliveau are not selection committee members either, but they have influential voices. Mahovlich serves in the Canadian Senate. Appointed by the Prime Minister, his term runs until 2012. Mahovlich and Beliveau admit to having been greatly influenced by Carnegie's play during their formative years. Has either man attempted to lobby the selection committee on Carnegie's behalf?

"I've tried to get a number of players elected," said Mahovlich, who would not name any. "I write a few letters from time to time. However, the decision-making is up to the [selection committee]. If I can influence them, I'll try. But I don't have a say in who gets in."

In September 2002, Mahovlich awarded Carnegie a Queen's Jubilee Medal, one of the highest civilian honours bestowed in Canada. Carnegie was among 2,080 citizens to be so honoured, as each of Canada's 104 Senators selected twenty recipients.

"Herb Carnegie should not go away forgotten," Senator Mahovlich said. "People should know he made a great contribution to the game of hockey. I think he should be in the Hall of Fame."

Why isn't he?

"He never played in the NHL and I think it's about playing in the NHL," Mahovlich said.

The most prominent Hall of Fame player never to have appeared in the NHL or its predecessor, the National Hockey Association, is Vladislav Tretiak, the goaltender from the former Soviet Union in the 1970s and '80s. The Cold War kept the renowned Tretiak out of hockey's major league. A racial cold war kept Carnegie from getting an invite to an NHL camp before his late twenties, and then only after Robinson had broken the colour barrier in baseball.

Beliveau took a Socratic stance, providing more questions than answers, in discussing the Hall of Fame prospects of his former Quebec Aces teammate. "Should Herbie be in? As a player? As a builder? Is it possible they cannot decide which one? Was his colour the reason the Rangers did not give him an NHL contract? I don't know. When I played with Herbie he seemed good enough to play in the NHL. But I would say in the Quebec League, he had time to look around and set up the plays. In the NHL, the league was much faster and he would not have had as much time to look around. I know there was some writing that he was too small, but I thought he was a very good hockey player."

Beliveau, an NHL legend, would have to declare Carnegie a *great* player, not merely a very good one, to put any heat on the Hall's selection committee. Not even in his foreword to Carnegie's 1997 autobiography did Beliveau advocate him as a Hall of Fame player.

Grant Fuhr, the goaltender on the dynastic Edmonton Oilers teams in the 1980s, became the first black Hall of Famer in 2003. Fuhr said he would be representing not only himself but also each of his progenitors, including Carnegie, as a Hall of Fame member—a statement Carnegie called "very kind." A selection in the builder category would appear to be Carnegie's best hope for enshrinement in the Hall. It did not happen in 2003. But other prestigious honours have not eluded him. In 2002, the year he received the Queen's Jubilee Medal, the former North York Centennial Arena was renamed the Herbert H. Carnegie Centennial Arena. The year before, he was inducted into the Canadian Sports Hall of Fame.

Breaking the Ice

The Hockey Hall of Fame has always paled in comparison to family in the Carnegie household. So Herb Carnegie, his hair made thin and grey, his body brittle by age, chuckles at the possibility that a grandson, eighteen-year-old Rane Carnegie, could someday skate in an NHL game. In the first round of the 2001 junior league draft, the Belleville Bulls of the Ontario League selected Rane Carnegie. He is a centre, like his grandfather, with soft hands and fine passing skills, also like his grandfather. "I've been in the rink a couple of times, but I have not seen him play," Herb Carnegie said. "That's a shame. I regret that I can't see him. How I wish I could see Rane play."

Glaucoma, which has deprived him of the joy of watching a grandson shine on a hockey rink, is the only regret Carnegie will give voice to these days. Not being able to see Rane's stride, his passing, puckhandling, slapshot and forechecking, to compare those skills to his own, is the regret. The glaucoma? Carnegie has found a silver lining even in that.

"Now, I have to be colour-blind," he said. "I only wish more people were."

Mike Marson, the NHL's second black player, certainly would have wished for the same.

Left wing Mike Marson became the National Hockey League's second black player—and its first in thirteen years—when he debuted with the expansion Washington Capitals in 1974.
London Life-Portnoy/Hockey Hall of Fame

Wrong Place, Wrong Time

If the sight of a black man such as Jarome Iginla or the dreadlocks-wearing Anson Carter on a hockey rink still raises eyebrows, just imagine what it was like three decades ago when people saw Michael Robert Marson. While still in his teens, Marson hit the ice as a member of one of the worst teams in NHL history and immediately stunned people. He was the second black player the NHL had ever seen, yet he was unlike anyone the league had ever seen. Everything about him was different, from the black Fu Manchu mustache and mutton chops to the four-inch Afro squeezed into a hockey helmet, to the rapidity with which he dropped his gloves and traded punches with opposing players, to his uncompromising decision to date and eventually marry a white woman.

Marson looked and lived this way in the mid-1970s, the era of "Black Power" and widespread civil unrest in America's major urban areas, including the area his team represented, Washington, D.C. Marson came along at a time when a black man's choice of hairstyle became a political statement, as did his preference in female companionship. He came of age at a time when an interracial marriage left him vulnerable to attack from both sides of a virulent racial divide. In Landover, Maryland., the suburban community in which his team played hockey—his first foray south of the Mason-Dixie line—he caught hell from those offended by the temerity of a black man loving a white woman. For this, he said, he received death threats. And the predominantly black community in Washington, America's capital, provided him no refuge because his decision to "cross over to the other side" made him "a traitor to the race." He came along at a time when blacks in all walks of life had freed themselves of the notion of turning the other cheek in the face of racial oppression. To turn the other cheek, they had learned, meant giving one's enemy another target to hit.

Marson fought early in his NHL career, and fought often. There was, in his mind, no shortage of legitimate reasons to fight. He played decades before hockey's major league ever dreamed of requiring mandatory diversity training sessions for every team to try to ease the transition of non-white Canadian men into the sport, and decades before anyone could have envisioned the necessity of a diversity task force to try to expand the talent pool from which future players would spring. Canadian men comprised 95% of NHL players in 1971. Three years later, when Marson debuted, he was the league's only Canadian man who was black.

An on-ice racial slur then did not merit severe disciplinary action from the league in the form of a hefty fine and suspension. When Marson first hit the NHL ice, taunts of "nigger," "monkey," "coon" and "spear-chucker" were just part of the cacophonous soundtrack that accompanied his games. Abuse from the other team's bench or the paying customers just came with the territory. Marson would view his attempt to negotiate his way through the NHL without any team- or league-mandated support system as being akin to walking blindly through a minefield. When he joined the NHL, no other player had to try to concentrate on the next faceoff or an opposing defense or the best way to beat a goalie to the short side while also having his ears singed by an insulting ditty:

"Marson's little baby loves shortnin', shortnin'
Marson's little baby loves shortnin' bread…"

That Marson failed to reach his potential as a hockey player was not at all surprising considering the force of the storm into which he skated for six professional seasons.

"I was the first contemporary black hockey player, so everywhere I went it was very novel and I felt like a target," he said. "The same people who were yelling, 'Niggers, go home!' to the black kids being bused to school in places like Boston were going to our games at night. Those people were racists to begin with and they would feel frustrated because they couldn't keep the government from sending black kids to school with their kids, so what did they do at the games? They let off steam yelling 'nigger' and every other name in the book at me."

Marson told this anecdote from three decades ago while sitting in a Thai restaurant in northern Toronto, not far from the bus depot where he works an early morning-to-afternoon shift. That's right, a bus depot. The same man who scored goals so prolifically in junior hockey that an NHL team drafted him three slots ahead of future Hall of Fame centre Bryan Trottier, the same man who tuned out racist slurs at Boston Garden and shared Star of the Game honours with legends Bobby Orr and Phil Esposito now had more in common with mythical working stiff Ralph Kramden.

Marson admits to harbouring some bitterness about the detour his life has taken. He was not the first black NHL player. That distinction belongs to Willie O'Ree, who debuted in 1958. But Marson was expected to be the NHL's first black *star*. It did not happen, despite a promising rookie season during which he scored sixteen goals for the Washington Capitals as a teenager. He would score just eight more goals in the next five NHL seasons. He would play more games in the minor leagues in those five seasons than in the NHL. After playing three games for the Los Angeles Kings in the 1979–80 season, he chose to retire at age twenty-five from the sport he once loved rather than accept another demotion to the minors. After what he had been through, it made no sense to endure another year of long bus rides from one nondescript minor-league town to another just to perform in undersized arenas before mean-spirited fans who got their jollies from raining verbal abuse, chicken bones and balls of cotton at the black man on skates.

"Looking back, there's some bitterness only because I feel that any mistakes that were made could have been avoided," he said evenly. "I felt that pro hockey was thirty or forty years behind on quite a few issues, particularly player development. For instance, a rookie should never go from the juniors [where players are still in their teens] straight to the National Hockey League without taking a course in life management skills, without letting a kid know, 'Hey, these are the kinds of people you're going to be dealing with in some of the places you'll be playing in. Not everybody you meet is going to look like or act like the people from your hometown. Not everybody is going to be sensitive to the things you say. In the evenings, this is the type of woman who is going to try to seduce you, and she could be linked to somebody who's trying to elicit information from you for betting purposes and your association with those people could be used against you.'"

Marson said shortly after he met with NHL executives in New York a decade ago the league implemented punitive measures against on-ice acts of racism. Racial slurs that once went unpunished now merit a ten-minute misconduct penalty as well as a fine and suspension. Good news for today's players, but decades too late for Marson.

That Marson felt wholly unprepared for the cauldron into which he entered in the 1970s is not something he blames solely on others. He also shoulders some blame.

"For me, the biggest problem was that I was naïve," he said with a shrug. "I watched the assassinations of Martin Luther King and the Kennedys in the sixties, as everybody did. But I believed coming through the hippie era in the sixties and seventies that the world was a better place and people had evolved to where you could love your fellow man and woman regardless of race, creed or colour. I mean, I really believed that. I believed that to the point of being *radically naïve*. That's what I call it: radical naïveté.

"For me, it seemed normal to be a hockey player. I grew up in Canada. I played hockey. A black hockey player? So what? But I found out that people looked at me like I was a martian. Not Mike Marson. Mike *Martian*. Because I was a black hockey player."

◆ ◆ ◆

Marson's tone was indignant. The expansive Afro he wore a quarter-century ago has given way to a clean-shaven pate. Despite a hockey life that included slugfests with Philadelphia's "Broad Street Bullies" and Boston's "Big Bad Bruins" and assorted other hired hands from the NHL and the minor leagues, his caramel skin is smooth and unmarked. At 5-foot-9 and 250 pounds, some fifty pounds heavier than in his playing days, he is as hard to move as a vending machine. Only after pouring himself another cup of green tea did he continue to reminisce.

"It seemed normal to me to be a high draft pick by the NHL because I had done so well in the juniors. It seemed normal to me to work so hard in the off-season because now I was playing against the best players in the world. I was the fourth player drafted going into junior hockey and no other junior league had drafted a black athlete that high before I went to the Ontario [Major Junior] Hockey League when I was sixteen. In that league, I played against guys who went to the NHL. But those guys didn't have to deal with the stuff I had to deal with. Those guys had the luxury to just play the game. I was never allowed to just play the game."

Marson watches the NHL today when time allows, and he wishes he had been afforded the same freedom of athletic expression given to today's black players. The Iginlas. The Carters. The Kevin Weekeses. While those players are not exactly performing in Shangri-La, they are not being subjected to racist sing-alongs from spectators, as Marson was. They are not being ostracized by teammates and club management because of the women they choose to love, as Marson was. They do not perform with a figurative bull's eye on their backs, as Marson did.

If a black player had to sacrifice his professional career to make the ice smoother for those of his race who followed, then Marson was the one. If ever an athlete seemed hopelessly ahead of his time, Marson, a first-round draft pick of the expansion Washington Capitals, was the one.

◆ ◆ ◆

Marson's days as a trailblazer actually began at birth, as the newest member of the first black family in the Toronto suburb of Scarborough. Born July 24, 1955, he was the first of Sidney and Jacqueline Marson's five children. Sidney Marson, a printer and the son of Jamaican immigrants, saw the move to Scarborough as part of the upward mobility his family had worked hard for and deserved. Scarborough today has a large, vibrant and thriving black community, which includes the parents of Anson Carter and Kevin Weekes.

Though a nonconformist in his adult life, Marson followed in childhood the path of other Scarborough boys: he played hockey and he dated white girls. The former activity would make him a star in his hometown; the latter would expose him to scorn. But the one thing he made clear in those days was hockey came first.

"I had a pair of toy skates when I was a baby boy, and whenever I needed real skates I got them," he said. "My parents never thought it was odd for me to be playing hockey. In Europe and South America, you play soccer with your friends; in Canada, you play hockey with your friends. That's it."

A bullish left wing, Marson emerged as an accomplished scorer and a fiery competitor for the Sudbury Wolves, the junior team he captained. Never before had the Wolves had a black captain. Never before had a black player in his league been targeted for professional stardom. At age seventeen, he had thirty-three points and 117 penalty minutes in fifty-seven games. The next year, he erupted for ninety-four points (thirty-five goals and fifty-nine assists) in sixty-nine games. He also picked up 146 penalty minutes and a reputation as a one-punch knockout artist, a Rocky Marciano on skates.

"I was right in that top 3% of players that you try to stay in to be a high NHL draft pick," he said, pouring himself another cup of green tea. "I was in that group all the way through the juniors and to stay in that group is difficult, especially for a person of colour, because there's often that incestuous hierarchy in the juniors, where a team brings in some player who's somebody's cousin or who looks like somebody's cousin, and suddenly that guy is getting more ice time at your expense."

Marson considered himself ready for the NHL at eighteen, and a rule change made sure he would get a chance to prove it. Eighteen-year-olds had not been eligible for the draft before 1974. But the NHL dropped the age of eligibility down from nineteen to try to stem the flow of hockey talent to the upstart World Hockey Association. The WHA had been drafting eighteen-year-olds since its inception in 1972, and raiding the NHL for veteran stars like Bobby Hull, Gerry Cheevers and Bernie

Parent. The NHL did not want to lose a player as promising as Marson, but would he have been better served in the juniors?

"I think so, yes," said Milt Schmidt, who, as general manager of the Capitals, drafted Marson. But Schmidt felt he had no other choice. "We were an expansion team, so we were short on material," the Hockey Hall of Famer said. "I had to take players that probably would have lasted a little longer in the NHL if they had another year of seasoning in the juniors. But if I hadn't drafted Mike, I probably would have lost him to a WHA team."

The Capitals were a typical expansion team in major professional sports, a motley crew of over-the-hill veterans and players with bad contracts, bad injuries and bad attitudes. Sprinkled among the also-rans were kids like Marson and defenseman Greg Joly, the first overall pick in the 1974 draft, who were thrown into the deep water too soon and told to sink or swim. Joly played nine seasons for the Capitals and Detroit Red Wings, but never fulfilled his potential for stardom. Neither, of course, did Marson.

"Unfortunately, Mike got rushed to the NHL," said Tony McKegney, the NHL's fourth black who played from 1978–91. "There was no support system in place for him as a young player, and especially as a young black player, and it kind of took its toll on him."

Washington drafted Marson with the nineteenth pick, three slots ahead of Trottier, who would have a Hall of Fame career with the New York Islanders and Pittsburgh Penguins. Just to make sure Marson would not spurn the NHL and join the WHA, the Capitals offered him a five-year contract worth $500,000. He signed it without hesitation. The $100,000 yearly salary was more than twice as much as many NHL veterans were making at the time. In hockey parlance, Marson had become a "bonus baby," an unproven talent whose high salary resulted from the intense competition for players between rival leagues. The hefty contract would sow seeds of resentment among his new teammates and, quite surprisingly to Marson, among his friends back in Scarborough.

"It bothered them that I had made it," he said. "They wondered why I was still talking to them. But friends should be friends forever, whether you wind up playing major-league hockey or digging a ditch."

Upon signing with Washington, Marson found that things rarely turned out as expected. He said he had encountered no problems with the parents of his white girlfriend, Patricia, whom he had met in a furniture store, until the young couple talked about marriage. Once talk of a wedding ensued, Marson found himself cast in the Sidney Poitier role in *Guess Who's Coming to Dinner?*

When Mike and Patricia relocated to suburban Maryland before the marriage and his first pro season, he was in no condition to play hockey.

"An incredible amount of money came our way," she said, referring to Marson's contract, "and we had no self-discipline. We lived high on the hog and didn't give two hoots about hockey. We cared more about parties. There was no self-discipline."

◆ ◆ ◆

The Hockey News, the international weekly, heralded Marson's pro debut with an ironically titled cover story, "Mike Marson First Black to Crack in 15 Years." Actually, Marson would become the NHL's first black in thirteen years, since O'Ree played his final game with Boston in 1961. Marson reported to Capitals' camp twenty-two pounds heavier than his ideal playing weight of 200. Schmidt, the general manager, said Marson would have opened the season in the juniors (although still under contract to the Capitals) had he not lost the excess weight and scored a hat trick in an exhibition game against Detroit. He rounded himself into shape for the 1974–75 season, but weighty issues dogged him throughout his career.

Said Bill Riley, the NHL's third black and Marson's Capitals teammate for parts of four seasons: "When Tom McVie coached the team [from 1975–78], he used to have a 'Fat Squad' for guys he would make practice harder because they needed to lose weight. Mike had to spend a lot of time on the 'Fat Squad.'"

Still, Marson had an encouraging rookie season—on the ice. With sixteen goals and twelve assists for twenty-eight points, he was Washington's third-leading scorer. Riley, who played with Marson on December 26, 1974—marking the first time in NHL history two blacks appeared in the same game—regarded him as a player of enormous potential. "Mike was built like a Brahma bull; he was a very, very powerful player," he said. "I called him 'Marciano' because he wasn't tall but he could hit like a heavyweight. And he was a great skater. He skated with such power. Man, he was so strong."

But the Capitals were anemic. Each NHL team played eighty games in the 1974–75 season, and the Capitals won eight, lost sixty-seven and tied five. They set dubious league records for fewest wins, most defeats, most consecutive defeats (seventeen) and most goals allowed (446). As if the deluge of losses was not dispiriting enough for Marson, he encountered antagonism and ridicule from his own teammates and indifference from team officials. The internal problems, he said, stemmed from lingering resentment over his contract and the insensitivity of white players who had never had a black teammate.

"There were guys on the team who thought it was funny to call me 'Uncle Ben,'" he said, declining to name names. "You know, humour is in the moment. But when you're constantly hearing insults and put-downs, then whatever humour there was loses its value. And you really resent it. I remember times when we used to pre-board an aircraft, and this was before teams started to charter their own flights, and a joke would be made, 'The black guy's not with us. We don't know him.' And the airline people would hassle me, make me take out my I.D. because they didn't believe a black man would normally be with all these white guys. The other guys would laugh, but I didn't find anything humourous about that at all. To me, I didn't enjoy being in a social environment with the other players. But in the interest of political correctness, I guess, everybody in the organization tried to pretend that I was the same as everybody else."

Schmidt, now eighty-five, found it surprising to hear that Marson felt alienated from his teammates.

"I don't know if he felt uncomfortable, and if he did he never mentioned anything like that to me," he said. "He was very well-liked by his teammates and there was no reason in the world he should have felt uncomfortable among his own players."

Told of Schmidt's comments, Marson leaned back in his chair at the Thai restaurant, threatening the stability of its wooden back legs, and emitted a loud sigh. "That's his opinion," he said finally. "Sometimes you don't know something because you don't want to know something." He then recalled another incident from his rookie season. The Capitals were filming television commercials to introduce players from the expansion team to the local community, and Marson was among those chosen to appear in the ads. This prompted Dave Kryskow, a journeyman who played for four teams in five NHL seasons, to say, 'If I get my face painted, will you pick me?'"

In another episode, a *Washington Post* reporter who had first sought out Marson after a game in Vancouver in which the player had been rendered unconscious by a stiff check was later upbraided by Capitals goalie Michel Belhumeur: "Why'd you run right to Marson? Was he the star of the game?"

Said Marson: "I always thought other people made far too much of my race when I played. I remember one night when we got destroyed in Boston, and the first thing the press did when we let them into the dressing room was crowd around me and ask me what it's like to be a black hockey player. This happened every time, in every city we played in, whether we won, lost or tied. We weren't winning many games, so the other guys weren't getting much attention. The press all wanted to talk to me. Let's just say that didn't help me in the dressing room."

Media accounts of Capitals' games in such NHL cities as New York, Boston, Pittsburgh, Detroit and Chicago included references to racial taunts from spectators directed at Marson and Riley.

"Man, we took a lot of abuse from the fans," Riley said. "But in the NHL, the stuff Michael had to deal with as a kid kind of destroyed him. We got called every dirty name in the book, and we were getting high-sticked and slashed and speared on the ice. We would both fight back, but those things just cut Michael's heart out. I mean, I loved Michael like a brother. I'd talk to him back then: 'Keep your head up.' 'Don't let 'em get to you.' But I'm five years older, so I think I could handle the abuse a lot better than he could as a kid. And he had to deal with things I didn't have to deal with."

Things like having the lug nuts on his tires loosened often enough to have to check all four tires every time he drove. Things like death threats. Marson's life was threatened before a game against the Flyers at The Spectrum in Philadelphia. He said when a Capitals' official took him aside before the game he assumed he had been demoted to the minors or there had been some sort of family problem back in Scarborough. Instead, he was told about the telephone threat.

"During the game, guys weren't sitting too close to me," he said with a faint smile. "Usually the linemates sit together on the bench—the left wing, the centre, the right wing—because we go on the ice together and come off together. But my teammates kind of made a joke out of it: 'Don't sit too close to that kid.' 'I'm not going out with you, kid.' It was that kind of insensitive humour that I was dealing with all the time in the NHL. When you have things like that taking place, they begin to mess up your mind. Now, I wasn't just playing against every opposing winger. I was playing against a sharpshooter who could be sitting in the stands at any one of my games."

Marson said he also got death threats by telephone to his hotel room and even to his condominium in Silver Springs, Maryland. He also got death threats by mail, including one he has kept for nearly thirty years, a letter with words from various sources pieced together to deliver a chilling message:

YOU'RE **skating** on *thin* **ICE BLACK** BOY…the **NIGGER** *is GOING* to **DIE** *if it* thinks **it** BELONGS in *a* **WHITE MAN'S** GAME.

"There was just so much garbage I had to deal with that I just wasn't used to," Marson said. "The accumulation of all that garbage just made me uneasy. Uncomfortable all the time. How can you perform at your best as a professional athlete if you're uncomfortable all the time? You can't. It's impossible. I was dealing with so much stuff that it's hard to articulate it.

"After one game, Patty and I went to a convenience store in Silver Springs. It was about 11 o'clock and we were getting milk and chips and pop, things like that. In the parking lot, two guys pulled up beside us in a van. I was driving my 1961 Jaguar Mark II: British racing green, cashmere ceiling. A nice car, eh? I left my wife in the car while I went in to get the stuff. As I came out, I could see that somebody had spit all over the car. And I could see terror all over my wife's face. These guys were calling her "nigger lover." So me and these two guys start talking. It wasn't a well-lit area. Not any other black people around. But I've got to deal with this issue and people had started gathering around. Anyway, the police show up and the situation only escalated because who were they looking at as the perpetrator? You know they're thinking, 'This black guy must have done something.' The police run a check on both vehicles and they found out I play for the Capitals and they know the Capitals' director of security is the head of the Maryland state troopers. One officer pulls me aside and he's very apologetic: 'We didn't know you play for the Caps.' And he tells me it's up to me to determine what happens to those two guys. He tells me I'm the judge and jury! I made the guys apologize to my wife and wipe the spit off my car with their jackets. That ended it, but it was very, very stressful. Stuff like that just wears on you. I remember going on vacation to Aruba with Patty and customs officers were going to strip search me because they didn't believe I was a hockey player. Black hockey player? No way. No such thing. That's what they said while interrogating me. The longer I played pro hockey the more I realized that I couldn't possibly live like a free man. People looked at me like I was a freak!"

Or a prized quarry. Marson remembered hearing from other players that some teams would award a bounty to anybody who could injure or cut him in a game. "Anybody who'd speak to me on the subject said, 'I'm going to tell you something, kid, but if I'm asked about it by the press or the league I'm going to deny it.' That was gutless. It's better they don't tell you there's a bounty on your head than to have you thinking about it the whole game." He said that whenever he mentioned a pay-for-pain bounty to Capitals' management or league officials, nothing was done about it.

Schmidt, the Capitals coach from March 23, 1975 to December 29, 1975 and general manager from their 1974 debut until December 29, 1975, said he never had a conversation with Marson about a bounty.

"If anything like a bounty ever happened to him, well, he kept it to himself," he said. "He didn't say anything to me about it. I wish he had because I would have told him, 'Hey, there's two sides to every street. Just go along as best as you possibly can. But don't take anything out there. If you have to defend yourself, do it.'"

Marson tried. NHL fans regarded him as one of the game's strongest fighters. But he entered the league not to become a featured performer on hockey-fight videos sold via the Internet. He expected to become a star, or at least an effective all-around player. But aside from flashes of excellence in his rookie year, he fell short. The combined weight of the indignities he suffered on and off the ice simply wore him down. In a 1977 exhibition game in Detroit, Red Wings forward Dennis Hextall broke his stick across Marson's chest. By then it was Marson's fourth pro season and the Capitals were phasing him out, yet he didn't know it. He now considers the *coup de grace* of his stint in Washington an interview his wife gave *The Washington Post* in 1976.

Gripes a hockey player holds against the team that signs his paycheque occasionally are relayed through the media. But more often than not, the player keeps his discontent cloistered within the team's dressing room. "Don't air your dirty laundry in public" is the way players, coaches and general managers sum up this code of silence. And since hockey men feel this way, they are usually circumspect about making sure wives, girlfriends and others of personal significance keep the lid on the hamper as well. Hence, it had to be stunning for the Capitals to see on the front page of *The Washington Post*'s sports section on January 17, 1976 a full airing of filthy, reeky laundry from inside the organization courtesy of Marson's wife.

"The overall attitude is bad. There is dissension among the wives and dissension on the team and I've got nothing to hide," said the woman Mike Marson called Patty, although the article referred to her as Dawne, her middle name. "I think the focal point of my unhappiness is that I know Michael is good and he's not being given a chance. I'm very discouraged, very peeved and I've spoken with [Capitals president] Peter O'Malley about my feelings. If you've grown up like we had in Toronto, completely involved in hockey, to come into the NHL and find false and empty promises is sad."

Responding to Patricia Marson's comments, Coach Tom McVie told the *Post*, "They shouldn't let the wives in the rink, and if they do they ought to put one in each section."

In the article, Patricia Marson also said the couple had contacted a lawyer in Toronto to try to determine whether Mike Marson's reduced ice time in his second season was "a racial thing, a conscious decision to rile up black fans in Washington to come out and support Michael." How any attorney could possibly prove such an assumption she did not explain in the story. But while *Post* readers must have had breakfast table snickers over the article, the Capitals were not amused. Marson remembers being in Buffalo for a game when he heard about his wife's rant.

"The guys showed me the paper and I was like, 'Oh, my God,'" he said, laughing. "That article pretty much put the biscuit in the basket for me. It really ended things for me in Washington. She told me she didn't say the things that were in the article. But I don't doubt that she felt strongly about whatever she said. And you just don't say the kinds of things she was quoted as saying in public. You just don't. The organization felt like they couldn't trust me after that. Whether the article was done to destroy me as a person, to put pressure on my career, to put pressure on my marriage, I don't know. But it was done to disrupt. At the time the team was on a losing streak, and [the article] just brought a lot of heat down on me. It caused a lot of trouble."

Marson spent more time in the minor leagues than in an NHL uniform after the *Post* article. He played a career-best seventy-six NHL games as a rookie. In his next five seasons, he played in the NHL for fifty-seven, ten, forty-six, four and three games respectively. From 1976–80, his final four pro seasons, he played two hundred eighteen minor-league games and sixty-three NHL games. The Capitals said Marson had defensive deficiencies and had lost confidence in himself.

"Quite often when you draft a player you expect him to improve with the better company that he's in," Schmidt said. "However, while Mike never lost his skating skills, he lost a little bit of his thoughts about playing with better company. He just didn't think fast enough."

◆ ◆ ◆

He just didn't think fast enough. Steam emanating from a freshly brewed pot of herbal tea at the Thai restaurant was weak compared to the steam seeping from the collar of Marson's white cotton warm-up jacket after he heard those words. Words that cut deeply. Words that he said affirmed his contention that he and Capitals management had been on completely different wavelengths during his career. Words that impugned his intelligence in the same manner white NFL coaches and general managers used in trying to justify the exclusion of blacks from the quarterback position, or white baseball general managers used in explaining the paucity of black field managers: they just lack the necessities, they just don't think fast enough.

While with the Capitals, Marson had taken courses at the University of Maryland rather than join teammates in what he derisively called "chicken wing-eating, beer-drinking, dart-throwing" sessions. For Marson, who as a teenager read books on the philosophies of leaders as diverse as Mao, Gandhi, Dr. Martin Luther King Jr. and Black Panther Eldridge Cleaver, hearing the line 'He just didn't think fast enough' resurrected the pain of a pro hockey career that he considered sabotaged from the outset.

"First of all, I never played with the 'better company' he's talking about," Marson said. "I played for the Washington Capitals. I played on some of the worst teams in the history of the league, and *nobody* looked good in that company, believe me."

The numbers don't lie. The Capitals had a combined record of eighty-four wins, 258 losses and fifty-eight ties in their first five seasons.

"What happened to me in the NHL was there was so much alienation that took place that I felt discontented. I lost my comfort zone, which every athlete needs to excel. When you lose your comfort zone, your play starts to diminish and maybe you start to spend too much time by yourself. It's easy to fall into a drinking pattern. And it's easy for that to become not a positive thing, but a negative thing, almost like an escape."

Marson admits he developed a drinking problem as his dreams of stardom died. "What I would say is there was a large amount of depression that took me down avenues where ordinarily I would not have gone. It was all because of the continuous barrage I faced in terms of how I was perceived. I saw myself as a hockey player. Everybody else saw me as *different*. Everywhere I went I was different. It was like being a sideshow, a freak show. A black hockey player. I might as well have been the first in the NHL because people acted like they couldn't imagine such a thing."

The Capitals gave up on Marson on June 9, 1979, trading the former "bonus baby" to the Los Angeles Kings for another left wing named Steve Clippingdale. Clippingdale played only three games for Washington. After Marson went scoreless in three games with the Kings and recorded fifteen points (seven goals, eight assists) in fifty-eight games for the minor-league Binghamton Dusters, he left hockey in 1980.

"Instead of working with Michael, the Capitals basically wrote him off," Riley said. "I know he was hurt by it."

◆ ◆ ◆

In athletic retirement at the age of twenty-five, Marson faced the question, "What will you do with the rest of your life?" He returned to Toronto, where he could have attended college. Instead, he applied for positions with the fire and police departments. That only exacerbated his pain.

"In those days, they weren't hiring minorities," he said. "It wasn't a written policy, but that's just the way it was. All I knew how to do was play hockey, but the politics of the sport made hockey too disillusioning. I wasn't going back there."

When Marson applied for a job driving a bus for the Toronto Transit Commission, he found his hockey background to be an asset because his first supervisor was a big fan. The green Jaguar Mark II with the cashmere ceiling was long gone, as was the prestige of being an NHL player in hockey-crazed Canada. Marson, married and the father of four, had become just another working guy. His outward appearance would change as completely as his outlook: Once a strapping 200-pounder, he ballooned to as much as 270 pounds and shaved every hair off his head. Whether he had altered his appearance so dramatically as to dissuade passengers from asking, "Hey, didn't you use to play in the NHL?" he would not say. But people sometimes recognized him anyway. He may be the only bus driver in Canada ever asked to sign an autograph. Still, alpine skiers have rarely faced a downward slope quite like the one that charted his working life.

"When you've been a hockey star and you've travelled all over the world and you've dined at the same restaurants as Henry Kissinger and heads of state and now you're getting up at three in the morning and you're carrying a change box onto a bus and you're driving people to work, and you're being spit on by people who don't have enough change and you can't let 'em ride, you start asking yourself a whole lot of questions. Like, what the fuck did I do to get here? What did I do to deserve this? Man, there really is a hell."

Marson punctuated his soliloquy with a full-throated laugh, one belonging to a man no longer consumed by the bitterness of an unfulfilled hockey career. He is today a man of forty-eight years who possesses the inner peace and sense of accomplishment that eluded him as a sports star. He found contentment, he said, in a most unusual place, in a most unusual way.

◆ ◆ ◆

The decade of the nineties brought profound changes to Marson's life. He divorced his wife of twenty years and married a black woman named Michelle and fathered his fifth child. He willed himself to shun alcohol and the nightclub scene. He began jogging regularly. On one such morning run through a Toronto park he met an old acquaintance from Scarborough, Gary Williams, who used to get bullied as a kid.

"Now he was a Canadian karate champion," Marson said, "and he was with his instructor. The instructor said to me, 'You're very strong. You should do more than run. You should train.' When you train in karate, I found out, you get your ribs broken, your fingers and toes broken, your nose broken. It's no joke. But what's that saying? That which doesn't kill you makes you stronger? It's that way with martial arts. It's made me stronger, in every way possible."

Marson has become a fifth-degree black belt and the developer of a style of self-defense called Mars-Zen-Do. The style incorporates hard and fast straight-line punches and powerful low kicks. He teaches the technique in Toronto-area fitness centres, and professional athletes are among his clientele. He has taught Rick Nash of the Columbus Blue Jackets, the number one pick in the 2002 NHL draft. Although Marson has high hopes for his martial arts business, he has not quit his day job. He still drives a bus and still satisfies the occasional autograph-seeker who remembers him on the ice in the seventies.

When Marson remembers himself on the ice of Washington's Capital Centre, the Montreal Forum, Maple Leaf Gardens and other NHL venues, he sees a vigorous and hard-charging player with speed and a blistering shot, but one who had neither the inner tranquility and discipline nor a league-authorized support system to help him endure the death threats, hate mail, racial slurs, catcalls, bounties and other pressures unique to the NHL's second black player. Were it possible to turn back the clock and unite Marson the self-possessed martial artist with Marson the teenaged talent, the result could well have been an athlete who stared down adversity as well as the NHL's first black player.

Regarded as "the Jackie Robinson of hockey," Willie O'Ree broke the NHL's colour barrier as a Boston Bruins left wing in 1958.
Imperial Oil-Turofsky/Hockey Hall of Fame

Unstoppable

Six decades after he acquired a reputation as one of the fastest skaters his sport had ever seen, Willie O'Ree still has not slowed down. Defying a birth certificate that confirms he turned sixty-eight years old on October 15, 2003, he travels relentlessly. Nary a week goes by during an NHL season that now stretches from October until mid-June that he doesn't give wife Deljeet a goodbye kiss and dash from his home in a suburb of San Diego to the airport for a business trip somewhere in North America. He's been to each of the NHL's thirty cities numerous times and to countless other places to spread the gospel of hockey in an effort to convert the young.

On a crisp early evening in November 1999, an audience of youngsters at the Martin Luther King Jr. Recreation Center in downtown Raleigh, boys and girls, ages five to fifteen who had never seen him before, abandoned their penchant for restlessness and stood at rapt attention as he spoke because they could sense they were listening to someone important. O'Ree, with grey hair thinned by age and fingers misshapen by decades of hockey, stood ramrod straight with posture that would make a major general proud. He began his presentation by showing the twenty-five youngsters the proper way to hold a hockey stick. Not a real hockey stick, such as the one he held on January 18, 1958 at The Forum in Montreal when he became the first black man ever to compete in an NHL game. Not the kind of stick he used as a left wing for eleven different professional teams in a career that spanned twenty-one years. For his young audience in Raleigh, he held aloft a four-foot-tall child-sized stick with a bright orange plastic blade—an appropriate visual aid for hockey neophytes. Perhaps none of the children would ever feel compelled to hold a hockey stick again. Or perhaps a future hockey professional or college player held a stick for the first time that day. The latter possibility is a large part of what drives him to bring hockey to the masses as, arguably, the most indefatigable ambassador in the sport.

Since 1997 he has served as director of youth development for the NHL/USA Hockey Diversity Task Force. He is, in effect, hockey's Pied Piper, an ideal role for a man whose zest for life and eternal optimism can be infectious, a man who would have uttered Ernie Banks' famous line about baseball—"Let's play two"—had he thought of it first. O'Ree had a Banksian passion for hockey. He still does, twenty-four years after his last professional game.

◆ ◆ ◆

When O'Ree tells youngsters stories about his life, whether at a hockey clinic on the lower East Side of Manhattan or at a summer camp in Calgary run by the NHL's MVP for 2001–02 Jarome Iginla, he does not tell them about the night racist spectators threw cotton balls at him during a game in Virginia, or the nights chicken bones were hurled at him from the stands, or the many days and nights he could neither eat nor sleep at the same establishment as his teammates but instead had to frequent other businesses with signs clearly marked COLORED. He doesn't talk about the spectators who mistook a hockey game for a Ku Klux Klan rally and yelled "nigger" until they were hoarse just to make sure he never got too comfortable at the rink. He doesn't talk about the avalanche of racial slurs to which he was subjected for daring to be different, for demanding to be accepted as the only black man on the ice and for refusing to leave if the acceptance never came. And he doesn't talk to the youngsters about how he managed to score more goals with one good eye than other players scored with two.

O'Ree would much rather expose youngsters to the joys of hockey, the importance of setting goals and doing the hard work necessary to achieve those goals, the value of being part of a team, the increased self-esteem one gets from learning new skills—especially those required to master a game once considered off-limits to those of his race. He was barely older than the children to whom he speaks at camps and clinics when he set a personal goal that took on the fervour of an obsession. "Ever since I was thirteen, I decided that nothing was going to keep me from getting to the National Hockey League," he said with typical enthusiasm. "And when I got to the NHL, I decided that no remarks about race were going to force me out of the NHL."

"He's a hero to every black player in the game today, no doubt," Carolina Hurricanes goalie Kevin Weekes said. "He paved the way for all of us, and I'm glad to see that he's getting the recognition now that he richly deserves."

The absence of a black role model to show O'Ree the way to hockey's major league proved no deterrent. Incidents of racial hatred in cities throughout North America, including the small city of Fredericton, from which he hailed, did not stop him. The systemic racial discrimination that wounded the psyches of many North American blacks, particularly during his formative years in the 1930s, '40s and '50s, did not stop him. It should come as no surprise, then, that a tragedy on the ice that robbed him of the use of his right eye did not stop him from leaving an indelible mark upon sports history.

So much of his time these days is spent in new-age hockey cities, like Raleigh, Tampa-St. Petersburg and San Jose where the short answer to why there are not more black hockey players is, "There's no place for us to play." He tries to convince those youngsters that a way to start playing is with a small plastic-bladed stick and a rubber ball on asphalt, grass or a hardwood floor. It's still hockey, he tells them, and it can be as much fun as the game he first played in Canada, in a more traditional setting.

◆ ◆ ◆

Born in 1935 in Fredericton, then a small city of 33,000, he could play hockey without leaving home whenever his father flooded the backyard and Mother Nature turned the water solid. He and his brother, Richard, used to fashion goalposts out of rocks and construct "skates" by attaching wooden blocks to the soles of their sneakers. "Double runners" the makeshift skates were called, and they would have to do until the boys could afford the real thing. Fielding two hockey teams in the O'Ree household was not that difficult since Willie was the youngest of thirteen children born to Harry and Rosebud O'Ree. He first took to the sport when he was three, and two years later he began playing every day from dawn till dusk.

Aside from his backyard "rink," black hockey players were scarce in New Brunswick, a province that along with Nova Scotia, Prince Edward Island and Newfoundland boards the Atlantic Ocean. Actually, black people were scarce in New Brunswick. O'Ree remembers only two black families in Fredericton and a few others in nearby Gagetown. But finding enough ice time or boys willing to play hockey was never a problem. There were eight outdoor rinks within a forty-minute walk from his home, and there was always the backyard.

"I really loved all sports when I was a kid," said O'Ree, who tends to speak in excitable bursts about matters athletic. "I played hockey, baseball, basketball, tennis, volleyball, rugby, swimming. Man, I was into everything." Following the example of a brother fifteen years his senior, O'Ree made hockey his number one sport. At least, his parents always knew where they could find him. Hockey was his best friend, his first love. He didn't date during his boyhood for two reasons: there weren't many black girls from which to choose in Fredericton and Gagetown and the social mores of the times made interracial dating almost a seditious act, and he couldn't be bothered with dating anyway when there was so much fun to be had on the rink.

O'Ree's parents and older siblings taught him to "stick with his own kind," but while that proved acceptable in choosing friends, he knew he would eventually have to "cross the line" to consummate his love affair with hockey. Becoming a professional player was his major goal, and he would have to compete against white boys to find out how good he was and to gauge the level of acceptance, or lack of acceptance, toward him on the ice. More than a decade before he was born, the mostly black Colored Hockey League of the Maritimes, which had fielded a team in New Brunswick, went out of business. The NHL, however, stood on solid ice and he decided not to let anyone or anything keep him from getting there.

While other boys liked to play hockey, O'Ree *needed* to play. Nothing else gave him as much satisfaction as leaving fast marks on an ice rink (from real skates, not "double runners") and using his stick to put just the right touch on a puck to produce a goal. Hockey had come to define him as a person: he would live it, eat it, drink it. His passion for the game would surprise everyone he encountered, even a fellow sports pioneer named Jackie Robinson.

◆ ◆ ◆

In 1949, O'Ree's youth baseball team won a tournament in Fredericton and received a trip to New York City, which included visits to the Empire State Building, Radio City Music Hall and the home of the Brooklyn Dodgers, Ebbets Field, where Robinson would greet the boys after a big-league game. As the Fredericton nine were ushered into the Dodgers' clubhouse, the man who broke baseball's colour line asked each one if he liked baseball. The boys typically nodded shyly and whispered assents until Willie spoke up:

"Yes, but I like hockey better."
"But there are no black men playing hockey."
"I play hockey, Mr. Robinson, and one day I'll play in the big leagues too."

O'Ree, then thirteen, still remembers Robinson smiling at the response and him beaming in return. In 1962, six years after Robinson retired from baseball rather than accept a trade to the rival New York Giants and while O'Ree played for the minor-league Los Angeles Blades, the two groundbreakers shared a dais at a sports banquet and laughed heartily at O'Ree's recollection of their first meeting.

Like Robinson, O'Ree would allow no amount of adversity to stop him. When a punishing check on an opposing player got him expelled from his high school team, he joined the Fredericton Junior Capitals of the New Brunswick Junior League. At seventeen, he scored eighteen points (fifteen goals, three assists) in twelve games before advancing to the Fredericton Capitals of the Senior League.

In his late teens, O'Ree became known in junior hockey circles as an exceptionally fast skater, one with powerful and effortless strides. He was 5-foot-10 and a sinewy 175 pounds with smooth copper skin, deep-set brown eyes and hands large enough for a man three or four inches taller. Players did not wear helmets in those days, so he proved impossible to overlook. But what hockey fans noticed second was his skating speed. He does not recall ever being timed for speed the way NHL players are today in the annual skills competitions. But what his contemporaries remember most fondly about him was the sheer rapidity and beauty of his skating.

"There were not too many guys who could keep up with him," said John Bucyk, a Hockey Hall of Famer and O'Ree's teammate for two seasons. "Willie could really motor. He was definitely one of the fastest skaters I've ever seen."

At nineteen, O'Ree joined the Quebec Frontenacs of the Quebec Junior League, two levels in quality below the NHL. However, Quebec coach Phil Watson, a former forward with the New York Rangers and Montreal Canadiens, told O'Ree his skills were of NHL quality. Watson also warned him that because of racist reactions to his skin colour he would be in for a rough time from other players and spectators. Regardless, O'Ree accentuated the positive. "I was really happy to hear this respected coach, this former NHL player, tell me that I had what it took to play in the NHL," he said. "He said I could get there if I kept working hard, and I was already determined to do that."

Buoyed by Watson's praise and mindful of his caveat, O'Ree signed in 1955 with the Kitchener Canucks, where he scored fifty-eight points (thirty goals, twenty-eight assists) in forty-one games. There's no telling how much better his statistics would have been had he finished the season. There's no telling how much greater an impact he would have had on hockey if not for a career-altering incident in a late-season game in Guelph, Ontario.

O'Ree certainly knew the risks that existed for a player of any hue in an organized hockey game, particularly in the 1950s when hardly anyone, not even a goaltender, wore any form of protection for the head or face. All were exceedingly vulnerable to injury from a puck, a vulcanized rubber disc that travelled at speeds approaching one hundred miles an hour. Not even the players' bulky gloves and padding—twenty to thirty pounds worth of padding for players and goaltenders today, nearly as much in O'Ree's day—could prevent injuries. He knew the risks, but he craved the potential reward, a chance to play among the elite in the NHL. To get to the NHL, he would need to show everyone his toughness. He would need to be tough enough to absorb crunching hits against the unforgiving boards and solid Plexiglas. As a black man, he needed to be tough enough to endure the racial taunting and deliberate attempts to injure about which Coach Watson had warned him. As a hockey man, he needed to be tough enough to propel his body into the path of a high-rising puck. Such rare acts of courage often are what the sport demands.

◆ ◆ ◆

The play began innocently. From his left wing position, he carried the puck deep into the offensive zone for Kitchener against the Guelph Royals. Having drawn the attention of the defense, he quickly passed the puck back to defenseman Kent Douglass at the left point. O'Ree then headed to the net, to create traffic in front of the goalie. This would mean putting his body directly into the line of a fired puck, but he had done that numerous times in his hockey life. Perhaps, he thought, he could screen the goalie and improve Douglass' chances of scoring for the Canucks. As Douglass, a future NHL player, unleashed a blistering left-handed slapshot, O'Ree felt himself being cross-checked by a Guelph defenseman. A cross-check is the illegal act of hitting a player in a thrusting motion with both hands on the stick. But things often happen with such rapidity in hockey that penalties often go uncalled. Such was the case with the cross-check against O'Ree. However, the blow spun his head around, toward the shooter. By this time, he could hear the crackling force of the shot and he glanced over his right shoulder to try to locate the puck. The hard rubber disc deflected off another player's stick, sprang upward and became a weapon that tore into the face of O'Ree with extreme force—breaking his nose, crushing his right cheekbone and shattering his right eye.

O'Ree lay in a pool of blood as stunned players and terrified spectators looked on. Teammates and opponents undoubtedly prayed for O'Ree, while also giving silent thanks that such immense pain had not befallen them. From stretcher to ambulance to hospital, O'Ree remembered none of it. He only remembered waking the next morning, after surgery, with a patch over his right eye and a sense of panic enveloping his body. Hysterical blindness would temporarily claim his left eye, before he would squint and blink furiously until his vision returned.

A doctor named Henderson visited O'Ree at his bedside and softly uttered these words: "Willie, I'm sorry to inform you that the puck did so much damage to your right eye that the retina in back of the eye is completely shattered. There is nothing we can do for you. You will never play hockey again." Only twenty-one, O'Ree's career had barely begun and now he was told it was over. He refused to believe it. How could his career be over before he had even reached the NHL? How could the game be over before he had been given a chance a win? He would do anything, absolutely anything, to make it to hockey's major league and compete against the best players in the world. His unyielding determination compelled him to ignore the pleas of his parents and siblings to seek other employment or pursue higher education back in New Brunswick. Eight weeks after the frightening episode in Guelph, he was skating again, bent on regaining his form.

"My legs were still strong and I didn't have any trouble maintaining my balance on the ice and I could still shoot the puck," he said. "The only problem I had was my eye. I wasn't wearing the eye patch any more, but I still couldn't see. No, I wasn't afraid to get back on the ice and take the hits and give out some hits. I had to play hockey again, because I had to make it to the NHL. That was always the goal, you see, ever since I was thirteen and I wasn't going to let anybody or anything stop me."

Despite O'Ree's iron will, his NHL dream would have died if not for the relative innocence of the era in which he played. He was allowed to cheat tragedy because Henderson, the doctor who treated him in Guelph, did not inform the Ontario Hockey Association Junior League that O'Ree had become legally blind in one eye. Neither the OHAJL nor the Ontario Hockey League, the league where he played in the 1956–57 season, attempted to ascertain the true extent of his injury. Given the vast amount of information shared today between professional hockey leagues and the various amateur and semi-pro leagues around the world, it is simply unimaginable that a player with vision in only one eye would be allowed to compete. The risks to the individual athlete would be too great, and the potential financial liability to the particular league too high.

But hockey players in the 1950s were not given eye exams as part of a pre-season physical examination. "It wasn't until around '64 or so when eye tests came into play," said Emile Francis, a Hockey Hall of Famer who tended goal in the NHL from 1946–52 before becoming a coach and general manager for three decades. "Before the eye tests came in, a player would be able to play as long as he looked like he was in shape and he wasn't falling behind the play in practice or in the games."

The NHL today requires each player to have full vision in at least one eye and a minimum vision of 20/400 in the other eye. The rule had been relatively obscure until a March 11, 2000 incident in Ottawa, when Toronto Maple Leafs defenseman Bryan Berard nearly lost his right eye when accidentally cut by the blade of a stick. Only after Berard became fitted with a contact lens that improved his right-eye vision to at least 20/400 could he resume his career in the 2001–02 season. All O'Ree had to do in the 1950s to remain eligible for hockey was keep the truth of his blindness to himself.

"Sure, I felt a little gun-shy at first when I stepped back on the ice," he said. "I wasn't as aggressive at first as I had been. But I had to get to the NHL."

Becoming the first black to compete in hockey's premier league was not the prime motivation for O'Ree, although he would be understandably proud of the accomplishment. But he would have been just as proud had he been the second black, or the third, or the tenth. For him, the stronger motivation was to achieve a boyhood dream. At a time when there were only six NHL franchises with twenty-one players per franchise—a total of 126 major-league jobs—O'Ree longed for one of those coveted positions. His courage may have been unmatched by any other athlete of his era. But even as he climbed the final two rungs and reached the apex of his hockey career, he was never again the same player.

◆ ◆ ◆

Playing left wing without sight in his right eye meant O'Ree had to turn his head as far right as possible and shift his body up to an additional 180 degrees to the right to field a pass or spot an opposing player in his area of the ice. Though still a swift and graceful skater, he began to get hit more frequently by players who would not have laid an elbow on him before. And passes that once had resulted in goals began to elude his stick or bounce off his blade before he could unleash a good shot.

As if he didn't face enough hardship as a one-eyed player, he also faced racial antagonism as a *black* one-eyed player.

"I heard 'nigger' so much on the ice, I thought it was my name," he said with a shrug. "But it went in one ear and out the other. Nothing was going to keep me from getting to the NHL, and when I got there, no racial remarks were going to force me out. The truth is, I never fought because of a racial remark I heard. I fought because I was speared, because I was butt-ended, because I was slashed. I *had* to fight because of those things. I fought because I had to, not because I wanted to."

O'Ree reached the professional ranks in 1956, signing for $3,500 a year plus a $500 signing bonus with the Quebec Aces of the Quebec Senior League. He wore no helmet or face shield and kept his head on a swivel. Not only could he keep his blindness a secret, he also knew how to bargain. Before agreeing to the $4,000 deal with Quebec, he extracted guarantees from Coach George "Punch" Imlach (a future Hall of Famer) of a $300 bonus if the Aces made the playoffs and another $300 if he scored twenty goals. O'Ree scored twenty-two goals that season and three more in the playoffs, pocketing an extra $600. A bachelor at the time, he made the $4,600 go a long way. He rented a comfortable apartment in Quebec City and also sent money to his parents so they could make a down payment on a house.

Prior to the blinding accident in Guelph, O'Ree played amateur baseball in 1956. A second baseman and shortstop with the speed and good hands that served him so well on the ice, he attracted the interest of a scout from Major League Baseball's Milwaukee Braves. The scout offered him a tryout at a Braves' camp for major-league hopefuls in Waycross, Georgia. It would be his first venture into the Deep South, with its blatantly segregated WHITES ONLY and COLORED ONLY water fountains, washrooms, restaurants, hotels, shops, schools and places of worship.

Canadian racism was of a gentler strain than that of the American South. O'Ree remembered not having as many career options or as much freedom of movement in Canada as a white man had. But Canadian racism was not overt, not thrust directly in his face, as it was in the U.S. Never was a choice of restaurant or hotel made for him until he arrived in Georgia. Never did he have to ride in the back of a bus, with other darker-skinned athletes, until he arrived in Georgia. A week into his visit, he and his black dormitory roommates sought refreshments at a drugstore after attending Sunday service at an all-black Baptist church. They saw no WHITES ONLY sign and occupied seats at the lunch counter, which infuriated a group of white male customers. A strong gust of racial insults drove O'Ree and his mates out of the drugstore.

"I tried my best into the second week of that baseball camp, but my heart wasn't in it," said O'Ree, who had also had enough of Deep South racism and not nearly enough of hockey. On the first three days of a five-day trek back to Canada, he had to sit in the back of the bus. But as the bus neared the Canadian border, he again could exhale and sit wherever he pleased.

Although O'Ree had been used to Canadian bigotry, that certainly didn't make it tolerable. Back on the rink, his ears burned from shouts of *maudit negre* ("damned nigger") from spectators at his games. Difficult as it was to tune out the ugliness and stupidity, he did so to keep alive his NHL dream. But whenever an opposing player struck him with an elbow, a fist, a knee or a stick, he struck back. Playing with one eye would not turn him into a pacifist. But whenever a spectator spat on him or doused him with a beer, he suppressed the inner urge to climb over the boards and beat someone senseless. Instead, he kept his eye on the prize. He believed himself on the cusp of an NHL career, and nothing would get in his way.

The Boston Bruins entered into a working agreement with the Quebec Aces beginning with the 1957–58 season, which meant an Aces player could be promoted to the major-league team at any time. Several of the more promising Aces, including O'Ree and Stan "Chook" Maxwell, a light-skinned black left wing from Truro, Nova Scotia, were invited to the Bruins' training camp in 1957.

"We saw right away that Willie was a fellow who could skate. He could do a lot of things we were looking for," Bucyk said. "Maxwell, the other black player in our organization, didn't quite have all the talent that was needed for the NHL. But he had ability, too. He could skate, but not like Willie could skate."

O'Ree did not have an eye test to worry about, and the Bruins were unaware of his handicap. Though he impressed Bruins general manager Lynn Patrick and Coach Milt Schmidt with his speed and athleticism, he began the 1957–58 season back in Quebec. Competition was fierce for a job on one of the NHL's six franchises—Boston, Toronto Maple Leafs, Montreal Canadiens, Detroit Red Wings, Chicago Blackhawks, New York Rangers. The number of NHL teams has increased fivefold since then. Had there been more opportunities for hockey players of any hue to reach the majors, Maxwell would not have had to spend an entire professional career in minor leagues. His NHL call never came. O'Ree's came on January 17, 1958.

The Bruins, beset by injuries at the forward positions, needed a winger for a weekend home-and-home series against Montreal. So without fanfare, without public attention even remotely comparable to Robinson's debut as the first black in Major League Baseball eleven years earlier, the Bruins promoted O'Ree from Quebec. He would don a black sweater with No. 22 on the back and skate in Boston's lineup on Saturday, January 18, 1958.

"The Montreal Forum was different and special that night," said O'Ree, who had played a minor-league game there two weeks before. "The lights were brighter and the ice was whiter. The fans seemed more elegant, and nobody called me any names."

◆ ◆ ◆

Leaving skate marks on the ice in an NHL game for the first time was, for O'Ree, the culmination of a childhood dream. Taking the ice as a black man in the NHL was a moment of historic significance. Yet his major-league debut generated few headlines. The first issue of *The Hockey News* after his initial NHL game carried no story on him. In the U.S. many newspapers ran a United Press International one-paragraph brief on his debut that began, "The Boston Bruins, with a Negro, Billy O'Ree, in the lineup for the first time in National Hockey League history...." Nearly everyone referred to him as Willie at the time, but it would take a while for the North American press corps to catch on. The game was televised on "Hockey Night In Canada," the long-running series that, in the pre-cable era of the 1950 and '60s, attracted about two-thirds of Canadian television viewers on Saturday nights. But to the North American media, he was not the story. He scored no points in the Bruins' 3–0 victory. Boston's surprising win over a Canadiens team that would win its tenth Stanley Cup was the story.

"Nobody made a big deal about the game at all," O'Ree said. "Not at The Forum, not on our team, not in the press. Nobody called me 'the Jackie Robinson of hockey.' But to me I was. I knew I had done something that no black man had ever done before. You bet, I was proud of it."

O'Ree knew in advance his initial NHL stay would be brief. The Bruins had told him he would return to Quebec after Sunday's game. Home-and-home weekend series, no longer in vogue in today's thirty-team NHL, used to be common. Teams often rode the same train, albeit in different cars, from Saturday's game site to Sunday's. Since Chicago was the franchise farthest west, each of the league's six teams travelled by train or bus.

Although O'Ree had no pivotal role Sunday in the Bruins' 6–2 loss to Montreal, he enjoyed an opportunity to play at Boston Garden in front of his parents as well as relatives who travelled to the game by train from Roxbury, a Boston-area neighbourhood with a sizeable black population. He received invitations to Bruins' training camp the next three seasons, but not until the 1960–61 season did he return to the NHL. The Bruins saw talent in O'Ree, yet they also saw a player who struggled to finish plays, one that repeatedly squandered golden scoring opportunities and took hits he should have been able to avoid.

"Willie couldn't see across the ice probably and we didn't know that at the time," said Bucyk, the Bruins captain. "When he was goofing up with the puck a little bit and losing it, we didn't know why. He was probably going by feel of the puck at the end of his stick to find out where it was. He couldn't see it the way another player could. When he had the puck on his stick, he was probably looking at the [opposing] player a little more than he should so he wouldn't get run over."

Schmidt, who in addition to coaching the NHL's first black also drafted the NHL's second black, Mike Marson, said he initially thought O'Ree was simply out of rhythm on the ice. "Willie's feet were just going too fast on the ice," Schmidt said. "He was a heck of a good skater, but he was skating too fast for the way he could think."

♦ ♦ ♦

Thought, or the lack thereof, had nothing to do with O'Ree's problem on the ice. Hockey is difficult enough to master with two good eyes. To try to compete against the best players in the world with only one eye was asking too much, even from someone with the fortitude of O'Ree. The decision to conceal his blindness, however, proved prescient. Had he not done so, his chance to achieve sports history would have eluded him.

"If I had known that he was playing with one eye, I don't think he ever could have been accepted," Schmidt said. "He kept that a secret as long as he could, because it looked to me at first that he was just too fast for his own good. He was a good team man but, no, he couldn't have played for us at all if we had known he only had one eye."

Coincidentally, O'Ree was not the only man with one eye appearing in NHL games during that era. Bill "The Big Whistle" Chadwick, a referee who worked more than 1,000 games from 1939–55, also concealed his blindness during his career. Chadwick, who invented the hand signals referees use to explain to spectators what penalty has been called, earned induction into the Hall of Fame in 1964.

O'Ree played forty-three games for the Bruins in 1960–61, netting four goals and ten assists. His brightest moment came in a New Year's Day game against Montreal at Boston Garden. With the Bruins leading 2–1 in the third period, he used his exceptional speed to stickhandle past defenders Tom Johnson and Jean-Guy Talbot on the left wing and challenge goalie Charlie Hodge on a breakaway. Hodge, whom O'Ree had faced in the minors, was 5-foot-6, so he usually tried to beat Hodge with a high shot. But Bruins teammate Bronco Horvath told O'Ree before the game to shoot low against Hodge, to beat him before he could hit the ice. O'Ree heeded the advice and beat Hodge with a skidding shot to the glove side. His first NHL goal triggered a standing ovation from a crowd of 13,909.

Fans treated O'Ree respectfully in the league's two Canadian cities. But he heard dirty names whenever he played outside Toronto and Montreal, and opponents in the American cities seemed to target him more often for physical abuse. This, he said, was never more evident than in his first trip to Chicago Stadium. He lined up against Blackhawks right wing Eric Nesterenko, one of the toughest customers ever to play in the NHL. In twenty-one seasons with the Blackhawks and Maple Leafs, the man nicknamed "Elbows" amassed 250 goals and more than five times as many penalty minutes (1,273). But as O'Ree remembers it, Nesterenko's toughness gave way to brutality in their initial meeting.

Breaking the Ice

On each player's first shift two minutes into the game, O'Ree remembers Nesterenko calling him "nigger." Then things really got ugly. "I didn't even have a chance to respond to what he had called me before he butt-ended me right in the mouth," O'Ree said. "He knocked out two of my teeth, he split my lip and he broke my nose. It was just a shock. I had never faced the guy before in my life! It had to be racial. It had to be. But I had to react, right away. I wasn't going to just stand there and bleed. I hit him back with my stick and I cut him. Now, we're both bleeding on the ice. So he grabbed me and pushed me up against the glass. He was a bigger and stronger guy, but I had a longer reach so I tied him up. He couldn't get a swing at me. That really frustrated him. I just made sure he couldn't throw a punch at me."

According to O'Ree, both benches emptied and fights broke out all over the ice. For several minutes Chicago Stadium staged a veritable mob scene, with players fighting and spectators spewing obscenities and launching cups of beer and debris. Once a semblance of peace had been restored, a bloodied O'Ree headed to the Bruins' dressing room.

"I got stitched up and I wanted to get back in the game, but they wouldn't let me," O'Ree said. "I had to stay in the dressing room with the trainer and there were two policemen stationed outside the room because the Blackhawks people said they feared there would be a riot if I came back out."

Nesterenko, now a ski instructor in Vail, Colorado, and Bucyk said they had no recollection of the incident. But neither attempted to deny it had occurred. When told that newspaper accounts of the game did not mention the brawl, O'Ree said the press had downplayed it and he was not sure why. Said Nesterenko: "If I elbowed a guy I would try to elbow him in the chest. I wouldn't have hit him in the mouth with my stick." Added Bucyk: "If there was a riot, it wasn't because Willie was black. Eric used to give it to anybody. He always skated with his elbows up and his hands up. If Eric gave him the butt-end of his stick, then the rest of us as Willie's teammates would try to protect him. We'd try to get even with him during the game. But I don't remember everybody coming over the boards and fighting."

O'Ree said he and Nesterenko had a chance meeting at an alumni function during the 1991 NHL All-Star Game in Chicago:

"Hi, Willie, how's it going?"
"Not bad."

That was it. No further discussion of an incident from the 1960-61 season that Nesterenko said he does not remember and O'Ree said he would never forget.

◆ ◆ ◆

Boston paid O'Ree $9,000 for the 1960–61 season. It would be his last in the NHL. At least he scored a goal in each of his last two games. Schmidt said the Bruins had become aware of O'Ree's blind eye but would not say how. He was traded to Montreal, a team rich in talent at every position, including left wing. The move effectively ended his major-league career. In a clear indication the Bruins felt betrayed by his deception, the team never called to inform him of the trade. A sports writer, seeking his reaction, broke the news.

"When we found out about Willie's eye, we were surprised just like everybody else," Bucyk said. "I was quite surprised that he even attempted to play in the NHL with one eye. But Willie was just like every kid back then who would do *anything* to play in the NHL. I mean, here's a guy who wanted to play so badly that he did it with one eye. That's amazing."

O'Ree would play in various minor leagues for another sixteen seasons, posting eleven seasons with at least twenty goals and five seasons with at least thirty goals. At age thirty-two and fresh off a thirty-four-goal season for the Los Angeles Blades of the Western League, he hoped for a major-league comeback in 1967. That year, the NHL expanded from six teams to twelve, with the Los Angeles Kings among the new entrants. But the Kings never offered him a tryout, nor did any other NHL club. O'Ree was selected by the WHA's Los Angeles Sharks in the February 1972 draft, but he never played in the fledgling professional league. No black appeared in an NHL game from 1960–61, his final season, until 1974–75, Marson's first season with the Washington Capitals. To the best of anyone's knowledge, no player with one eye competed in the league during that period either.

The urge to play hockey remained strong, however. He performed in the minors past the age of forty, although he never made more than $17,500 in any season. Some of his less-gifted teammates made more than twice as much, because an NHL team owned their playing rights. The NHL had forgotten about O'Ree after the early 1960s. Still he soldiered on, through the minor-league circuit, despite being pelted with cotton balls, chicken bones and racial slurs in some cities and being slashed and speared by journeymen who would never know the feeling of scoring a goal in the NHL. He played into his forties in part because of an undying love of the sport and in part because of a lack of employment opportunities within the sport for a retired black player. A chance to coach or scout talent would have appealed to him, but the opportunity never came. "I tried and tried, but those doors never opened for me," he said.

After scoring forty-six points at the age of forty-three for the San Diego Hawks of the Pacific Coast League in 1979, he put away his skates. Married for the second time and the father of three, he settled in the San Diego suburb of LaMesa and worked as a security officer, first for a company that guarded the NFL's San Diego Chargers and then for the swank Hotel Del Coronado. Just when it appeared his only connection to hockey would be the occasional alumni event or autograph show, he got a call from the NHL's first-ever black executive, Harvard-educated Bryant McBride who had become the league's vice president of business development, and had a plan for O'Ree.

"I thought Willie would be a great resource," McBride said. "He's a guy who would inspire people. I thought he would enjoy working with young people, and he would benefit the league by helping us reach out to groups of people who weren't really familiar with hockey."

McBride devised the concept for what is now known as the Willie O'Ree All-Star Weekend. At the first such event in 1996, two dozen youngsters chosen from youth hockey programs geared toward racial minorities came to Boston to meet O'Ree, learn about his life, receive on-ice tutelage, play in their own game and watch an NHL game. The event has occurred every February since then, in a different NHL city (Minneapolis-St. Paul in 2003). It is entirely possible a future major-league player could emerge from the ranks of those invited to the O'Ree All-Star Weekend.

"What I love most about the job is the excitement I see on these kids' faces when they're on the ice," he said after a 2002 clinic in New Rochelle, New York. "It's just great to see young people get as much joy from playing hockey as I did at their age."

As per usual at an O'Ree public appearance, he placed a hockey card into the hand of each boy and girl, a photograph the NHL has had printed by the thousands of him skating up the ice in a Boston Bruins uniform. The hope is the tangible evidence of a black man in hockey's elite league long before the youngsters' *parents* were born will inspire the children to dream big and strive to become unstoppable. Just as that man's presence on the ice and tireless promotion of hockey to this day inspires every black player who has followed him.

Edmonton Oilers right wing Georges Laraque is considered by many to be the National Hockey League's toughest fighter. Laraque, the son of Haitian immigrants, often had to fight against racism while playing youth hockey in Montreal.
Dave Sandford/Hockey Hall of Fame

A Brand New Game

Because January 15, the birthday of Dr. Martin Luther King Jr., fell on a Tuesday in 2002, American institutions chose not to honour the life of the slain human rights leader until the following Monday, when it could become part of a three-day holiday weekend. So it was left to hockey, that most Canadian of institutions, to provide an appropriate, albeit unplanned, tribute to King's ideals on his actual birthday. Thanks to serendipitous scheduling, the NHL slate for that day featured the only meeting of the 2001–02 season between the St. Louis Blues and Edmonton Oilers. That meant seven black players would be on the ice at Savvis Center in downtown St. Louis, more blacks than had ever appeared in a single game in the history of the league.

"Unbelievable!" said Edmonton forward Georges Laraque, one of the Significant Seven. "For a long time there wasn't even one black player in the whole league, and that night there were seven in one game!"

"You always hoped to see something like this, but I didn't know if it would ever happen," said Willie O'Ree, the man who broke the NHL's colour barrier forty-four years earlier. The NHL, recognizing the game's significance, invited O'Ree to St. Louis along with Grant Fuhr, the former goalie on the dynastic Oilers teams in the 1980s and the first black inducted into the Hockey Hall of Fame. O'Ree and Fuhr watched an Edmonton quartet of Laraque, Anson Carter, Mike Grier and Sean Brown and a St. Louis trio of Jamal Mayers, Bryce Salvador and Fred Brathwaite claim a piece of sports history. Not one of the seven players was new to the NHL, but their coming together on one rink provided a profound example of the changing face of hockey.

"It was pretty cool," said Mayers, a forward noted more for defense and aggressive hitting than goal scoring. "I remember growing up and looking up to guys like Grant Fuhr and Tony McKegney. They're both black and they both played for the Blues. Guys like them showed me what was possible. Those are the guys I looked up to, a goalie and a goal scorer. But now, everything's completely changed. There's every type of black player to choose from."

Hockey fans today are seeing Carter and Jarome Iginla making indelible marks as goal scorers; Brathwaite and Kevin Weekes winning games as goaltenders; Brown, Salvador, Jason Doig and Jean-Luc Grand-Pierre earning their keep as defensemen; Grier and Mayers battling in the corners and along the boards as power forwards; and Laraque, Peter Worrell, Donald Brashear and Sandy McCarthy punishing opponents as on-ice enforcers.

Since the NHL began in 1917 as an offshoot of the National Hockey Association, thirty-eight blacks have played on its teams. That number pales in comparison to the thousands of whites who have played, in part because the pool of available black talent in Canada, the sport's birthplace and prime spawning ground, has been so shallow. In 1971, the last year the Canadian census included a specific question about race, 34,445 citizens identified themselves as "Negro." That equalled 0.16% of Canada's total population of 21,568,000.

Between 1917–18, the NHL's first season, and 1977–78, only three blacks appeared in league games. But since 1978–79, thirty-five blacks have appeared in the NHL. Virtually all of them have been the sons or grandsons of Canadian immigrants from the Caribbean or Africa. According to 1991 Canadian census figures, about 300,000 of the country's 27.3 million citizens were black—1.1% of the total population. And the 1999 Canadian Global Almanac listed 2%, or 573,860, of the total population as black. With more black families calling Canada home has come the inevitability of more blacks taking up the national pastime of hockey and developing enough proficiency in the sport to make a living at it. And never before have all children in Canada had as many black men in professional hockey to consider as role models.

◆ ◆ ◆

"It's good to show kids who are getting into hockey now that they can be any kind of player they want to be, instead of just one kind," Mayers said while sipping an iced tea at Winged Foot Golf Club in Mamaroneck, New York on a sun-kissed August afternoon in 2002. He was among more than a dozen current and former NHL players attending a fundraising golf outing at Winged Foot, site of the 1997 Professional Golfer's Association of America Championship. On this day, Winged Foot opened its gates to Ice Hockey In Harlem, a non-profit organization that provides instruction in academics and hockey to inner-city youngsters in New York City. The IHIH youngsters had been in need of a positive and creative outlet for their energies, much as Mayers himself once had been.

Mayers' familial roots extend to the Caribbean island of Barbados, as do those of Carter, Brathwaite, Weekes and Worrell.

In Barbados, the birthplace of his paternal grandparents, the Mayers name occupies three pages in the phone book. Yet Mayers, whose father is black and whose mother is Irish, grew up in Toronto. His parents separated when he was two and, he said, he never got to know his father. Before his mother married an Englishman twelve years later, money was tight, too tight to satisfy an affinity for hockey shared by Jamal and his brother Allan.

"It's unfortunate that hockey is so expensive," Mayers said. "Skates cost $500 a pair now. It's ridiculous. Kids are growing every year and it's not easy for parents to put out $500 a year for skates and hundreds of dollars more for the other equipment you need. It's really too bad because every kid should have an opportunity to play the game."

Usually, just one Mayers boy could afford to play hockey while their mother, Doreen, spent money on food, clothing and shelter—the necessities. And usually, Allan got to play because he was older. Jamal mostly watched from the stands and hoped for a chance to someday play regularly. His brother's sacrifice eventually made it possible.

"What happened was I was ten and my brother was sixteen and I didn't play at all that year because there wasn't enough money," Mayers said. "But the following year, Allan ended up quitting hockey because he knew how much I really wanted to play. During the year that I couldn't play I went to every game of his, and he knew how much I missed it. I definitely feel indebted to Allan. The type of gesture he made is something I will never forget."

With the resumption of Mayers' hockey pursuits at age eleven came an introduction to racial taunting from opponents. The tan-skinned Mayers stood out on the ice because of his colour and bigots tried to make him uncomfortable. He combatted the taunts by heeding the advice of his mother: "The best way to get back at them is to score a goal."

Mayers grew into the kind of hockey man a bigot would be reluctant to confront face-to-face. He's a well-muscled 6-foot-1 and 212 pounds. His head is clean and slick as a bowling ball, his eyes piercing and light brown, his eyebrows dark and bushy. He earned a hockey scholarship to Western Michigan University and, after being drafted by the Blues with the eighty-ninth pick in the 1993 draft, spent two-and-a-half years with St. Louis' top minor-league club in Worcester, Massachusetts. In those days, he fancied himself a scorer, however the Blues had a different role in mind.

"Jamal's got an aspect for us that we need," Blues general manager Larry Pleau said. "The bump and the grind and the speed and the strength." Mayers has embraced the physical side of hockey, earning his teammates' respect and the nickname "Jammer."

"Ever since I've played hockey, I've always given a 100% effort because I was never the most talented player on my team," he said. "I tell kids, 'Look, I made it in pro hockey because I worked hard and got the most out of my talent.' If you look around the NHL, there are only so many first-round draft picks playing in the league. The rest of the guys made it because of their perseverance and work ethic."

Mayers, who made $800,000 in the 2002–03 season, represents a group of hockey men often referred to as "lunchpail guys." Theirs is a blue-collar, unglamorous approach to the game. Every successful team has such players, men who relish the opportunity to bang bodies along the boards for possession of a loose puck, who forecheck aggressively without a coach having to demand it, who seek to wreak havoc in front of the opponent's net, who willingly throw their bodies in the path of fired pucks and who watch teammates score goals and grab headlines. Although lunchpail guys earn the respect of their peers and astute fans, the downside to their ultra-physical style of play is a heightened susceptibility to injury. Mayers became a case in point in the 2002–03 season when, in the Blues' fifteenth game, he tore the medial collateral ligament and anterior cruciate ligament in his right knee, ending his season.

The extensive period of rehabilitation has not slowed the efforts of Mayers to find unsung young heroes in the St. Louis area, children with the altruism of Allan Mayers, the delivery-service worker in Toronto whose decision to forego hockey helped Jamal reach the NHL. Mayers and teammate Salvador, who made $520,000 in 2002–03, honour such youngsters through a foundation called Jam and Sal's Community Stars.

"Students up to Grade 8 are eligible and they have to be nominated by someone other than a family member," Mayers said. "Bryce and I recognize something the kid does. It could be as simple as sticking up for another kid who's getting picked on on the bus, or a girl we recognized who heard about kids who had lost their hair because of chemotherapy and she donated her own hair to Locks of Love so wigs could be made for the cancer patients. We started the foundation because kids nowadays are being pushed so hard to succeed and Bryce and I felt that somewhere along the way the message was being lost that it's important to be a good kid. Not everyone is going to be a professional athlete, a movie star, a doctor, a lawyer. Being a good kid is important, too. Last season [2001–02], our foundation brought 110 kids to our games, kids that maybe had never seen hockey before. And we gave them goodie bags and had a skating party at Savvis Center, where the kids and their parents could come and spend quality time with us."

Breaking the Ice

◆ ◆ ◆

Since his NHL career began in 1998–99, Mayers has been active in Ice Hockey In Harlem events, as has Carter, who moved much closer to the organization's home base on March 11, 2003. The New York Rangers, a team desperate to end a five-year playoff drought, used their vast resources to pry Carter from the cash-poor Edmonton Oilers in a four-man trade that also brought defenseman Ales Pisa to New York and sent winger Radek Dvorak and defenseman Cory Cross to Edmonton. Carter was in the final year of a contract that paid him $2.4 million in 2002–03, and the Oilers apparently considered themselves unable to re-sign him after the season. Only the Oilers didn't say that to their fans. Carter remembers hearing general manager Kevin Lowe say on an Edmonton sports-talk radio station that he had asked to be traded. Carter, packing his bags in Edmonton at the time, could not believe his ears. "I called the station that day because I had to go on the air and defend myself," said Carter, who speaks as rapidly as he skates. "No way did I ask to be traded. I never brought up the subject of a trade. It was their decision, but you know what? I'm better off with the Rangers."

The Oilers were unwilling to admit to fans the trade was made strictly to cut their payroll, although the trade would likely weaken the team in the long run. "Of course, the Anson trade was not even," Laraque said. "Anson had twenty-five goals and Radek had six [at the time]. But the team wanted to keep players' salaries down. The team could not afford to pay Anson."

Besides, Carter had had enough of the sniping from Oilers management during his two-and-a-half seasons there. Some in the organization did not like Carter's choice of fashion: leather and suede casual wear from the Sean John collection of hip-hop entrepreneur Sean "P. Diddy" Combs instead of the Western wear favoured by many Edmonton residents. And many in the organization did not like that Carter dashed out of Edmonton as soon as the season ended and headed to a home in Marina Del Rey, California. But bright lights and big cities have always appealed to Carter, a Toronto native. Marina Del Rey is where his personal trainer, T.R. Goodman, has a thriving business with clients including such other hockey stars as Chris Chelios of the Detroit Red Wings, Rob Blake of the Colorado Avalanche and Rem Murray of the Nashville Predators. And Carter knew Chelios, Blake and Murray were not catching any flak from their teams about spending time among the beautiful people and hard bodies in Southern California. Furthermore, Marina Del Rey puts Carter in close proximity to Los Angeles, where he has made contacts with musicians, actors, singers, producers and other show business types. Carter values these contacts because he has studied the landscape for blacks in hockey and knows how exceedingly difficult it has been for former black players to get hired as coaches, general managers, talent scouts and broadcasters. Hence, he's making contacts with an eye toward a post-hockey career in the entertainment industry, most likely as a producer.

"I'm musically challenged," he said with a laugh, "but I admire people who have artistic talent and I'm eager to meet as many of them as I can to learn more about what they do. I'm eager to express more of my creative side." He'll have ample opportunities to do it in New York City, the world's media capital. But hockey comes first, and Carter joined a Rangers team trying to qualify for the playoffs with only eleven games left in the regular season.

"Anson makes a lot of unique plays," Rangers general manager and coach Glen Sather said. "He skates well. He shoots hard. He can score. He's played all three forward positions (centre, left wing, right wing). He should really help us." Carter led playoff-bound Edmonton in scoring with twenty-five goals and thirty assists for fifty-five points (more than any Rangers player) at the time of the trade. But excelling in Edmonton nowadays is almost akin to excelling in obscurity. Rarely were Carter's accomplishments noticed outside of western Canada, rarely were they publicized in the U.S. Thus, a move from the NHL's twenty-ninth media market (out of thirty) to the league's number one market energized him.

"I'm going to bring offense to the table," he said. "I'm trying to instill more grit to my game here in New York. I'm going to try to create balance on whatever line I play on, whether it's offensively or defensively. I'm going to try to bring a lot of energy to the locker room and the bench."

After years of vigorous workouts with Goodman in Marina Del Rey, Carter arrived in New York at 205 pounds, having added forty pounds of muscle since joining the league in 1996. When he possesses the puck, defenders find it difficult to separate him from it. But strength, energy, speed and balance are not the only areas in which Carter stands out. In a league where many players appear nondescript, Carter is someone whose appearance merits attention. With smooth dark chocolate skin, dreadlocks and a ready smile, Carter would surely have been mistaken on the old game show *What's My Line?* for the front man of a reggae band. But once a puck is dropped, the power forward looks right at home. Hockey seems to come easy to him, but it didn't always.

Born June 6, 1974, Carter had to sell hockey to his parents, Horace and Valma, part of the influx of Caribbeans to Toronto in the 1960s and '70s. His parents thought ice hockey much too rough for a boy so thin he had nicknamed himself "Slim." At age five, Carter began playing "foot hockey," more like a form of soccer with a tennis ball, on streets and in parks. Not until he turned eight did he step onto the ice, with embarrassing results.

"I couldn't skate," he said, laughing. "The other kids were saying, 'Maybe soccer's your game, man.' I could weave through all the other kids and score goals in foot hockey, but when I first went on the ice and had to be conscious of staying on my feet and keeping my head up I had trouble. And wherever there was a big commotion on the ice with a lot of kids going after the puck, I'd sort of stay out of the way so I wouldn't get knocked down."

Fortunately, a new pair of skates, a Christmas gift from his parents in 1982, transformed Carter's game as if they were magic slippers. Soon, his boyhood rivals on the ice became familiar with the Carter of foot hockey—the shifty moves, the speed, the goal-scoring prowess. It all had returned. That's when Horace and Valma Carter, an accountant and government worker respectively, cobbled together the hundreds of dollars it would cost annually to nurture their son's hockey ambitions.

"Every kid in Toronto wants to be a pro hockey player, even if he likes other sports and plays other sports," said Carter, whose boyhood pursuits also included baseball and basketball. "My parents didn't grow up with hockey, but I did. In Toronto, you couldn't turn on the TV or radio or read a newspaper or go next door to your neighbor without seeing or hearing something about hockey. Sure, I started to think about playing in the NHL someday. All the kids did."

Yet as Carter advanced through the ranks of amateur hockey, he found almost no other boys who looked like him. That didn't matter, he decided. He just wanted to play. But his colour became an issue in 1988 at a Christmas tournament in Guelph, Ontario. Anson played that year for the Don Mills Flyers in a bantam league game against the Detroit Little Caesars.

"We were in the stands watching the game, the whole family, when all of a sudden we see these people, so-called adults, waving bananas at Anson," Valma Carter said, the pain still evident in her voice. "I mean, these people brought bananas to the game to wave at a fourteen-year-old boy because he's black? That's so sick you wouldn't believe it unless you saw it with your own eyes, and I saw it. My husband and I, we talked to Anson about it because we knew he was upset. We told him that there are going to be very prejudiced people that are going to be jealous of you because they see you accomplishing your goals. But you can't let those people stop you. You can't let those people win. And you can't go down to their level. You are better than they are. Don't let them win. We told Anson to be *more* determined to win from now on. And I can say he was stronger and more determined to succeed in hockey after that tournament."

Added Anson: "You have to know there are people who are just ignorant and they're going to say or do [racist] things to you. If you think racism doesn't exist, you've got another thought coming. We've got a long way to go as a society. Unfortunately, there's a lot of ignorance out there."

The buzz about Carter as a future NHL player began when he was sixteen, but he had a weightier issue on his mind. "I was so skinny then, 6-1 and about 130 pounds," he said, shaking his dreadlocks from side to side. "I had a choice in 1992, to go to major- junior hockey or go to college. College was definitely the right move. I needed to get stronger."

The Quebec Nordiques selected him with the 220th pick in the 1992 draft, but he accepted a hockey and baseball scholarship to Michigan State University. He said the agility, quick reflexes and hand-eye coordination needed in hockey also helped in baseball—unless a tough curveball pitcher was on the mound; then, he was at the pitcher's mercy. After a freshman season of year-round sports in the Big 10 Conference and a full academic course load, Carter, a right-handed pitcher and shortstop and a hockey centreman, felt exhausted. He decided to focus solely on hockey, and his game flourished. As a sophomore, he had thirty goals and fifty-four points for the Spartans before winning a gold medal with Team Canada in the World Junior Championships. Each year, six players (two defensemen, three forwards and one goalie) are voted to the All-America team. They are considered the six best players in U.S. college hockey. As a junior, Carter had thirty-four goals and fifty-one points and was voted a second-team All-America. As a senior team captain, he compiled twenty-three goals and forty-three points. He weighed only 160 pounds as a senior—a "before" picture compared to the chiselled physical specimen he is today. But Carter's skills were NHL-ready. His draft rights were traded to the Washington Capitals in April 1996, and after nineteen games with the Capitals he was traded to Boston in March 1997.

A fan favourite in Boston, where teammates and autograph hounds called him "A.C.," Carter nonetheless enjoyed a surprising anonymity away from the rink. "It took me six minutes to walk from my apartment to the FleetCenter (the Bruins' home rink), unless I stopped for a bagel on the way, and people really didn't notice me," he said. "I could go pretty much wherever I wanted in Boston and not be recognized. I guess people didn't think a black guy walking around town with a baseball cap on backward was the same guy who wore Number 33 for the Bruins." His relative anonymity even extended to Barbados, where only those with satellite dishes can watch hockey. "I usually go to Barbados ever summer with Kevin Weekes, and people down there don't really know me because I don't go around pumping myself up," he said. "I did a TV interview down there one time and people had no idea I was Valma and Horace's boy."

Yet Carter, who wore his hair in a conservative short-cropped cut as a Bruin, seemed destined for superstardom in Boston, particularly after a strong 1998–99 season. He scored twenty-four goals despite playing in only fifty-five of a possible eighty-two games because of injuries and a contract dispute. Only two Bruins scored more goals than Carter: Dmitri Khristich, with twenty-nine, and Sergei Samsonov, with twenty-five, and each man played in seventy-nine games. In coach Pat Burns' tight-checking, zone-trapping, defense-oriented system, Carter emerged as a solid, two-way player and an exuberant performer. He punctuated his goals during home games with a celebratory leap into the Plexiglas attached to the corner boards. Since the FleetCenter's naming rights are owned by Fleet Bank, Carter christened his goal celebration "The Vault."

In the opening round of the 1999 Stanley Cup playoffs, Carter quelled the Carolina Hurricanes with a sensational, series-shifting goal in Game 5 in Greensboro. With the series tied at two games apiece and Game 5 tied 2–2, the clock edged past midnight as the teams battled into a second overtime period. Just when triple overtime seemed inevitable, Carter pounced on a loose puck in the neutral zone, swept past Carolina winger Ray Sheppard along the right wing boards and raced toward goalie Arturs Irbe on a breakaway. Carter, showing uncommon speed for a man in the fifth period of a gruelling playoff game, kept the puck on the forehand side of his stick and patiently waited for Irbe to commit himself. When Irbe went down in anticipation of a low forehand shot, Carter deftly switched the puck to his backhand and swept it past Irbe and into the net for the game-winner. Since he wasn't in Boston, Carter eschewed "The Vault" and celebrated with a twenty-foot belly flop along the ice. Within seconds, he disappeared under a mound of jubilant Bruins.

"That's the biggest goal I've ever scored in the NHL," he said. "It gave me a lot of confidence knowing that I could score a big goal like that." Buoyed by the emotion of the Game 5 winner, Carter scored an insurance goal, his third tally of the series, in Boston's decisive 2–0 victory in Game 6.

But things turned sour for Carter in Boston because of another contract dispute after his twenty-two goal, forty-seven point season in 1999–2000. Contract squabbles were hardly unusual in Boston, where president and general manager Harry Sinden held the purse strings as though clinging to life on the edge of a cliff. Two other stars from the 1999–2000 Bruins, centre Jason Allison and goalie Byron Dafoe, eventually left the team after contract disputes. As he would do during his impasses with Allison and Dafoe, Sinden used the Boston media to portray Carter as someone who put his own financial wants ahead of the team. Once the rift became irreconcilable, the Bruins traded Carter to Edmonton for winger Bill Guerin, a former Boston College star.

"I've been traded before and I know hockey is a business," Carter said. "I certainly didn't like [Sinden] saying in the newspapers that I wanted too much money, but I've had to grow up fast in this sport." Carter's mother took the trade harder. Asked about Sinden, she said, "We don't even speak that man's name in this house. I really don't think they wanted a black player in Boston. But instead of admitting to that, they tried to make it look like Anson was greedy."

A trade can be a shock to one's system, even if the player has been traded before. There's an indeterminate period of adjustment, particularly if the player had felt comfortable in his surroundings. Carter, a bachelor, did not have a wife or children to transport to western Canada. Still, the trade jolted him. He had felt a bond developing between him and Bruins fans. He was only twenty-six, coming off consecutive twenty-goal seasons and people had even begun to recognize him away from the rink. "I was being looked upon more as a role model," he said. "I didn't realize it until I would walk down the street and see a young black person who would say, 'Hey, you're Anson Carter.' That was starting to happen a little more often."

Not much was happening in Edmonton. By the year 2000, Gretzky was a statue outside the arena where he had led the Oilers to Stanley Cups in the 1980s. Fuhr, Mark Messier, Paul Coffey and Jari Kurri were also long gone. The dynasty was history. The 2000–01 Oilers were a small-market franchise with 536,000 television homes, fewer than every other NHL city except Calgary (493,000 television homes), and with no national television presence in the U.S. In the NHL, Canadian teams pay player salaries in U.S. dollars and collect revenue in weaker Canadian dollars, which poses an extreme challenge for Edmonton on its balance sheet and in the league standings.

Carter slumped to sixteen goals in sixty-one regular-season games, although he rebounded for three goals in a six-game playoff series loss to the Dallas Stars. In 2001–02, he scored a career-high twenty-eight goals. He also made $1.9 million, making him the fourth-highest paid Oiler. That season he would have been only the tenth-highest paid player on the Rangers, whose top-grossing player, defenseman Brian Leetch, hauled in $8.6 million. Strictly in terms of money, not performance, the Rangers represent the NHL haves, Edmonton the have-nots. The Oilers knew Carter would have commanded a multi-year contract worth about $3 million annually as a free agent after the 2002–03 season, and they wanted no part of that bidding contest. Edmonton, then, made what it considered its best deal, getting Dvorak, who made $1,575,000 in 2002–03 and was due $2 million in 2003–04—considerably less than Carter's salary. The Rangers, with a bloated league-high payroll of $84 million, certainly could afford Carter, whom they hoped would help them avoid a sixth straight non-playoff year.

"As a hockey player, you like this kind of challenge," he said. "You want to be in a situation where a lot is expected of you, as a player and as a team."

Should Carter excel in media-rich, playoff-hungry New York, he would stand little chance of walking down the streets of "The Big Apple" in anonymity. Hardly the introverted type, he assumed temporary residence in The Hotel Pennsylvania, across the street from Madison Square Garden and Macy's Herald Square and one block north of Broadway, until he could find more comfortable digs elsewhere in Manhattan. Although the Rangers practice in suburban Westchester County and most players choose to live there, Carter enjoys the excitement and dynamism of New York City. Shortly after the March 11 trade, he had dinner with Academy Award-winning actor Cuba Gooding Jr. and looked forward to meetings with a pair of Academy Award nominees, actress and rap singer Queen Latifah and filmmaker Spike Lee.

As for the 2002–03 Rangers, they earned for the sixth consecutive season the dubious award of Worst Team Money Can Buy. They missed the playoffs (again) despite a cast of marquee names including Messier, Leetch, Eric Lindros, Pavel Bure, Bobby Holik, Petr Nedved, Alexei Kovalev, Mike Dunham and Carter. Eleven games is hardly enough time to develop chemistry with a new team, so Carter scoring only one goal with New York was not shocking—but it undoubtedly contributed to the ire of fans who booed the Rangers off the ice after they lost their last three home games. However, Carter did not let the disappointment linger. While the Stanley Cup playoffs went on, he suited up for Team Canada and led his country to a gold medal at the World Championships on May 11, 2003. In his crowning moment as a professional, Carter scored thirteen minutes and forty-nine seconds into overtime to give Canada a 3-2 win over Sweden and its first world title in six years. Carter scored on a wrap-around shot after goalie Mikael Tellquist blocked his shot from the right circle. Carter's teammates poured onto the ice before the referee signalled the goal, which prompted a five-minute video review. But Team Canada's celebration began anew once Carter's goal became official. Following the World Championships, an extended spring and summer amid the neon lights of Broadway gave Carter a chance to feel right at home. Grier, another former Oiler, also had a homecoming of sorts in 2002–03 when Edmonton traded the NHL's first African-American star to the Washington Capitals.

A football brat, Grier was born January 5, 1975 in Detroit because that is where his father, the respected pro football talent evaluator Bobby Grier, worked as an assistant coach with the Detroit Lions. But Mike Grier spent his formative years in Boston while his dad served as director of player personnel for the NFL's New England Patriots. Bobby Grier's keen eye for talent helped the Patriots win the American Football Conference championship in 1997. When Patriots coach Bill Parcells left the team after the season following an unsuccessful effort to secure more decision-making authority, he exited with a memorable quote: "If they want me to cook the meal, the least they could do is let me pick the groceries." The comment was a veiled swipe at Bobby Grier, the man who picked New England's groceries for a meal the team savoured all the way to the Super Bowl.

As natives of Detroit, a.k.a. Hockeytown, and residents of hockey-mad Boston, Mike Grier and his older brother, Chris, soon became immersed in the sport. In youth hockey Mike opted for scoring goals as a forward, Chris for stopping them as a goalie. Mike also played basketball, baseball and soccer. He wanted to play football, but a weight restriction prevented him from competing in the Pop Warner League. Nobody in Boston would do a double-take if a black boy played organized baseball, basketball or football. But hockey? The reactions of others at the Grier boys' hockey games proved too much for their mother, Wendy, to stomach. She stopped watching from the stands because of the torrent of racial insults directed at her sons. Chris also abandoned hockey, in part because of slurs from opponents and spectators. He would later become a scout for the NFL's Miami Dolphins.

"When we would go to tournaments, there would be name calling," Wendy Grier said. "But we used to tell Mike, 'Just put the puck in the net and answer them that way.'" Mike Grier persevered in hockey, fortified by the universal response of the parents of a black player: convert the insults into fuel and let that fuel drive you as far as your talent will take you.

Grier still battled weight problems, but his hockey skills earned him a scholarship to Boston University, where the right wing improved his conditioning and embraced the city's rich hockey tradition. For three years he competed for the Beanpot, an always-intense annual tournament involving Boston University, Boston College, Northeastern University and Harvard University. The St. Louis Blues drafted him with the 219th pick in 1993, but Grier stayed with college hockey. He placed himself firmly on the NHL's radar screen in 1994–95, leading Boston U. to an NCAA championship with twenty-nine goals and fifty-five points. He was a finalist for the Hobey Baker Award, given annually to the best player in American college hockey, and he won the Gridiron Club of Boston's Walter Brown Award as the top American-born player in New England.

By that time, the NHL had never had a black star born and trained in the U.S. Valmore James, who was born in Florida and reared on Long Island, N.Y., debuted as the NHL's first black American with the 1982–83 Buffalo Sabres. The left wing appeared in only eleven games and went scoreless. Art Dorrington, a Canadian-born black who became an American citizen, signed a minor-league contract with the New York Rangers organization in 1950. He starred in the Eastern League, but never reached the NHL. Grier had a chance to take James' and Dorrington's accomplishments a step further.

"My going to the NHL is not etched in stone," he said in a 1995 interview with a *New York Times* reporter who assumed no American-born black had ever played in the league. "I hope it comes true. As for being the first black this means a lot to me. I regard it as an honour. It's something to take pride in…. I like to think if there are some young kids out there seeing another black having fun playing hockey, then they might give it a try."

After college, Grier's NHL rights were obtained by Edmonton and he made his pro debut October 4, 1996. A fifteen-goal rookie season and a solid twelve-game playoff run were encouraging signs. Grier, at 6-foot-1 and 227 pounds, cut an imposing figure on the ice. His dark brown skin was what people noticed first, but his ability did not go unnoticed for long. He developed into a power forward that punished opponents along the boards, opened up skating room for linemates, forechecked purposefully, excelled on defense, finished scoring plays and led by example on the ice. In 1998–99, his first twenty-goal season, he received Edmonton's "Unsung Hero" Award. The next season, Oilers fans voted him their top defensive forward. A year later, he equalled his career-best total with twenty goals. And he undoubtedly won new fans because of the grace with which he handled an ugly racial incident on November 8, 1997.

As the final horn sounded that night, Grier noticed teammate Doug Weight, the Oilers' best player, being manhandled by rugged Capitals winger Chris Simon. When Grier came to Weight's aid, he and Simon traded shoves and exchanged words. One of Simon's words was "nigger." Game officials prevented a fight on the ice, but Simon later was fined and suspended for three games. Grier said he accepted Simon's face-to-face apology three days later, "because there have been times when I've done stupid things or said things that I regret in the heat of the moment. I understand it from that point of view. But at the same time it's something I don't feel should be said when you're out there playing a game."

Grier relished being part of a 2001–02 Oilers team that had an NHL-record four black players, with a fifth black, goalie Joaquin Gage, in Edmonton's minor-league system. He said the unique distinction could prove inspirational to youngsters who might be inspired to take up hockey. "I don't mind talking about the subject of being a black in hockey," Grier said. "We need to get the message out." He's in a much better position to do it now as a member of the Washington Capitals. Unlike 1970s black Capitals Mike Marson and Bill Riley, who played home games in suburban Landover, Grier's Capitals play in downtown Washington, D.C., at the MCI Center, mere blocks from The White House. Grier, who made $1.48 million in 2002–03, now plays in an area with a black community so vast the residents themselves call it "Chocolate City." With Grier in the U.S. national capital and Carter in the world's media capital, the visibility of both black stars has never been higher.

◆ ◆ ◆

Although Rumun Ndur did not play in the NHL in 2002–03, the defenseman reached the major league in 1998 from a unique starting point. Born in Zaria, Nigeria, Ndur (pronounced EN-dur) immigrated to Toronto at six months old as his father, a pediatrician, and mother, a nurse, escaped the African nation's political unrest. Toronto was not the Ndurs first choice, but visa problems kept them from moving to Austin, Texas. Since Rumun (pronounced Roman) grew to 6-foot-2 and 220 pounds, he probably would have aspired to play on "Monday Night Football" instead of "Hockey Night In Canada" had he been reared in Texas.

As a boy, he dreamed of playing for the Toronto Maple Leafs, but the Buffalo Sabres, New York Rangers and Atlanta Thrashers would have to do. Prior to his becoming the NHL's first African-born player, Ndur fought his way through the minors and heard racial slurs on and off the ice. "You hear it and it kind of surprises you because you think people are beyond that," he said. In three seasons with Buffalo's top farm team in Rochester, he accumulated 795 penalty minutes. The fists were always willing, but his skills lacked polish. After three games with the Sabres, the Rangers claimed him on waivers. But stops in New York and Atlanta were also brief. His overall game needed work—skating, puck-handling, passing and positioning. He returned to American-based minor-league teams in 2001 and '02 and played in Europe in 2003.

At the end of the 2001–02 season, the Oilers had four black players. At the end of 2002–03, they had only one. Grier, Carter and Brown had been traded and Gage, the minor-league goalie, played pro hockey in England. That left Laraque, whom some regard as the major league's best fighter. He is one of two NHL players of Haitian descent. The other is Jean-Luc Grand-Pierre, whose name hardly conjures the image of a black hockey player. A Formula One auto racer? Perhaps. An alpine skier? Maybe. But not a caramel-skinned defenseman for the Columbus Blue Jackets, an NHL franchise born in 2000.

Because the Blue Jackets are Columbus' first major professional sports team, all the players are beloved in the community, including the 6-foot-3, 207-pound Grand-Pierre, who seems almost too handsome for such a rough-and-tumble sport, what with his chiselled features, smooth skin, bright brown eyes and short curly black hair. He would apparently have little difficulty challenging Tyson Beckford and other black male models for photo shoots and runway work were he so inclined. A player noted for crunching hits, Grand-Pierre knows he would never have found hockey had his parents not emigrated from Haiti to Montreal to pursue careers in medicine. His father, a radiologist, and his mother, a nurse, both graduated from the University of Montreal.

"There's a really big Haitian community in Montreal and everybody speaks French and Creole there," Grand-Pierre said. "I spoke French first, then Creole. I picked up English when I was nineteen. I knew I'd be coming to the States to play hockey and I thought I'd make the NHL, so I started taking English lessons." His English is fluent and precise, free of the double negatives and other syntax errors that mar the speech of many who claim English as their mother tongue. He bypassed college and played major-junior hockey for the Val-d'Or Foreurs in the Quebec League for three seasons. The St. Louis Blues picked him on the sixth round of the 1995 draft, then traded his rights to Buffalo. The need to learn English arose when the Sabres assigned him to their top farm club in Rochester, New York.

"Learning English wasn't difficult at all. I just worked at it the way I worked at my hockey," he said. "I didn't have black role models in hockey, except for Grant Fuhr, and I knew I didn't want to be a goalie like him. I always wanted to play defense. You get to hit more than you get hit."

Grand-Pierre, whom teammates call "Lu-key," said as a boy he idolized former Montreal Canadiens defenseman Chris Chelios. "It means a lot to me now when a black kid or the parent of a black kid comes up to me and tells me that I'm an inspiration. I thought about being somebody that kids could look up to when I was coming up in the sport. That's what kept me working so hard at it. I didn't have any racial incidents coming up, but I heard about that happening to some other black guys. But when kids ask me about that, I tell them the important thing is that the guys I know who had racial things happen to them didn't let those things stop them from playing."

Grand-Pierre makes time during the off-season to attend clinics and summer hockey schools because, as he said, it's important for youngsters, *all* youngsters, to meet a black player and know what possibilities they have. He served as the Blue Jackets' host in 2002 at the Willie O'Ree All-Star Weekend. Grand-Pierre, who made $600,000 in 2002–03, said he is recognized in Haiti as a professional hockey player, but he's not as well-known there as Georges Laraque, another Haitian Montrealer who has been in the NHL longer. Grand-Pierre and Laraque have followed a path charted by Claude Vilgrain, a native of Port-au-Prince who played on the Canadian Olympic team in 1988. He also played eighty-nine games in an NHL career that began with the 1987–88 Vancouver Canucks and ended with the 1993–94 Philadelphia Flyers. Vilgrain, who lives in Calgary, played right wing. So does Laraque.

When Laraque took up the sport, he looked not to another hockey player, but to baseball legend Jackie Robinson for motivation. At age seven, Laraque, forbidden by his parents to watch television or play video games on school nights, read a book about Major League Baseball's first black player and found a hero. The story of how Robinson triumphed over racial prejudice struck a responsive chord.

"I was going through as a kid what he was going through, but in hockey, so right away he became my role model," said Laraque, who made $1 million in 2002–03. "It was important to me to have somebody I could look up to because getting through the hockey games was so hard."

Laraque was always big for his age, and he constantly heard racial slurs at youth games in Sorel-Tracy, a community in Quebec, because he was black and he hit like a truck. "The kids were calling me 'nigger,' the coaches were calling me 'nigger,' the parents in the stands were calling me 'nigger.' It was unbelievable. I cried a lot when I was a kid. Not that I would cry in front of the other kids because I had a lot of ego. But I would go home and cry."

Laraque's parents, Edy and Evelyn, an engineer and a nurse respectively, stopped going to the games because of the torrent of racial abuse heaped upon their son. They urged Georges to quit hockey. He refused. Why? Because Robinson did not quit baseball.

"I felt that if he did it, I should be able to do it too," he said. "I think that it became a mission for Jackie Robinson to make it in baseball, to shut all those people up, and it became my mission to make it in hockey—all the way to the NHL. All those people who were calling me 'nigger,' they pushed me. I remember people calling me 'nigger' when I was on my bike with my hockey equipment over my shoulder going to the games. Those people, they pushed me. They pushed me with their racist comments."

Laraque who grew to 6-foot-3 and 250 pounds, is not one to be pushed, because he has always had a tendency to push back—harder. Faced with racial hostility on a daily basis, his mind proved as strong as his physique. Fluent in French, Creole and English, he used French to describe his boyhood determination to reach hockey's major league. He considered it his *raison d'être*, his reason for being.

Hockey, he readily admits, was never his favourite sport. He preferred to play soccer, especially the goal-scoring position of striker. He even enjoyed football more, where his size at running back made him a Canadian grade-school version of Jerome Bettis, the Pittsburgh Steelers' punisher known as "The Bus."

"I used to run through people on the football field, and many people urged me to stick with football," he said. "It's funny. Danny Maciocha was my football coach when I was sixteen and now he's [an assistant] coach for the Edmonton Eskimos [of the Canadian Football League] and he tells everybody how good I could have been in football. I could have had a scholarship to play college football in the United States. He was really shocked when I told him I would stick with hockey. He said to me, 'Hockey? You have no chance to play [professional] hockey. You don't see any blacks in hockey.' But I was on a mission. If I played football or soccer, I would be just another black kid. But I was determined to make it in hockey, so everybody could see that it's not the white man's game anymore. Hockey can be everybody's game."

Laraque said he urges young blacks at hockey clinics and in youth leagues to persevere in the sport, as he did and as his idol had done in baseball. "I tell them, 'We need you to play hockey because we need more role models. You don't have to play in the NHL. If you play in the Quebec Major Junior League or college hockey or the minor leagues in the pros, you can still be a role model and encourage more black kids to play,'" he said. "But I still hear from black parents, 'Oh, I won't let my boys play hockey. They'll play soccer, football, basketball, baseball. Anything but hockey. That's the white man's game.' That's still a problem for black kids, convincing the parents to let them play."

What Laraque also stresses to youngsters is that a black player cannot be mediocre and reach the NHL. He has to be exceptionally good. He has to command attention, and scoring goals is not the only way to do it. Laraque is among the most physically imposing players in the NHL, and proud of it.

"I see it as my job to be a physical player," he said. "It's not like I can't play any other way. This is the way I choose to play. The way I help my team is to bring the physical aspect to the game. I play about ten minutes a game, and when I'm on the ice I'm a physical player."

In junior hockey in 1994–95, he scored nineteen goals for the St. Jean Lynx of the Quebec League, but the statistic that commanded the most attention was his 259 penalty minutes. He made his NHL debut with the Oilers in 1997–98, quickly winning over Edmonton fans with his hard-hitting style. They appreciated having an on-ice enforcer, a player who could protect his teammates and intimidate opponents. Fans voted him the most popular Oiler in the 1999–2000 season, and not just because his relentless and vigorous hitting sent opponents bouncing away as though made of rubber. Community involvement, including reading books to children, is a pastime for Laraque. The story of Robinson, his own role model, is one he shares with those who could easily draw motivation from him.

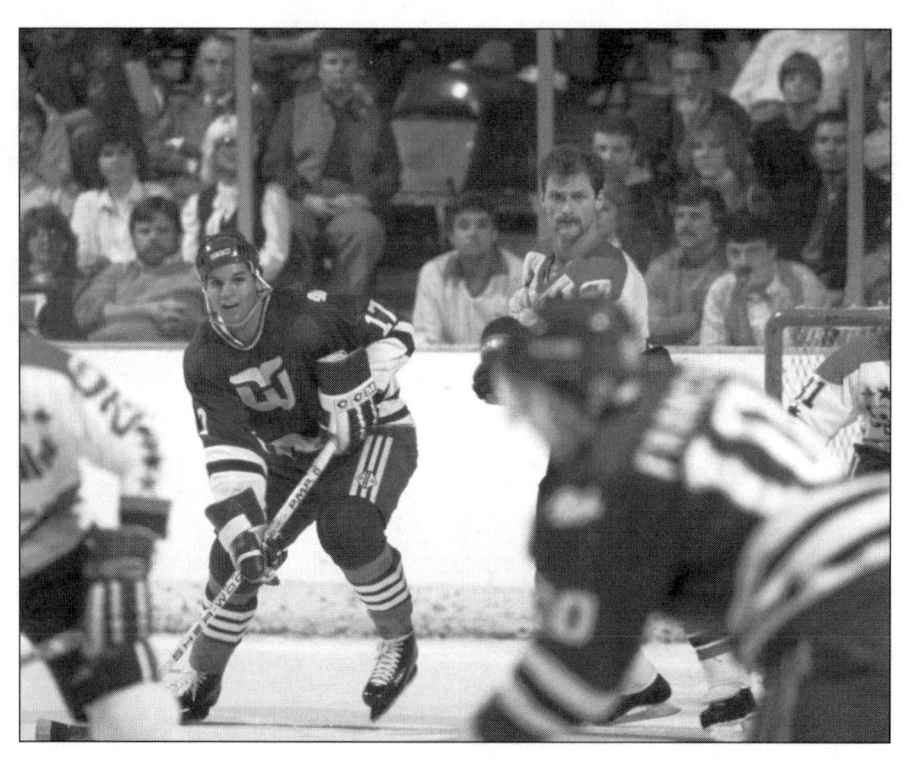

Right wing Ray Neufeld (No. 17) combined with centre Ron Francis (No. 10) to form a potent scoring duo for the Hartford Whalers from 1982–85. The helmet-less player to Neufeld's left is Washington Capitals defenseman Rod Langway, a 2002 inductee into the Hockey Hall of Fame.
Paul Bereswill/Hockey Hall of Fame

Somebody Always Wanted Me

You're twenty years old and black and you've just signed a lucrative contract to play professional hockey in an aggressive and exciting young league, in a city with a sizable black population. Now, imagine having that contract withdrawn by the team owner because so many white fans in the city vowed to cancel their season tickets if a black player joined the team.

The above scenario is not the storyline of a provocative new film by Spike Lee entitled "Hate, American Style." Actually, the scenario is far more troubling because it happened in real life. It happened in 1978 to Tony McKegney, the NHL's fourth black player.

"That week was probably the worst of my life," said McKegney, who went from potential franchise player to *persona non grata* in Birmingham, Alabama, in less than seven days. "I had been close to signing with Birmingham the year before and throughout the discussions with the team my parents were very worried about me going down to play hockey in the Deep South. I had never been to that part of the world and neither had they. We were Canadians. But they knew about all the problems that had taken place in the Deep South during the civil rights movement—the rioting, the violence, the racism. But I always thought of it as just a hockey situation."

How else would a hockey-savvy but not worldly young man have looked at it? McKegney was used to being in demand by teams. Birmingham had been just the latest team to clamour for his services. He had almost always been the only black player on the ice since taking up the game as a boy, and had almost always been the best player on the ice. The racial slurs he would hear at every stop along the road to professional hockey would be converted into the stimulus that helped him to silence or thoroughly outplay his tormentors. And in 1978, he had the first opportunity to reap dividends from his considerable skills.

The NHL faced fierce competition for talent at that time from the World Hockey Association. The WHA—born in 1972, dead in 1979—had already raided the NHL for such world-class talent as "The Golden Jet" Bobby Hull, Derek "Turk" Sanderson, Dave Keon and "Mr. Hockey" himself, Gordie Howe. The bidding war between the leagues, coupled with the advent of players' unions, had lifted salaries to a level previously unimagined. McKegney thought himself to be the right player in the right place at the right time.

He could not have been more mistaken.

"I just looked at Birmingham as a hockey city, the only pro hockey team in the state," he said. "The NHL wasn't in Alabama. The closest team they had to Alabama was the Atlanta [now Calgary] Flames. My ultimate goal was to play in the NHL because of its tradition and it was still clearly the best league. But I thought the WHA would be a good stepping stone. Put in a year or two there, then join the NHL. And the money Birmingham was offering was pretty darn good."

John F. Bassett Jr., son of Canadian beer baron and former Toronto Maple Leafs part-owner John Bassett, owned the Birmingham Bulls. The younger Bassett offered McKegney a two-year deal worth $75,000 annually plus a $75,000 signing bonus. McKegney had no reason to believe Bassett would renege on the deal. Bassett already had established roots as a pro sports franchise owner in the American South and acquired a George Steinbrenner-like reputation as a businessman unafraid to spend big bucks to generate publicity and create excitement for his product. As owner of the World Football League's Toronto Northmen—a franchise he would relocate and rename the Memphis Southmen—Bassett stunned the sports world in April 1974 by luring a trio of stars away from the NFL's Miami Dolphins. He signed running backs Larry Csonka and Jim Kiick and wide receiver Paul Warfield to three-year contracts worth a combined $3 million. At the time, Bassett's deals were the highest-priced player contracts in pro football history. Now, he would dip into his deep pockets to pay McKegney. This time his parents could not convince him not to flirt with Bassett. A friend of McKegney's, a feisty centre named Ken "The Rat" Linseman, had played for Birmingham in 1977–78 and endorsed the city's laid-back Southern lifestyle. However, Linseman is white and could not see Birmingham, or be perceived by Birmingham, the way a black man would. McKegney, a left wing, and Linseman had clicked as linemates in junior hockey and a reunion would afford them an opportunity to rekindle the magic, and be paid handsomely for it.

The same week McKegney put his name on a Birmingham contract Linseman announced he would leave the WHA and re-submit his name into the NHL draft. He went on to sign with the Philadelphia Flyers. That turned out to be the lesser of McKegney's problems. He would learn from

Bassett that white Bulls fans had expressed disgust over the signing of a black player and threatened to cancel their season tickets. By 1978, blacks were playing football for Paul "Bear" Bryant at the University of Alabama, although the legendary coach had been among the last in major college football to recruit black talent. Blacks were playing football and basketball at Alabama, at its intra-state rival Auburn and at every other school in the Southeastern Conference. But a black man on skates with a stick in his hand evidently conjured frightening images in the small minds of certain Bulls fans. The possibility of season-ticket holders and an untold number of other fans boycotting an integrated Bulls team so intimidated Bassett he declared McKegney's contract null and void. Even though McKegney had a signed and enforceable contract and could have fought the issue successfully on legal grounds, he decided—once his head stopped spinning—a divorce from Birmingham would be in everybody's best interest, especially his.

"It was an extremely stressful time for me," said McKegney, a calm and easygoing type. "I don't ever remember having a heated exchange with my parents before, particularly my mother. But the stress was so great that we actually had a couple of heated discussions with her saying things like, 'See, I told you so!' I was just kind of shell-shocked. I had never come up against anything like this before. Politics, racial politics, had never played any part in hockey for me before."

After some deliberation with his parents and his agent Alan Eagleson, McKegney reaffirmed his decision not to challenge the Bulls in court because, he said, he no longer wanted to go to Birmingham and he felt defeated by the whole controversy. He never even got his $75,000 signing bonus. He suspects it may have been pocketed by Eagleson, the erstwhile head of the NHL Players Association who pled guilty in 1998 to three counts of mail fraud in Toronto and three counts of mail fraud in Boston. In a startlingly blatant conflict of interest, Eagleson ran the NHLPA while also serving as the agent for about 150 players, including legendary defenseman Bobby Orr. In addition to committing fraud, he siphoned funds from players' pensions and disability cheques.

McKegney, eager to put the Birmingham fiasco behind him, entered the NHL draft and was taken with the thirty-second overall pick by the Buffalo Sabres.

"Another thing happened to me that I've never spoken to anybody in the press about," he said. "I wasn't returning phone calls during the whole thing with Birmingham because I didn't know how to react or what to say. But, you know, a quote from me ended up in a Toronto newspaper. It basically said, 'Everything is O.K. I'm not upset about this. I'm just going to go forward.' And that wasn't what I was feeling and that's not what I would have said. The truth is, I didn't know what to say about it. So on top of everything else, I was having quotes made up about me in the newspaper."

♦ ♦ ♦

Buffalo would be the first stop on a winding journey through professional hockey for McKegney, who holds the unique distinction of being the NHL's fourth black player and his family's second NHL player, even though his older brother was not among the league's first three blacks. Ian McKegney, a former Chicago Blackhawks defenseman, is white. Tony McKegney, born February 15, 1958 in Montreal, was adopted at age one and reared by a white family in Sarnia, Ontario. McKegney remembers Sarnia as a town of 50,000 dominated by petroleum factories. Hockey players were plentiful, blacks scarce. No more than twenty lived in the town. His father, a retired chemist, and his mother, a homemaker, adopted five children (four boys and a girl), and each one had easy access to hockey every winter at McKegney Outdoor Arena.

"My parents built a rink in the backyard," McKegney said. "Typically, it would last from about Christmas until the middle of March. Not only did we have ten to twelve straight weeks of hockey in the backyard, we had a lit rink. My father strung up lights along clotheslines and he put up some flood lights on the back of the house." As long as McKegney played hockey, as long as he did what other Sarnia boys did, he felt accepted. Growing up in an otherwise all-white neighbourhood didn't make him feel different, he said. Success in youth sports made him popular in town. He became known in Sarnia, not as "the black kid," but as a local star, the best player on the team. His level of acceptance also made it possible to date white girls without incurring the wrath of white males.

"In those days I also played basketball, baseball and football," he said. "I used to love watching the flashy basketball players, like "Pistol" Pete Maravich and Earl "The Pearl" Monroe. But being in Canada, we didn't read about any Canadians in the 1970s making it to the pro leagues in those sports. I knew I wanted to be a pro athlete so I stuck with what was more realistic for me, and that was hockey."

McKegney brought a measure of Pistol Pete's potency to the ice, with the rapidity in which he scored. In hockey, the objective on defense is to limit the time and space of an offensive player, but McKegney needed precious little time or shooting room to put the puck in the net. In this respect, McKegney's game was a precursor to that of Jarome Iginla, the NHL's MVP for 2001–02. Both are comparable in size: McKegney, a six-footer, played at an even 200 pounds; Iginla plays at 6-foot-1 and 202 pounds. Neither can be considered an elegant skater possessing the sort of long and powerful strides that move fans to the edge of their seats. But give each man an opening, or the opportunity to create one, and the defense would pay dearly. Give each man a chance to snap off a quick wrist shot and the goalie would invariably have to fish a puck out of the net.

McKegney played thirteen seasons (1978–91) during an era when professional hockey had more of a free-flowing style, when an end-to-end dash by a gifted and graceful puckhandler was not the source of surprise it would be today. He scored more than three hundred goals and had eight twenty-goal seasons, yet he was not a dominant player. Had he been the NHL's first or second black, his game would have garnered more attention. But while historians are apt to focus on fourth heads of state, they tend to overlook fourth blacks in professional sports leagues. Still, McKegney is deserving of wider recognition, for his career far surpassed those of Willie O'Ree, Mike Marson and Bill Riley, the NHL's first three blacks. While there are no All-Star Game appearances on McKegney's resumé and he cannot be mentioned in the same sentence with the game's superstars, he was the NHL's first black star, the first black to reach the forty-goal plateau, the player today's NHL blacks quickly mention as a source of inspiration.

"Tony McKegney showed me it was possible for someone like me to play in the NHL," Iginla said. "He set the example. He was a role model."

McKegney became a role model without having one for himself. "Sometimes I would ask myself why I was trying to be a pro hockey player when there were no black players to look up to," he said. "But I'm proud that I stuck with it and I was the first black to really establish myself in the NHL." O'Ree, an NHL player in the 1957–58 and 1960–61 seasons, was before McKegney's time. And neither Marson nor Riley set the league afire. So McKegney found his inspiration elsewhere. "I used to draw strength from what black athletes were doing in other sports," he said. "In the sixties and seventies blacks were making their marks in every sport but hockey. I looked to people like Muhammad Ali. I was a huge fan of his. And I was a big fan of the NBA: Walt Frazier, Earl "The Pearl," "Pistol" Pete, Bob Lanier, Kareem Abdul-Jabbar. Willie Horton and Earl Wilson of the Detroit Tigers were my favourite players in baseball. Bob Hayes of the Dallas Cowboys was a favourite of mine in football."

In junior hockey, McKegney was a fan favourite in Sarnia. Prolific scoring can do that for a player, even the only black on the team. At age sixteen, he had forty goals and fifty-five assists for the Sarnia Black Hawks. In three seasons of major junior hockey with the Kingston Canadians, he netted twenty-four, fifty-eight and forty-three goals respectively. Being a teenage hockey star in the 1970s put McKegney on the NHL's radar screen. He would not have to face a strain of racism as debilitating as that which plagued black hockey pioneer Herb Carnegie in the 1930s, '40s and '50s.

"When people saw me in youth hockey, it wasn't like I had been shot out of a cannon," McKegney said. "I played at the top level of junior hockey in Canada for four years in the 1970s. I played on junior-league All-Star teams for Canada. I had articles written about me in *The Hockey News*. People had heard or read about me. That helped a lot. Willie O'Ree's situation in the '50s must have been more like Jackie Robinson's situation. Had I come into the NHL out of college, where not many NHL players might have heard of me, that would have made it a more difficult segue. In the juniors, I played against guys who would become high draft picks and stars in the NHL. On every NHL team I played against in my career I faced maybe four of five guys I either played with or against in the juniors, because at that time the majority of NHL players were drafted out of the Ontario Junior League. I'd say 80% of the players came out of the Ontario League as opposed to the Quebec and Western leagues. This was before many NHL players came from Europe, and there were very few American-born players."

With the St. Louis Blues in 1987–88 he had forty goals and thirty-eight assists, the best offensive season by a black NHL player until Iginla posted fifty-two goals and forty-six assists for Calgary in 2001–02. McKegney's 320 career goals and 319 assists, if done with one franchise, would have been more impressive. But the significance of his numbers has been diluted somewhat because of the frequency with which he changed uniforms. He played for eight teams in thirteen seasons. His seven trades inspired one sports writer to give McKegney a nickname that he still treats like a rash: "Suitcase Tony."

"The first time I heard that, I had been an NHL star two years previously, so I don't know how you go from being a star to a journeyman in that space of time," he said, a rare edge to his voice. "The thing that affected me was that it's fine to say a guy has been traded, but I scored forty goals in the league and when you've done that it's unfair to make it seem as if a guy is being traded because of a lack of production. I was never traded because of a lack of production."

McKegney played his first five seasons with Buffalo, his longest stint with any NHL club. "The one oddity for me when I joined the Sabres [at age twenty] was I was exposed to a lot of white people who had never been exposed to a Canadian black person," he said. "I was speaking differently from what they expected to hear: like a Canadian, not like the kind of black American they were used to. And they automatically expected me to be a great dancer. A lot of them didn't know what to make of me. But they got used to me." McKegney so enjoyed the Buffalo area that he lives there today with his wife, Susan, and their sons, Daniel, 17, and Robert, 16. He saw plenty of North America during an NHL career that included stays in Quebec, Minnesota, New York, St. Louis, Detroit, Quebec again and Chicago. And the gentlemanly McKegney felt welcomed at every stop.

"I was treated well by NHL fans because I had the ability to treat people well," he said. "I was always interested in what people had to say. And hockey fans are very complimentary. They're very loyal. They remember things about your career, about your team. That's why I stayed in the Buffalo area, even though I had been traded away and came back to beat them in the playoffs with Quebec two years in a row. People were still genuinely nice to me."

Buffalo traded McKegney after the 1982–83 season, which was the second-most productive in his career: thirty-six goals and thirty-seven assists. Although the Sabres cited a hockey-related reason for the deal—they wanted to acquire younger players and used McKegney as trade bait to get a first-round draft choice from Quebec—he suspects the trade may not have been just about hockey.

"Assistant coach Jimmy Roberts actually came up to me in Buffalo at a time when I was dating a white girl who would become my wife and he said, 'Do you think maybe you could start dating a black girl?'" McKegney said. "That question struck me as odd. I think it must have come down from the team's ownership group. I don't know if [Sabres coach and general manager] Scotty Bowman would have been involved in that decision at all. I would have to assume that he really wouldn't have cared who I was dating. I think it was just an image thing. I was very high-profile. It must have been an oddity to team management to see me dating a white girl, even if it was a white girl from Buffalo.

"Did the Buffalo Sabres want a black player to be their leading scorer? I don't know. I would hate to think race was a factor because the ownership group was very friendly with me and my parents. But when you see other players have off years and not get traded, you wonder."

McKegney had been told Quebec would not have parted with its first-round pick had he not been part of the deal. He also had been told Buffalo wanted to overhaul their roster and get younger. But McKegney was only twenty-five, and a thirty-six-goal scorer at that age is a rare commodity. He was the Sabres' leading scorer, yet they chose not to build the team around him. He headed to Quebec for two seasons, then to the Minnesota North Stars for two seasons, then to the New York Rangers for part of the 1986–87 season, then to St. Louis for two seasons, then to Detroit for part of the 1989–90 season, then back to Quebec for two seasons and finally to Chicago in 1991.

"Of course, I wish I hadn't been traded so often," he said. "But I always took the view that somebody always wanted me. My attitude was to turn it into something positive and try to prove the other team wrong."

◆ ◆ ◆

At least McKegney never got traded to the Canadian franchise closest to his hometown, the Toronto Maple Leafs, the NHL's only Ontario-based franchise at the time. Sometimes, the worst thing that can happen to a professional athlete is to play in his own hometown. The self-imposed pressure to excel can become too unnerving, the daily reviews of one's performance from family, friends and acquaintances too critical, the degree of disappointment when things don't go well too debilitating. The ongoing struggle to write "Local Boy Makes Good" headlines in the city that knows him best could cause a player to lose something much more important than games. He could lose himself. Ray Neufeld knows. It happened to him.

"If I had not been traded from Hartford to Winnipeg, I know I would have had a different career, different as in better," said Neufeld, the NHL's sixth black player. "I would have been able to play longer with Ron Francis in Hartford, and people don't realize what a great hockey player he is. He's going to the Hall of Fame. Instead I got traded to my hometown team, and it seems like after nine seasons in the NHL and four twenty-five-goal seasons, my claim to fame is that I was once traded for Dave Babych."

Neufeld allowed himself to laugh at the irony of his comment, but for many years he would find no humour in those words. For many years after retiring from hockey in 1990, a rink was the last place he wanted to be. He's in Winnipeg now, happily married and the father of three, although he nearly lost everything because of an inability to handle a three-year stint with the Winnipeg Jets that he compared to playing hockey in a straitjacket with a hangover.

Neufeld, born in 1959, is a self-described "country boy" from St. Boniface, Manitoba. He grew up in Winkler, a dot on the map about seventy-five miles south of Winnipeg, after being adopted by a white family.

"I was the only black in the whole town," he said. "My dad, William, was a pharmacist. He owned the drugstore in Winkler for twenty years. My mom, Elise, was a stay-at-home mom. They had six kids on their own and adopted two more—one of my sisters and me. But most of my parents' kids were getting older when they adopted me. They already had a son who was around my age, and I guess they wanted to give him somebody to pal around with.

"I don't remember race being an issue for me when I was growing up. But to this day, I'm still not as comfortable in a room full of blacks as I am around whites. I'm just not used to it. I've associated with some black friends, but the funny thing is the other blacks I know are in the same situation as me. They grew up in a white environment."

Neufeld's size and hockey prowess helped to defuse potential racial problems in Winkler. "I was a big kid and really overpowering, and most kids were probably afraid to say anything bad to me," said Neufeld, who grew to 6-foot-3 and 210 pounds. He began playing hockey at age nine, and within three years his talent surpassed his brown skin as an object of attention.

"I remember my mom asking my high school coach what my potential was in hockey, and he told her that if I worked hard I could play as a professional. From that moment on my parents bought me everything I needed for hockey and they sent me away to hockey camps."

Neufeld's parents let him live with a billet family while he starred for the Flin Flon Bombers in the West Coast Junior League. There, he got an initiation to racism. "Guys used to skate behind me, hitting me with their sticks and calling me 'nigger,'" he said. "That happened to me in the juniors and in the minors. I have to admit it was intimidating. I was scared. But I never complained to the referee. Not once. I never heard white players complain to the referee about names they were called. So why should I?

"At one game I remember some [spectators] brought a basketball with them and they were passing it around and yelling at me, 'Hey, Neufeld, you're in the wrong sport. You should be up here playing ball with us.' But stuff like that I found easy to ignore."

Only five blacks had played in hockey's premier league before Neufeld. He proved gifted and tough enough to join their ranks after posting sixty-nine points and 224 penalty minutes in seventy-two games for Flin Flon in the 1977–78 season, and fifty-four goals in fifty-seven games the following season for the Edmonton Oil Kings of the Western League. The Hartford Whalers chose him with the eighty-first pick in the 1979 draft and he made his NHL debut a year later.

"Ray was a real solid two-way player for us, aggressive in the corners and a tough guy to handle in front of the net," Whalers general manager Emile Francis said. "Oh, he was a big, strong, tough guy without an ounce of fat on him."

When centre Ron Francis (no relation to Emile) joined the Whalers in the 1981–82 season, he formed a potent combination with Neufeld at right wing. Francis, a consummate playmaker still excelling in his forties with the Carolina Hurricanes, consistently got Neufeld the puck when and where he needed it, and Neufeld used his physical style to create skating room for Francis and discourage opponents from trying to rough up the finesse centre. Both men posted impressive numbers from 1982–83 through 1984–85:

	Neufeld			**Francis**		
Season	Goals	Assists	Points	Goals	Assists	Points
1982–83	26	31	57	31	59	90
1983–84	27	42	69	23	60	83
1984–85	27	35	62	24	57	81

Things were going swimmingly for Neufeld. Rare is the NHL player who records three consecutive twenty-goal seasons by the age of twenty-six. The only on-ice problem he recalled during that period occurred in a game against the Canadiens in Montreal, when his crunching check sent defenseman Chris Chelios wobbling off the ice, producing a cacophony of racial slurs from the Montreal bench. Neufeld still remembers the soothing response from Canadiens forward Ryan Walter in the face-off circle: "Just relax, Ray. Don't worry about it. We've got more important things in life to be concerned about, like family." Walter was a member of Hockey Ministries, a group of Christian players that would come to Neufeld's aid several years later.

Although highly productive on the ice, Neufeld felt himself losing a private battle to alcohol. A symbiotic relationship has long existed between beer and hockey. Beer companies have owned and continue to own sports franchises, and are among the biggest advertisers of sports events. For hockey players, beer is ever present and readily available at the arena after games and at the nightspots they frequent upon leaving the rink. Some find it difficult not to overindulge.

"Alcohol was a big challenge to me," Neufeld said. "I knew I was drinking more than I should. But when guys get together after the games or on the road, they drink. A lot of guys can handle it, some can't."

Neufeld managed his life well enough until November 21, 1985, the day he was called into Emile Francis' office. The general manager needed to find a way to turn the Whalers into a Stanley Cup contender. Despite the prolific scoring of Neufeld and Ron Francis from 1982–85, Hartford failed to make the playoffs in any of the three seasons. The team needed a multi-skilled defenseman to orchestrate its power play, a quarterback on the ice who would play half the game and increase Hartford's overall potency on offense. Dave Babych, a 6-foot-2, 215-pounder whom the

Winnipeg Jets had taken second overall in the 1980 draft, was obtainable, but for a high price. Emile Francis rolled the dice and made the trade: Neufeld straight up for Babych.

"I always felt there should have been more players included in that deal," Neufeld said. "I was traded for a guy who was a first-round draft choice and very popular in Winnipeg. The Jets were already loaded with talent, but the perception was that I was the missing piece in the puzzle, the tough and strong winger they so desperately needed. But I was not a fighter. I never played that role in Hartford. I was a strong, grinding winger who could handle himself along the boards, in the corners, in front of the net. But I wasn't going to fight all the tough guys in the league. That wasn't the way I played."

Neufeld said he wondered for years if word of his struggles with alcohol had filtered back to Emile Francis and been a factor in the trade. But Francis denied that.

"I honestly didn't know he was having trouble with [alcohol]," Francis said. "This was strictly a hockey trade. We had a chance to get a top defenseman and improve our team. John Ferguson was the general manager of Winnipeg at the time. He was a tough hockey player himself [with Montreal from 1963–71], and he wanted Neufeld."

The Neufeld he got never adjusted to an ill-fitting role. Neufeld shined when playing alongside a playmaking centre such as Ron Francis. Neufeld had the size of an enforcer, but playing the heavy amounted to a subjugation of his talent. And despite being back home, he felt no love from Jets fans. They missed the dynamic Babych, who would help the Whalers to six straight playoff seasons from 1986–91, although they'd advance past the first round only once. And Jets fans couldn't understand why Neufeld could no longer score twenty-five goals a season *and* clean the clocks of the league's other enforcers.

"No matter what I did I could never do enough to satisfy Winnipeg," he said. "We made the playoffs every year I played for the Jets, but we got knocked out by Calgary (once) or Edmonton (twice). And each year the team that eliminated us went to the Stanley Cup finals. But I was always pointed at as the reason that Winnipeg never reached the next level. It took a long time for the players in the dressing room to warm up to me. The fans? They never warmed up to me in Winnipeg."

So Neufeld drank. More than he ever had in Hartford. The drinking, he admits, threatened the stability of his marriage to wife Dawn. The drinking also led to an undeniable erosion of his hockey skills. In his first three seasons in Winnipeg, his goals and points declined while his penalty minutes skyrocketed:

Season	Games	Goals	Assists	Points	PIM
1985–86	60	20	28	48	62
1986–87	80	18	18	36	105
1987–88	78	18	18	36	169

PIM—penalty minutes.

He didn't like his role. Jets fans didn't like him. He didn't like the game anymore. So he drank, until the player wearing No. 28 in Winnipeg white was but a shadow of his former self. Fortunately for Neufeld, teammates Doug Smail and Laurie Boschman intervened—not soon enough to resurrect his career, but soon enough to rectify his life and salvage his marriage.

"They were involved in Hockey Ministries and they encouraged me to get involved," he said. "They said, 'Ray, you don't have to drink to try to fit in or escape your problems. Drinking is not the solution to what you're going through. God is the solution you're looking for.' I wasn't a believer in Christ until then. But thanks to those guys, I became a believer and it turned my life around."

A life that soon would not include hockey. He managed but seven points in thirty-one games for the Jets in 1988–89 before they traded him to Boston for a journeyman winger named Moe Lemay. A year later Neufeld was out of the NHL and back in Winnipeg, but in a role he desired—concerning himself with more important things in life, like family.

"I put hockey behind me for a long time," said Neufeld, who since 1991 has managed St. John Ambulance, a company that offers paramedic training and first aid. "I didn't even want to go back to the rink for a long time. I just didn't want to turn those rocks over again and see how ugly things were. Under different circumstances, I know I would have had a much better career. My best memories in hockey came before I got traded to Winnipeg from Hartford. But my best memories in life came after I got traded to Winnipeg and got involved in Hockey Ministries."

The inner strength acquired through faith has convinced him to give hockey another chance. He put out feelers two years ago and was offered a chance to coach a team in the Manitoba Junior Hockey League, but declined the job because he didn't want to move farther north. He then applied for the job of commissioner of the MJHL, but did not get it.

"I'd like to get back into hockey," he said. "My kids are getting older and I don't have as many responsibilities. If the right opportunity to coach came along, I'd consider it."

Neufeld still thinks about how much better his career would have been had he been allowed to consistently be the power forward and two-way player with a knack for goal scoring of his Hartford days rather than the George Foreman on skates he was forced to become in Winnipeg. Still, he knows he did not just pass through hockey's major league. He left an ineradicable mark on the ice.

"A lot of people look at hockey as a white man's game, and I guess it is, but that doesn't mean other people can't play it," Neufeld said. "I scored twenty-five goals four times in the NHL, so I proved I could play it, and other blacks have proved it too."

◆ ◆ ◆

Blacks such as McKegney who, like Neufeld, had the potential for NHL greatness spoiled by that dreaded five-letter word: T-R-A-D-E.

For McKegney, a 1989–90 stint in Hockeytown lasted fourteen injury-plagued games. He unwittingly reduced his value to the Red Wings by coming back too soon from a groin injury. His performance suffered as he tried to play with pain. "I made a mistake a lot of players made then: I did whatever I could to get back into the lineup," he said. "Now you would take a doctor's advice and not even think about going back on the ice until the groin is 100% healed. What players do today is smarter. The money is so big in hockey now and all the players have their own insurance on top of what the teams already provide. A player now isn't going to try to play through a serious injury because that decision could cost him $2 million or $3 million down the line."

Asked if he thought any of his seven trades were racially motivated, McKegney paused for nearly twenty seconds. Finally he said, "My parents thought that a lot." What he thought he would keep to himself. Four times he was traded during an NHL season, and two of those trades occurred shortly after his sons were born. In-season trades are the most problematic, for they can separate a player from his family for many weeks, if not months, until the season ends. Tony and Carol McKegney always decided not to pull their sons out of school in the winter or spring and move them to an unfamiliar city where they would have to make new friends.

Sandy McCarthy, a Boston Bruins forward who has been traded three times during an NHL season and four times in all, said his family handles the situation differently and democratically. "We vote on what to do as a family," he said. "If my wife and kids want to move with me to another city right away, we do it. If they don't, then I go alone. When I was traded from Philly to Carolina [in March 2000], my wife wanted to come, my kids wanted to come, so we all went together."

McCarthy's four trades make him experienced. McKegney's seven trades make him an authority. If any hockey player ever acquired an expert's perspective on the relative differences between performing for an American-based team and a Canadian team, it is McKegney. "Once you leave the rink in a place like St. Louis or New York, you sort of meld into the community and you sort of disappear," he said. "But in a city like Quebec or Montreal or Toronto, you're reminded every day why you're there and what your job is and how you did last night. In Canada, the focus is always on hockey and that makes it a great experience."

Of all the trades he endured, St. Louis' decision to send McKegney to Detroit in June 1989 stung the most. Raw statistics seemed to justify the Blues' decision because his numbers in the three major offensive categories plummeted from the previous season.

Season	Goals	Assists	Points
1987–88	40	38	78
1988–89	25	17	42

But he cited an unexpected, and unjust, demotion from the Blues' number-one line in 1988–89 as an underlying cause for his decreased production.

"The season after I scored forty goals, I started the year on the third and fourth lines," he said, still annoyed by the memory. "Brian Sutter, who was a teammate in my forty-goal season and a left wing like myself, was basically forced into retirement by the ownership. They wanted him to coach the team. He still wanted to play. The reason they wanted him to retire was because of my scoring as a left wing. (Sutter had fifteen goals in 1987–88.) The following year, I must have played 30% less than I had the year before. That was out of my control. When your ice time is cut by that much you're not as involved in the flow of the game and you end up playing with different linemates. I wasn't one who could take the puck from end to end and score a goal. I needed to play with other offensive-minded players. When I didn't get that opportunity, the drop-off in goals and points showed."

Ice time has always been a bone of contention for hockey players. Rare is the player who does not believe he should be on the ice more often. How a coach dispenses ice time is the surest indication of a player's status on a team. Yet sometimes ice time has little to do with a player's ability and more to do with who's making the most money or which player was drafted higher. Hockey is unlike baseball, basketball and football in that a team's best lineup does not necessarily start the game. It may take a shift or two before the best players hit the ice. Even in football and basketball, where player substitutions are frequent, a team's best players start the game. The constant and rapid substitutions in hockey, generally at intervals of thirty to fifty seconds, allow a coach to seek the most favourable matchups for his team (e.g., one team's best defensive line against an opponent's best offensive line). But regardless of who starts, a team's best players invariably log the most ice time. In McKegney's view, a first-year coach in St. Louis stifled his progress on a team for which he had just produced the best season of his career by limiting his ice time. He does not know if race was a factor, but he does know it would have been extremely difficult to prove such a charge, because virtually every player, black or white, considers himself deserving of more ice time.

Being traded seven times could not have inspired in McKegney much faith in the judgment of NHL general managers. But he said that was not the reason he said *arrivederci* to the league and signed with HC Varese of the Italian League in the 1991–92 season. If a black in the NHL is unusual, a black in professional hockey in Italy is an August snowstorm. McKegney, however, called it "a great experience."

"My body had become a bit ravaged (at age thirty-three), and the NHL had gotten to the point where teams were often playing three games in four nights. The NHL had figured out that Thursday, Saturday and Sunday nights were when they could really draw good crowds. So we ended up with a lot of three-games-in-four-nights stretches. By the fourth night, my knees ended up having to be drained and shot with cortisone. I was toward the end of my career and my knees couldn't take it. And I knew from other players who had gone over to Italy that the schedule was easier: forty-five games, shorter practices. Italy was perfect for my body at the time. I'll tell you this: I averaged thirty minutes of ice time a game in Italy. I wanted to see how good I could be playing that much hockey."

With more ice time and fewer games each week against lesser competition, he felt rejuvenated. He tallied thirty-three goals and twenty-seven assists in thirty-three games. The Italian League season lasted six months, a far easier workload than the NHL schedule of eighty games (now eighty-two) spread over seven months followed by up to two months of playoff games. The quality of Italian hockey, he said, was a notch below that of the American Hockey League, which is the highest level of minor-league hockey in North America. But of more importance to him, Italian fans embraced him. The more knowledgeable ones knew of his NHL pedigree and were eager to see him in person. While NHL fans had never been hostile toward him, he felt what he considered an unusually high level of personal comfort playing in Italy, and not only because few, if any, of his opponents were of NHL quality. He got ice time befitting a star in Italy and wished he could have experienced that on a consistent basis in hockey's major league. Buoyed by his season in Italy and his 1992 stint on the Canadian national team, he attempted an NHL comeback, but was unable to get an invitation to a training camp. His pro career ended in the minors in 1993 with the San Diego Gulls of the International League. Coincidentally, O'Ree and McKegney, the first and fourth blacks in NHL history, both ended their careers as minor leaguers in San Diego.

McKegney now works as an account executive for a Michigan-based registration company that audits businesses. He keeps a close eye on the NHL today and enjoys watching the progress of contemporary black stars like Iginla, Anson Carter and Kevin Weekes about as much as he delighted in the exploits of a goaltender who would become hockey's first black Hall of Famer.

Kevin Weekes established himself as an NHL star during the 2002 Stanley Cup playoffs, leading the Carolina Hurricanes to a first-round series win over the New Jersey Devils.
Dave Sandford/Hockey Hall of Fame

Masked Men

Kevin Weekes is a number-one goaltender for an NHL team, something he once thought might never occur. His doubt had nothing to do with his ability to stop a puck fired in anger at speeds above one hundred miles per hour. His doubts about ever becoming The Man for an NHL team stemmed from his being passed around the league like an old coin earlier in his career. From Miami to Vancouver to New York to Tampa to Raleigh before his twenty-eighth birthday, Weekes had seen far more of North America than he had cared to, and with each stop he wondered if the term *black goalie* was too much of an oxymoron for team executives.

All Weekes wanted to do was become anchored in one place long enough to prove his worth. The opportunity finally came in the spring of 2002 when he turned a supporting role into a bravura performance as the leading man in a first-round playoff series that propelled the Carolina Hurricanes to a wholly unexpected berth in the Stanley Cup finals. Yet his euphoria dissipated because of two cruel reminders of how fleeting success can be: first, a spectator in Montreal threw a banana at him during a playoff game; then, after his team played a sub-par first period in the next game, he found himself back on the bench.

Weekes, the Hurricanes' starter in 2002–03, is only the second black to become a bonafide, clear-cut number-one goalie in the history of a league that dates to 1917. The 2002–03 season tested his resiliency after he suffered a seizure on the ice during the first week of training camp.

"It was just a case of exhaustion," he said with the precise pronunciation of a network news anchorman. "The medical testing showed I hadn't been getting enough rest going into camp."

The hockey gods would not snatch away his opportunity to play his team's most pivotal position. He would again be able to don a kaleidoscopic mask, one dominated by the Hurricanes' colours of red and black with a viewing space wide enough for him to scan the entire rink and for spectators to clearly see that indeed the goaltender is black. Being a leading man had been his primary goal ever since he embraced hockey as a boy in the Toronto suburb of Scarborough. His major goals now are the usual ones for a man in his position: make the All-Star team; receive the Vezina Trophy, an award presented annually to the best goalie in the sport; have his name engraved on the Stanley Cup, an honour reserved only for members of a league championship team; and become immortalized in the Hockey Hall of Fame. His goals, in short, are to achieve each of the career highlights of his progenitor, the only other black man to consistently start games and consistently excel as an NHL goalie, Grant Fuhr.

"I'd like nothing better than to sit down with Grant and pick his brain," Weekes said, sounding like a graduate student in physics yearning for an audience with Albert Einstein. "He played this position, he was a winner, he was a champion and he's a black man. He definitely was an inspiration to me."

"Somebody gave me Kevin's phone number recently," Fuhr said, "and I'd really like to get together with him and talk about things."

Both men would have plenty of intriguing thoughts to share. Fuhr, born in 1962, came into the NHL a generation before Weekes, at a time when the league's black population could be counted on four fingers (Fuhr, Tony McKegney, Ray Neufeld, Bernie Saunders). But Fuhr buoyed the hopes of Weekes and every other black boy who dreamed of major-league hockey stardom. The notion of playing hockey for a living would no longer seem far-fetched to those boys because there, beginning in the 1981–82 season, was Fuhr, a cocoa-skinned man, stopping pucks and helping his Edmonton Oilers team become a dynasty.

"Fuhr was always fun to watch, always very humble, never bragged, supported his teammates and was accountable for his own game," Weekes said. "He just wanted to be a part of his team, play hard and make saves."

◆ ◆ ◆

Fuhr won Stanley Cup championships with the Oilers in 1984, '85, '87, '88 and '90, teaming with such greats as Wayne Gretzky, Mark Messier, Jari Kurri, Paul Coffey and Kevin Lowe. He repelled pucks while wearing the type of bland white plastic mask with almond-shaped eye holes and tiny punctures for breathing that was prevalent in the 1980s, the kind of *Friday The 13th* mask that prevented casual observers from noticing the Edmonton goalie was black. Yet playing incognito was something the media-reticent Fuhr hardly minded at all. As long as his teammates knew who was behind the mask and respected his work, nothing else really mattered.

"Grant was not a guy motivated by statistical success," said Glen Sather, the Oilers coach and general manager during the Cup-winning years. "Grant was always more interested in winning than being noticed. We were an offensive team. We weren't as concerned about the defensive part of the game because winning was more fun when you scored a lot of goals. But the only way that style of play could work was if you had a goaltender that you knew could make the big saves and always give us a chance to win the game at the offensive end. Grant was that goaltender for us."

Fuhr could remind Weekes of the sixty-six Stanley Cup playoff games he won in the 1980s when Weekes was a youngster—fast-paced games from an era when hockey seemed more exciting because of the swift frequency with which Gretzky or Coffey carried the puck the length of the ice and dissected defenses to trigger a goal, or Fuhr responded to a two-on-one or three-on-two rush with a spectacular kick save or a sprawling one-handed stab of the puck.

"Our teams were built to play wide-open hockey, so it wasn't unusual for us to win 5–4 or 6–4 or 7–4," Sather said. "We'd be ahead 7–2 or 7–3 and Grant would let in a goal or two because it didn't really make a difference. But if the score was 3–2 or 4–3, that was when Grant was at his best. He made the big saves. He stood up well in the net and had a great glove hand. He was an important goaltender and a tremendous competitor."

A competitor who always raised his level of performance at playoff time. In each of Edmonton's first four Cup-winning seasons, Fuhr allowed far fewer goals in the postseason than he had during the regular season. The following chart shows how his goals-against average (GAA) improved in the playoffs:

Season	*Regular season GAA*	*Playoff GAA*
1983–84	3.91	2.99
1984–85	3.87	3.10
1986–87	3.44	2.46
1987–88	3.43	2.90

Fuhr had a 3.89 goals-against average in Edmonton's Cup-winning 1989–90 season, but he missed the playoffs. The goals-against average is the result of multiplying the number of goals allowed by sixty and then dividing the total by the number of minutes played.

"On those teams nobody wanted to be the weak link, especially at playoff time," Fuhr said. "We did whatever we had to do to win in the playoffs. If guys had to check, they would check. If I had to tighten up my game, I would tighten it up. The whole deal was about winning. It was no different from what my parents taught me when I first put on the skates: everything you do in this sport, you do as part of a team.

"My father played [amateur] hockey. It seemed like all the men I knew played hockey. Being from Canada, hockey was the main game. I was kind of lucky to get caught up in the excitement of the game when I was three. Before I was ready to go to school I was already playing hockey."

Fuhr has always been a trendsetter. In 2003, the year he turned forty-one, he enjoyed his first year as a hockey immortal when he earned induction into the Hall of Fame. He strode through the Hall's doors in Toronto in his first year of eligibility.

"It's fantastic, not so much being the first black in the Hockey Hall of Fame, but being the luckiest black to play the game," Fuhr said, his expression of extreme understatement yielding to a dignified acknowledgement of his predecessors. "You look at guys like Willie O'Ree, Herb Carnegie, Mike Marson, Bill Riley, Tony McKegney—black guys who came along before me and made it easier for me to play in the National Hockey League. You look at those guys and you feel lucky. I really feel like I'm representing all those guys in the Hall of Fame."

Each of his progenitors can share in the pride of Fuhr's accomplishments. Aside from his five Stanley Cup titles, he won the Vezina Trophy in 1987–88, appeared in six NHL All-Star Games, made the 1987 Canada Cup All-Star team, shared the William Jennings Trophy (for lowest team goals-against average) with Buffalo Sabres teammate Dominik Hasek in 1993–94, set an NHL record for goalies with fourteen points in 1983–84 and overcame injuries and adversity to play nineteen seasons in hockey's major league.

Although Weekes is familiar with most of Fuhr's statistics, Fuhr could teach the young man a lesson about the dangers of excess, the potential for peril in hockey's fast lane. Fuhr was suspended by the NHL for six months in September 1990 after admitting to past cocaine use.

"An ex-wife brought it up when I was going through a divorce, so I admitted to the league that I had done it," he said. "Instead of being bitter about the whole experience, it made me a better person because I got the help I needed."

Sather, his former coach and general manager, thought the NHL dealt with Fuhr too harshly.

"When Grant was suspended, the league was a lot different from what it is today," he said. "There were never any drug charges brought against Grant. There were never any drug tests done. The league didn't really have a drug policy then. If you admitted you used something then, you were out of hockey. No treatment program. Nothing."

However, Fuhr acknowledged at the time that he had an addiction. He told the NHL he had used cocaine for six years. "I was young and foolish," he told *The New York Times* in 1991. "I had no regard for the rules. I thought about why I did it, but I try not to dwell on the subject. Sometimes you just sit there and wonder, 'Why?'"

Fuhr paid for his own drug treatment during the suspension, and the journey back to the NHL was at times publicly humiliating. During a

1991 stint to sharpen his skills with the minor-league Cape Breton Oilers, he faced unmerciful heckling from spectators at a game in New Haven. Among the non-obscene chants was "Just Say No," an anti-drug catchphrase popularized in the 1980s by U.S. First Lady Nancy Reagan. He also heard this ditty, performed to the tune of "Camp Town Races":

"Grant does it up his nose...
Doo-dah, doo-dah..."

Another spectator waved a bag of white powder at him whenever he skated on or off the ice.

"It was definitely no place for a sensitive person, but I knew it would happen," he said. "It was a bit of a character assassination but all you could do is laugh. I heard some old lines and some new ones. They went through the whole routine."

Fuhr's game lost some of its lustre after the suspension, and the stability he once enjoyed in Edmonton disappeared as well. In his final nine seasons he played for five different teams: Toronto Maple Leafs, Buffalo Sabres, Los Angeles Kings, St. Louis Blues, Calgary Flames. He retired quietly as a Flame after the 1999–2000 season, in contrast to his meteoric rise to the NHL as a nineteen-year-old.

◆ ◆ ◆

At seventeen days old, Fuhr was adopted by Robert and Betty Fuhr, a childless white couple in Spruce Grove, Alberta. He has never met his birth mother. He talked to his biological father once, for five minutes in a bar. The Fuhrs are the parents he knows, the parents who showed him love, the parents who introduced him to sports. He grew to be 5-foot-10 and 200 pounds, about average size for a goalie or a baseball catcher, which he had also been as a teenager. The Pittsburgh Pirates selected him in the 1979 Major League Baseball draft, but he opted for junior hockey and joined the Victoria Cougars of the Western League. In two seasons he established his NHL credentials, posting seventy-eight wins, twenty-one losses, one tie, a 2.43 goals-against average and six shutouts. Both years he made the Western League All-Star team and he led the Cougars to the league championship in his second year.

Edmonton chose him with the eighth overall pick in 1981, the highest a black goalie has ever been drafted. The Oilers sent him on the ice immediately, and as a rookie he won twenty-eight games, lost five, tied fourteen and had a 3.31 goals-against average. But in the midst of a sophomore slump caused by poor conditioning, Fuhr was sent to the minor-league

Moncton Alpines for ten games. The demotion might have lasted longer if not for an assist from Bill Riley, the NHL's third black player.

"Grant came to camp about 25–30 pounds overweight, so the Oilers sent him down to get in shape and as a disciplinary action," Riley said. "They felt that if he spent some time with me I could help him 'cause I was a player and assistant coach with the Moncton club in the Edmonton organization. Grant had been with us for seven games and he had a reputation then for not always saying the right thing to the right people. Anyway, Grant stood on his head [played a great game] one night in Baltimore. And afterward, I came out of the shower and a reporter said to me, 'Grant, you really played well tonight.' I did the entire interview as Grant Fuhr. To this day, that reporter doesn't know the difference. Of course, I said all the right things when the reporter asked me, 'Are you pissed off at Edmonton for sending you down?' I said, 'Nope. Basically I was sent down because I deserved to get sent down. I was overweight and out of shape. But I'm working hard now and I'm going to keep working hard until Mr. Sather sees fit to bring me back to Edmonton.' Well, geez, a few days later Grant got called back to Edmonton! I helped him get back! He owes me a percentage of his money for helping him get back!"

Once Fuhr returned to Edmonton in the 1980–81 season, the building blocks of a hockey dynasty—Gretzky, Messier, Coffey, Kurri, Lowe, Fuhr—were in place. Three seasons later, the NHL's youngest team would also be its best, and Fuhr would play a pivotal role in the ascension.

"Grant had a great attitude for the game," Sather said. "Nothing seemed to bother him. He was the kind of guy that would let anything that was bad just roll down his back. He was very adaptable, a great team guy. He got along great with his teammates. The players treated everybody as players. It didn't really matter what colour you were or where you were from. What mattered was could you play hockey."

Respect from the other Oilers came easily to Fuhr, Sather said, because of his considerable skills. Any man whose role was central to a team's ability to win games and league championships was not going to be ostracized by teammates because of a difference in skin tone. His teammates nicknamed him "CoCo," a jocular reference to his colour, and he laughed right along with them. Fuhr, a legend in Edmonton, where he still resides, also helped his country win titles in the Canada Cup series in 1985 and '87.

"I was lucky, I think, not to experience any racism in hockey," he said. "I've been on teams where the guys respected me for what I could do and I respected them for what they could do. We just went out and played the game. I was a hockey player first and foremost. The only racism I ran into was at a private golf club in Buffalo while I was playing for the Sabres (February 1993 to February 1995). I wanted to join this club so I could play golf there regularly because it was a very good course. But they wouldn't let me join the club because of my colour. The club had no black members and they didn't want any. It actually surprised me more than anything. Up until then, it had been pretty smooth sailing. Basically all peace and harmony. I ended up joining another club in the Buffalo area and playing golf there. But that experience with racism at the other club was a real eye-opener. That was the first time I ever played for a team in the States. That incident was…well, nothing like that ever happened to me in Canada."

Yet racial incidents have happened to Weekes in Canada. He could tell Fuhr all about them, starting with the 2002 Stanley Cup playoffs.

◆ ◆ ◆

A time out had been called during Game 3 of the second-round series between the Hurricanes and Canadiens on Montreal's home rink, then known as the Molson Centre. The one-minute time out, which occurs once per period, is hockey's version of the NFL's two-minute warning: a device used to allow television networks to air more commercials. During the breaks, fans at the arena generally are treated to video montages of spectacular goals or bone-jarring hits. Carl Weekes attended the game and remembers that a video had been playing on the giant screen, but of what he could not recall. However, he'll never forget what else he saw during that time out: a banana hurled from the stands in the direction of his son, Kevin.

"Man, that's disgraceful that somebody would do a thing like that in this day and age," said Carl Weekes, who works at a chocolate factory in Toronto. "My reaction? I was shocked. Kevin noticed it. It was thrown at him. But he's a professional. He's into the game. I knew he wouldn't let it hurt his game. Man, that's not funny. Throwing a banana at a player because he's black?"

The vile act might have been one of gamesmanship, surmised Georges Laraque, a black NHL player who grew up in Montreal. "Of course, it was wrong to do that, but the way the fans are in Montreal I'm sure they were trying to rattle Kevin Weekes," he said. "He was playing great and somebody might have said, 'He'll be very rattled if I do this and he'll let in some goals.'"

Montreal won Game 3 in overtime to take a two-games-to-one lead in the series. Weekes insisted his play had not been adversely affected by the banana incident. That Carolina won the series in six games gave him a measure of revenge. But his parents had taught him long ago to steel himself against possible acts of racism if he wanted to excel in hockey.

Carl and Vadney Weekes emigrated separately to Canada from Barbados. They knew next to nothing about hockey, but enough about human nature to conclude, correctly, that their only son would face unique challenges as a black in the sport.

"We let him know that it wasn't going to always be easy for him because of some of the people he might encounter and some of the things he might hear," Carl Weekes said. "But he knew from the start that he would always have the full support of his family. We weren't going to pull him out of hockey as long as he wanted to play. And let me tell you how much he wanted to play. When he was six he wrote a book, *My Hockey Book*, that was published by the McMurrich School when he was in the second grade. And he said in that book that he was going to play in the NHL. We knew then he was serious, and we told him we were behind him all the way."

Kevin began playing street hockey in the shadow of his family's apartment in Toronto. Because he was several years younger than his cousin and most of the other boyhood players, Kevin became the goalie by default. Although he had to stay anchored in front of the net and couldn't roam about the concrete "ice" like the others, he enjoyed playing goal.

"I was fascinated by the position, all the goalie's masks and sticks and gloves and pads and blockers. All my favourite pros were the goalies," he said. "We used to use a street hockey ball and I'd have on my winter coat, a baseball glove, a goalie stick with a plastic blade and rubber boots. When I first played on the ice, I still wore rubber boots. Not having skates didn't matter much then because being a goalie I didn't have to move around a lot. I just had to stop the puck. But the game became even more fun when I could finally play with skates and a real goalie's glove."

Weekes persuaded his parents to let him join a youth hockey program at St. Michael's, an indoor rink that has spawned the professional careers of many NHL players. Among his teammates at age eight was Michael Peca, now the captain of the New York Islanders, and Anson Carter, a New York Rangers winger. As Weekes progressed in youth hockey, black teammates like Carter became harder and harder to find. "I never thought anything of being the only black kid on the team at that time," he said. "It was never an issue for me. Not with the other kids. Not with the coaches. I'd sleep over at Mike Peca's house. White kids would sleep over at my house. It was no big deal. I think with my parents coming from Barbados, where tourism is the primary industry, they showed me a world where it's common to interact with people from all different backgrounds and different countries. That's the world I was born into."

His world narrowed somewhat, as did the minds of some people he encountered in youth hockey, from the peewee league to the bantam league to the juniors as a teenager. "When I got older my race started to become an issue—for everybody else," he said with a shrug. "Not necessarily for my teammates, but when we played against teams from outside Toronto or against certain teams from the States. I'd hear whispers like, 'Hey, look at that kid.' As if they're at the zoo looking at somebody in a cage. That started when I was maybe eleven or twelve and became more of an issue in the juniors and the minors."

In 1995, at a junior-league game in Kitchener, a spectator yelled at the nineteen-year-old Weekes: "Nigger, you should be playing basketball. The NCAA tournament is going on. You're taking a job away from one of our Canadian boys." Never mind that Weekes was born and reared in Toronto, making him "a Canadian boy." To that weak-minded spectator, a black boy did not qualify as a real Canadian. Yet rather than be scarred by such a racist remark and abandon hockey, Weekes vowed that he would never be run out of the sport.

"I've always known how deep my love is for hockey," he said. "If I had quit, I would have figured, 'Well, I'm just creating an easy victory for these people who are trying to drive me away from the game I love.' They would want me to live my life on their terms and deny me the opportunity to realize my ultimate goal, which was to play in the NHL."

Having realized his dream, Weekes said the biggest drawback he faces now is the occasional dumb query from the press. "I get silly questions like, 'How does it feel to be a black goalie?' I don't really know how it feels. I've never been anything different," he said with a laugh. "I started playing hockey when I was six and I was always a goalie and I've always been black. That's what I know. Sometimes the questions are innocent and people really just want to be educated. But with other people, the questions and the comments have a stigma attached to them. Those people have a preconceived negative stereotype about what a black athlete is expected to do and what sport he's expected to play. But again, everybody has their own social consciousness. Sometimes you just get silly questions and narrow-minded perspectives."

Weekes, as thoughtful and well-spoken a man as there is in hockey, should be one of the players the NHL uses to market the sport to all fans, particularly racial minorities. But what would raise his profile considerably throughout North America would be another lengthy playoff run by the Hurricanes, but this time with him starting most of the games, something that did not occur in 2002.

One topic he could seek Fuhr's counsel on is how to inspire enough confidence in one's coach to become a number-one goalie in the post-season after splitting time with another top-notch goalie in the regular season. On Edmonton's first three Cup winners (1984, '85, '87), Fuhr appeared in 135 regular-season games and Andy Moog, a highly regarded NHL goalie from 1980–98, appeared in 123. But in those same three seasons, Fuhr played in fifty-three playoff games to Moog's eleven. When the games mattered most, Fuhr got the call. That has yet to happen to Weekes in the playoffs.

In 2002–03 he played the final weeks with a broken left thumb (on his glove hand) and underwent surgery after the season, a non-playoff season for Carolina, whose defense gave him virtually no support. However, he is in a much better position now than in his first four-and-a-half NHL seasons.

Weekes is six feet tall and 195 pounds with smooth dark brown skin, almond-shaped brown eyes and black hair cut down to the scalp. He plays bigger than he is because of uncommon quickness and athleticism, which allow him to cover more of the net than goalies of comparable size. Like Fuhr, he has an excellent glove hand, and the fierce competitiveness and ability to shrug off the last goal that the position demands. While Fuhr said he was not subjected to racial comments on the ice, Weekes admits to having heard a few choice words.

"Guys say things out there that are not always clean," he said. "Some guys, opponents or teammates, will go to any length to try to get under your skin and gain an advantage for themselves. Some guys have tried to use those tactics against me, but I'm not going to let myself get beaten like that. Most guys I've competed against are pretty understanding and pretty mature about knowing there's a certain line you don't cross." Weekes remembers the scene from the broadly satirical 1977 hockey film, *Slap Shot*, in which Paul Newman, portraying the ribald captain of a minor-league club, so offended the opposing team's goalie with remarks about his wife that the goalie left the net and chased Newman around the rink while Newman's team scored the winning goal. Weekes certainly has never seen anything so extreme in the NHL, but he said he's always careful to maintain his cool in the face of a verbal attack because any loss of concentration, however temporary on a goalie's part, could cost his team the game.

A second-round pick of the Florida Panthers in 1993, Weekes spent four seasons in the minors before making his NHL debut. After eleven games in Florida he was traded to Vancouver. Thus began a series of address changes that had him worried he might become an NHL journeyman: always desired by somebody but never with one team long enough to truly establish himself. He played thirty-one games as a Vancouver Canuck, thirty-six games as a New York Islander, and one-and-a-half seasons for the Tampa Bay Lightning before the team signed veteran free-agent goalie Nikolai Khabibulin and traded Weekes to

Carolina in March 2002. He had been told the Canucks traded him because they wanted a veteran goalie. But shortly after acquiring veteran Felix Potvin, the Canucks traded him and installed as their new starter Dan Cloutier—a goalie one year *younger* than Weekes whom he had outplayed in Tampa Bay. Not only has Weekes been traded often, he has been traded from one bad team to another. His appearance in the 2002 Stanley Cup playoffs was the first of his career. He considers race a factor in the frequency with which he has changed teams.

"It's an issue, of course," he said. "I don't know how comfortable other people are sometimes with having someone like me as the starting goaltender. The position is a pretty important one, if not the most important position in the game. It's like the quarterback position in football. If you look at football, it's only been since the late '90s that a lot of the people in charge of [NFL] teams have been comfortable enough to have a black quarterback—a Donovan McNabb [Philadelphia Eagles], an Aaron Brooks [New Orleans Saints] or a Kordell Stewart [Chicago Bears] in the same position as [white quarterback] Brett Favre [Green Bay Packers]. For me, hockey is a great game. But I've been in situations where I didn't get the chance to show I could be a full-time starting goalie."

The chance has come in Carolina, thanks to Hurricanes president and general manager Jim Rutherford, a former NHL goaltender for thirteen seasons who had fancied Weekes for some time. "I started watching Kevin in the juniors when he was sixteen and I liked him then," Rutherford said. "Fundamentally, he was good. He still had things to work on, but everybody does at that age. He has good size, takes up a lot of the net, and has exceptionally good reflexes. The fact that he moved to a few teams in his early twenties doesn't tell me anything other than a few teams pushed this young goalie too soon."

Weekes found a supportive environment in Carolina with Rutherford, Coach Paul Maurice, former All-Star goalie Arturs Irbe and a dressing room of players hungry to prove something. The Hurricanes won the Southeast Division in 2001–02 but garnered little respect around the league because of the weakness of the division's other teams (Washington Capitals, Florida Panthers, Tampa Bay Lightning and Atlanta Thrashers). As a division champion, the Hurricanes claimed the No. 3 seed in the Eastern Conference playoffs, even though they finished with the eighth-best record in the East. Conventional wisdom had the sixth-seeded New Jersey Devils, the defending conference champions, eliminating Carolina in the best-of-seven-game, first-round series. But because of a brilliant relief effort by Weekes, Carolina made a mockery of conventional wisdom.

After getting wins in Games 1 and 2, Irbe, a 5-foot-8 goalie from Latvia, struggled with his positioning and confidence in Games 3 and 4 in New Jersey, prompting Maurice to yank him during each game in favour of Weekes, a playoff neophyte. "I wouldn't have made the switch if I had not had complete confidence in Kevin," Maurice said. "I'd seen him play ever since the juniors and there was no doubt in my mind that he could do the job."

"The change in goaltenders was the singularly most important move of the entire series," said award-winning broadcaster Mike Emrick, who described every game of the Hurricanes-Devils series on American television. "The Devils knew they could beat Irbe, and after seeing Weekes in a few games they knew they were going to need a pretty good shot to get one past him."

Although the Devils held onto leads built against Irbe to even the series at two games apiece, Weekes provided airtight goaltending and stood up to the Devils' efforts to physically intimidate him on hard runs at the net. Maurice had seen enough positive signs from Weekes to start him in the crucial fifth game in Raleigh. In the hockey equivalent of the Broadway musical, *42nd Street*, Weekes made his first playoff start as an unheralded understudy and skated off as a star.

All of his athletic gifts were on full display—the speed that few of his contemporaries can match, the anticipation that enables him to take away a shooter's angle, the rapidity with which he moves from one goalpost to the other, the quick reflexes, the strong glove hand and steady puck-handling, and the use of his body to cover the net as though he were 6-foot-6 and 230 pounds instead of six feet and 195 pounds. Weekes matched Martin Brodeur, Canada's 2002 Olympic gold medal-winning goalie, save for save and Game 5 moved into overtime with the score 2–2. The next goal would decide the game, and New Jersey had two golden scoring opportunities. Both were denied when Weekes entered that rarefied place of athletic supremacy known as "the zone."

Devils winger Stephane Richer, who had scored four game-winning overtime goals in his career, fired at Weekes a whistling shot from point-blank range only to be repelled on a sprawling save with the left skate that demanded the full extension of his body and left him prone on the ice. Fans at the arena in Raleigh barely had time to absorb the enormity of the save because another threat loomed. The puck lay still and tantalizingly free in front of the net when New Jersey's John Madden pounced on it and fired from ten feet away.

"Paul Maurice would tell me after the game that when he saw the puck on Madden's stick, he took one foot off the bench and was heading to the dressing room. He thought the game was over," Emrick said. "Had that been Arturs Irbe in goal, with all due respect to him, I think it would have been a goal and the game would have been over."

Breaking the Ice

It wasn't. Weekes, in an act as improbable as grabbing a fistful of water, contorted his body 180 degrees to the right, snatched the puck out of the air while prone and then held it aloft in triumph. Madden, thoroughly dumbfounded, could only bury his head in his hands while a capacity crowd of 18,000 chanted "Weekes! Weekes! Weekes!"

"When you're on that ice, things are happening at such warped speed as a goalie that you're basically just reacting," he said. "After the save on Richer, I saw Madden closing in so I knew I wasn't going to have time to actually get back to my feet. If I had tried to get up, he would have put the puck in the net. So I basically rolled back over toward him, to my right, and put everything I had in front of the puck. Fortunately, I made the save."

Weekes also was fortunate his virtuosity had not been in vain. Josef Vasicek scored four minutes later to give Carolina a 3–2 win and a 3–2 series lead. Weekes, a winner in his first playoff start, left the ice to a thunderous ovation—the newest star on the only major professional sports team in town.

"I've seen a lot of great saves in hockey, but I have never seen back-to-back saves like that, ever," Rutherford said, echoing the sentiments of thousands.

Weekes stayed in the zone in Game 6, repelling every shot and staring down a rabid New Jersey crowd in the Hurricanes' series-clinching 1–0 win. A hockey game lasts sixty minutes of clock time. Weekes, however, looked so impenetrable it appeared he could have shut out the Devils for six hundred minutes.

"I liken playing goal to playing a video game or a pinball machine," he said. "You keep playing it and playing it and then when you get better the game kind of slows down for you. Things are still happening as fast as they always did, but your reactions are so much quicker and your anticipation is so much better that the game slows down."

Hockey remained at a comfortable speed for him when he defeated Montreal in Game 1 of the Eastern Conference semifinals in Raleigh. The Canadiens won Game 2 to tie the series, and then took a 2–1 series lead with an overtime goal against Weekes in Game 3—The Banana Game in Montreal. Nevertheless, his job as Carolina's starting goalie seemed secure. Carolina had had critical defensive breakdowns in the Game 2 loss, and an ill-advised icing infraction against usually reliable defenseman Glen Wesley in Game 3 led to the faceoff deep in Carolina ice on which Montreal scored the decisive goal. But Game 4 proved to be Weekes' final playoff appearance.

Carolina trailed 2–0 after the first period. While Weekes could not be specifically faulted for either goal, he did not do anything spectacular in the period, either. With Carolina in danger of falling behind 3–1 in the best-of-seven-game series, Coach Maurice reinserted Irbe to start the second period in the hope that it might spark the team.

"I had said throughout the Montreal series that I had confidence in both goaltenders and I was going to go with the guy who I thought would give us the best chance to win," Maurice said. "I didn't feel that Kevin was playing poorly. He just got some bad breaks on both those goals in the period. So I made the change for the exact same reason I had taken Arturs out in Games 3 and 4 against New Jersey."

Weekes felt blindsided by the goaltending switch, but he was too much of a team player to say so publicly. "He just told me he was going to make a change," Weekes said. "I got hit on my collarbone [with the puck] pretty hard in that game, and we had a couple of funny bounces and we were down 2–0." Sore collarbone or not, he admitted he could have stayed in the game. Indeed, he wanted to stay in.

"A lot of times when a goalie gets pulled, people think the coach is upset with the goalie or he doesn't think the goalie is playing well," Rutherford said. "But for the most part, when Paul pulls the goalie, it's not for either reason. It's more to relieve the pressure on the goalie or just to change things up a little bit."

Montreal went ahead 3–0 in the second period of Game 4 before the Hurricanes staged a remarkable rally. They stormed the net and tied the score, 3–3, on Erik Cole's goal in the final minute of regulation time, and won Game 4 on Niclas Wallin's slapshot in overtime. Whether Carolina could have staged what is remembered as "The Miracle at Molson" with Weekes in goal is impossible to know. But the comeback occurred with Irbe in goal, and Maurice stuck with him for the remainder of the playoffs. Irbe had been tending goal for Maurice in Carolina since the start of the 1998–99 season, Weekes for only two months. A certain comfort level already existed between the coach and the incumbent goalie that Weekes had not had time to attain. As a newcomer, albeit a gifted one, on a team in uncharted playoff territory, Weekes had been told in figurative terms to wait his turn. The man who had almost single-handedly won the New Jersey series rode Carolina's bench in the team's final thirteen postseason games.

"The momentum went Irbe's way at the start of the playoffs, then it went my way and then it went his way again," Weekes said diplomatically. "I really can't complain because momentum is what got us to the Stanley Cup Finals." On its maiden trip to the Finals, Carolina lost to the Detroit Red Wings four games to one. Still, Weekes took solace in his performance in the New Jersey series and carried the momentum into the 2002–03 season, when he decisively outplayed Irbe and seized the starting job.

Breaking the Ice

◆ ◆ ◆

Weekes, who made $1.5 million in 2002–03, still longs for an audience with his goaltending idol, Fuhr. But he had to figure out on his own how to emerge as The Man on an NHL club: never stop working to improve your game, physically and mentally, and hope to find a team somewhere that believes in your talent as much as you do. Fuhr found that team in Edmonton.

Fuhr has also found a sense of bliss in Edmonton, where he lives with wife Candice. He's the father of three daughters and an eleven-year-old son who plays peewee hockey, although he lives with Fuhr's ex-wife in California. "I wouldn't mind if he becomes a hockey player when he grows up, but I'm leaving that up to him," Fuhr said. "My parents didn't push me into hockey. It was there for me and I took to it. That's the way it was for my son."

Had the boy remained in Edmonton, Fuhr might have coached him during the 2002–03 season, a time he spent guiding a youth team in preparation for what he hopes will be an NHL coaching gig someday. "I want to coach hockey at the highest level because I have some definite ideas about how I think the game should be played," he said. "But I want to start coaching at a lower level, a minor league or a junior league, to kind of get established. I'm sending out the resumés and I'll see what I can get."

After his retirement, he spent the 2000–01 season as a roving goaltending instructor in the Calgary Flames' system and the following season doing corporate work for the Flames. However, the pull to get back on the ice—or in this case, behind the bench, has proved strong.

"I know as a former player that players prefer a more wide-open style of hockey, and I really believe that's the way a team can achieve its best results," he said. "If you look at the NHL now, there are a lot of teams playing a tight-checking style, which can get you into the playoffs, as the Minnesota Wild proved [in their third season, 2002–03]. But you're not going to win a Stanley Cup, I don't believe, playing that style of hockey. Players will tell you a more wide-open style of hockey keeps you in the game mentally. It keeps you more alert, and it's much more fun to play and much more entertaining for the fans."

Since shedding his mask and the other tools of the goaltending trade, he has become closer than ever to sports fans as a participant on the professional celebrity golf tour. He plays up to twelve tournaments a year throughout North America against former stars from Major League Baseball, pro football, pro basketball and other sports. His 2003 season began May 1 with a tournament in San Diego. Three days before the Hockey Hall of Fame Induction Class of 2003 was announced, he competed in Mario Lemieux's annual tournament in Pittsburgh. Fuhr's goal is to finish the year ranked in the top five among the eighty golfers on the celebrity circuit. In 2002 he finished in the top fifteen, not bad but well behind the top hockey player on the tour, Dan Quinn, a former centre who played for eight NHL teams in fourteen seasons.

Quinn has certain physical advantages over Fuhr, however. His right knee has not been operated upon ten times, as Fuhr's has. And his shoulders are not constantly barking—an inevitable result of placing them in front of fired pucks for nineteen years in hockey's elite league—as Fuhr's do.

"I gave some serious thought to playing another season before I retired in 2000," he said. "But my body finally convinced me to stop. My body hurt every day. The doctors said if I had tried to play one more year, I would have needed to have my right knee replaced. A forty-year-old with a knee replacement? That was not something to look forward to."

When he finally sits down with Weekes, Fuhr said he'll advise the twenty-eight-year-old on the importance of taking care of his most valuable asset: the body. Considering Weekes' seizure in September 2002, a breakdown born out of insufficient rest, the young man had better be listening.

"Kevin is a goalie who could be around for another ten years because of his focus and athletic ability. I really admire those things about him," Fuhr said. "He can make saves a lot of goalies can't because of his athleticism. Now that he's a number-one goalie, the only advice I would give him is to relax and enjoy it. When you have the bad days, just roll with it. Because when you're a number-one goalie in the National Hockey League, not every day will be good. And some are going to be really bad."

But not as bad, Weekes should hope, as March 18, 2003 was for goalie Fred Brathwaite. On that day, just three weeks before the post-season, the playoff-bound St. Louis Blues released Brathwaite, an Ottawa native who, like Weekes, was born of parents with roots in Barbados. The release was but the latest setback for Brathwaite, who had teamed with Fuhr for parts of the 1998–99 and 1999–2000 seasons in Calgary. The 5-foot-7 Brathwaite made his major-league debut with the 1993–94 Oilers, after signing as an undrafted free agent, and has been a reluctant passenger on an NHL-minor league roller coaster ever since.

"Wherever Freddie has gone he's played well, but size has been his biggest downfall," Fuhr said. "Teams just don't think he can play because of his size."

Brathwaite, who made $1.15 million in 2002–03, appeared in thirty games for the Blues and had more than respectable statistics: twelve wins, nine losses, four ties (a goalie is not credited with a win, loss or tie in every appearance) and a 2.75 goals-against average. But he always had to look over his shoulder.

"From day one of the season, everybody was saying the Blues' weakness is their goaltending," Fuhr said, "and that gave St. Louis an automatic excuse if they didn't win. If they didn't win their division: blame the goaltender. If they didn't win the Cup: blame the goaltender."

The Blues replaced Brathwaite as the occasional starter and made Brent Johnson the number-one man until he played himself out of the job. But rather than go back to Brathwaite, the Blues traded for Chris Osgood, who won consecutive Stanley Cups with Detroit in 1997 and '98, the latter year as the starting goalie. Two days after acquiring Osgood, St. Louis fired Brathwaite.

In 1999–2000, Brathwaite's most active season, he played in sixty-one games for the Flames and won twenty-five with five shutouts. Three years later, the Stanley Cup playoffs went on without him and he looked for his next job in hockey. He found it on June 2, 2003 when the Columbus Blue Jackets signed him to a one-year deal.

"If you're a goalie in the NHL, black or white, you're going to have your ups and downs," Fuhr said. "Nobody stays on top forever and you've got to learn how to deal with the bad days and keep coming back. You can't have a long memory. That's what I would tell Kevin. That's what I would tell any goalie."

And Fuhr would say, "Keep the faith" to every black goalie trying to play his way into the NHL, including Tyrone Garner, Joaquin Gage and brothers Pokey and Smokey Reddick. Eldon "Pokey" Reddick, a backup on the 1989–90 Stanley Cup-winning Edmonton Oilers, also has played for the Winnipeg Jets and Florida Panthers. He tended goal for the minor-league Fort Wayne Komets in 2002–03. Stan "Smokey" Reddick has yet to play in the NHL. Married to a Slovenian, he played pro hockey in her country in 2002–03. Garner, a former Flame, and Gage, an ex-Oiler, hope to leap from minor leagues into the NHL in 2003–04.

◆ ◆ ◆

As Weekes worked his way toward leading-man status in the NHL, he once shared a Florida Panthers dressing room with John Vanbiesbrouck. The precipitous fall from grace of Vanbiesbrouck, a goaltender-turned-minor league coach, is another subject Weekes and Fuhr could discuss. It's the subject of how one man's distinguished two-decades long playing career went up in flames because of an utterance of hate that shed light on professional hockey's silent shame.

Tony McKegney, shown here as a Quebec Nordiques left wing, was the first black offensive star in the National Hockey League. He scored forty goals for the St. Louis Blues in the 1987–88 season.
O-Pee-Chee/Hockey Hall of Fame

The N-Bomb

Trevor Daley is on the magical track that carries players to the NHL. In the 2002–03 season, he was the nineteen-year-old team captain and star defenseman of the Sault Ste. Marie Greyhounds of the Ontario Hockey League. Excelling for the Greyhounds in the city known as "The Soo" puts Daley in select company. Hockey icon Wayne Gretzky starred for the junior-league team, as did probable Hall of Famers Ron Francis and Paul Coffey. Wherever Daley goes in The Soo—a restaurant, a shop, a gas station—he receives warm greetings from townsfolk, people who admire his talent as well as his poise and precocity. That Daley is a black hockey player, or more accurately, the brown-skinned offspring of an interracial union between a black Jamaican-Canadian man and a white Canadian woman, did not seem to colour anyone's perception of him. That is, until he truly got to know his coach.

John Vanbiesbrouck, himself a former Sault Ste. Marie Greyhound, assumed the duties of coach and general manager of the team in 2002 after a noteworthy twenty-year career as an NHL goaltender. Vanbiesbrouck was still learning the ropes as a hockey executive on March 7, 2003 when he uttered the word with which he hanged himself. While visiting the billet home of white Greyhound players Mike Amodeo and Jeff Doyle after a loss that night, Vanbiesbrouck referred to Daley on more than one occasion as a "nigger." Amodeo and Doyle were shocked, according to an associate of Daley's agent, Hall of Famer Bobby Orr, and approached Daley the next day. "Trev, we've got to tell you something," the teammates said.

Daley, taught by his parents the credo of Dr. Martin Luther King Jr. that each person should be judged not by the colour of his skin but by the content of his character, was stunned and deeply wounded by what he had heard. "Trevor asked me what he should do and I told him he should go home," Orr said. Daley returned to Toronto the next day, but not before meeting for two-and-half hours with OHL commissioner Dave Branch. "I saw a very hurt young man," Branch said, "who wants no part of this and didn't ask for it."

Vanbiesbrouck coached the Greyhounds game on March 9. It would be his last. The next day, the former Greyhounds standout and NHL All-Star resigned in disgrace. He also announced plans to sell his 25% stake in the team. "I did use the N-word. That is the truth," he said. "I used it in the heat of the moment. I don't know where it came from. It was wrong. I'm the first one to admit it."

◆ ◆ ◆

Vanbiesbrouck is hardly the first one to use the slur, and Daley is not likely to be the last black hockey player to be smeared by it. The slur is so regrettably common that it has its own euphemisms (e.g., the N-word). Willie O'Ree, the NHL's first black player, said he was called "nigger" so often on the ice he thought it was his name. Black players who came before O'Ree, such as Herb Carnegie, often heard it too. Efforts have been made by the NHL, professional minor leagues and major-junior leagues such as the OHL to sensitize players to the psychological damage of racial slurs, particularly "nigger." The NHL made each of its thirty teams attend a racial diversity seminar, at which O'Ree spoke, during the 1999–2000 season. The OHL posts a harassment and abuse policy statement in the dressing room of each of its thirty teams. However, no league can regulate human behaviour, or misbehaviour. And too many hockey men, even a forty-year-old like Vanbiesbrouck, simply have not come to grips with their latent racism.

"John said he said it in the heat of the moment? That just means it was in his heart the whole time," said Boston Bruins winger Sandy McCarthy, who is black and Irish. "You don't just say something like that about somebody unless you were already thinking it."

Said Carolina Hurricanes goalie Kevin Weekes, a black who played with Vanbiesbrouck in the Florida Panthers organization in 1997–98: "It leads me to now wonder what he thought about me the whole time that I was in the [Florida] system. It makes you wonder. People ask, 'Why don't more minorities play hockey?' Well, what are you going to play for? Are you going to play just to get substandard treatment or be treated foolishly or unfairly?"

In an ironically worded comment, Boston Bruins defenseman Sean Brown, who is black, said, "I don't know John Vanbiesbrouck, but I've heard from people that he's actually a nice guy. But because he was stupid for three minutes, he's going to be wearing a black mark for the rest of his life."

With Vanbiesbrouck excised from the body of the Greyhounds, Daley rejoined the club March 13 and finished out the season. Daley, a second-round draft pick of the NHL's Dallas Stars in 2002, embraced hockey at age two while watching youth games in his Toronto neighbourhood, games that featured his uncle Don Harris and future NHL players Weekes, Anson Carter and Michael Peca. It is ironic that Daley has been subjected to a racial slur in hockey because of the extent to which his family tried diligently to de-emphasize the issue of race.

"The way I raised him and the way he sees himself, he thinks he should get to wherever he has to go because he worked for it, not because he's Trevor Daley," his mother, Trudy Daley, said. "Trevor doesn't care what colour you are and he doesn't think colour should have anything to do with anything."

Yet Trudy Daley and Trevor Daley Sr. understood that their son would eventually encounter people who were not as open-minded about matters of race. "What his father and I stressed to him was that we know who you are. But when you go out on that street you're just another black kid. That's how you'll be treated. They'll stereotype you. But think less about what certain people think of you and think more about who you really are."

Nevertheless, no amount of positive reinforcement can totally erase the pain of a black person subjected to a racial slur, particularly one uttered by someone in a position of authority, someone who could affect your quality of life. The slur is an attack on one's personhood, an attempt to damage the psyche and wound the soul. And for a black in the overwhelmingly white world of hockey, no slur cuts deeper and instills more pain than "nigger."

◆ ◆ ◆

"Nigger" is what made a Boston Bruins player tackle a New York Ranger on the ice during a game at Madison Square Garden. "Nigger" is what made a college hockey player chase an opposing player into his own dressing room after the post-game handshake. "Nigger" is what ignited a horrific scene at Detroit's Joe Louis Arena where players swung sticks at each other's heads.

"I always thought that word was the worst one because it was associated with slavery. Black people were the only group brought to America to be slaves," said Tony McKegney, the NHL's fourth black player. "Some nasty things are said on the ice in the heat of battle, but when somebody calls you that, that's just over the line. You're not going to respond by calling him 'fathead' or something like that. You're much angrier than that. But what are you going to do about it?"

McKegney, usually a mild-mannered type, swung his stick at the head of Joey Kocur, a Detroit Red Wings forward, who called him "nigger" during the 1987–88 season. McKegney, whose swing missed Kocur, surmised the slur might have been an attempt to destroy his groove since he scored a career-high forty goals for the St. Louis Blues that season. "Kocur and I got into a shouting match. He called me 'nigger' and got a gross misconduct (a game suspension and $10,000 fine) and I got a ten-minute misconduct for swinging my stick. We swung sticks at each other. Things just got completely out of hand."

Just to prove that hockey, like politics, makes strange bedfellows, McKegney and Kocur became teammates when Detroit acquired McKegney in a trade before the 1989–90 season. "We ended up becoming friends in training camp," McKegney said. "We both sort of came to each other. With me being new to the team, I certainly wanted him to feel comfortable being around me. I think I realized then how badly he felt about it."

Fines and suspensions are handed down by the NHL to players found guilty of racial slurs, a far cry from the verbal *laissez faire* that existed on the ice when O'Ree played for the Boston Bruins in the 1957–58 and 1960–61 seasons and Mike Marson, the league's second black, played for the Washington Capitals and Los Angeles Kings from 1974–80. "I was called 'nigger' and every other bad name in the book along with stuff that I didn't even know was in the book," Marson said.

According to one player in the OHL, the league in which Daley plays, racism remains unchecked. "Guys have called me a spear-chucker before," said Oshawa Generals forward Colt King, an aborigine. "I know [referees] have heard me being called it, but they really don't do anything." Sean McMorrow, a black player with the American Hockey League's Rochester Americans, said he heard racial slurs as an OHL player in the 2001–02 season. "You go to battle every night for your teammates, owners and managers. It's a slap in the face," he said.

Black players on any level of hockey who feel blatantly disrespected by an opponent will sometimes respond in kind. John Saunders, the versatile ABC and ESPN sportscaster who serves as studio host of NHL telecasts on both networks, can attest to that. Saunders, the brother of Bernie Saunders, the NHL's fifth black (Quebec Nordiques, 1989–91), was a hockey star at Ryerson College when a white opponent slurred him.

"We were playing Royal Military College, which is the Canadian equivalent of the U.S. Army, Navy and Air Force teams all rolled into one," Saunders said. "The Royal Military team was not real good. We were beating them badly one day, so they started cutting a few of our guys. And I, in my craziness, said I was going to exact some revenge. During a faceoff, I went after a guy who had just cut one of our guys. I told our centreman, 'Just hold his stick so he can't go anywhere.' I came toward him and brought my stick up and cut him. Because there was a big collision or commotion, the referee didn't see it or didn't care. There wasn't even a penalty. Nothing happened until the end of the game when players shook hands at centre ice, as they do in college hockey, win or lose. On the handshake line, the guy I cut said to me, 'We won the battle 'cause we cut more of your guys.' I told him where to go and he called me a 'nigger' and bolted off the ice. I chased him into his own locker room and went after the guy. I ended up with a suspension for that. Even though I knew what he was trying to do by using that word, it had reached the point in my life—I'm a young man now, in college—where it was totally unacceptable to hear that. I guarantee there are black guys in the NHL right now who hear it and it doesn't even faze them. They just say, 'Consider the source' and just skate away."

◆ ◆ ◆

Carter, a New York Rangers winger, handled the slur that way as a collegiate star at Michigan State. He laughed in the face of a Michigan player who called him 'nigger' during a game between the Big 10 Conference rivals. He laughed, he said, because he knew where he was going—the NHL—and he knew his antagonist lacked the talent to ever get there. He considered the slur the act of a "desperate" opponent.

McCarthy represents the opposing viewpoint. The hard-fisted winger was playing for the Philadelphia Flyers in April 1999 when he became enraged by a slur in a playoff game against the Toronto Maple Leafs. After a fierce battle for the puck along the boards in Game 1 of the series, McCarthy at 6-foot-3 and 225 pounds, continued to bang bodies with 5-foot-10, 200-pound winger Tie Domi, who is nicknamed "The Albanian Assassin." Long after neither man was in any position to play the puck, they still seemed intent on pummelling each other. Only the intervention of on-ice officials prevented it. But in the Flyers' dressing room after Toronto's overtime victory, a seething McCarthy told reporters, "Tie Domi dropped an N-bomb on me. For him to say a thing like that was totally out of line."

Domi vehemently denied the charge and accused McCarthy of spitting on him during the game. A league investigation, which consisted of the NHL asking on-ice officials and players from both teams if they had heard or seen anything to substantiate either charge, cleared Domi and McCarthy. However, bad blood lingered between the two players for the next three seasons, during which McCarthy changed teams twice. He and Domi, two of the more willing fighters in the NHL, reached a détente only after a chance meeting in February 2002 in, of all places, the Bahamas. While the NHL was on hiatus during the Winter Olympics, the two ran into each other at a resort and they finally talked things over, man-to-man.

"I know he regretted what he said," McCarthy said, "but I think he was trying to play a smart game for his team and get me frustrated without taking a penalty for his team. I think he regretted saying what he said right away, even if he denied it at the time. He's Albanian, so I'm sure he understands what it feels like to have a word used to try and hurt you."

The N-bomb, as McCarthy calls it, has irritated him ever since his formative years as an interracial child in a predominantly white section of Toronto. "I heard a lot of name-calling from the kids at school. But I always stood up for myself and never let anybody push me around. I got into a lot of fights over it, but in the long run I ended up prevailing. I would say grade six was the first time I started having to fight because of something said to me. And I went on fighting other kids until people saw how well I defended myself and then I didn't have to fight those kids anymore."

Fights in youth hockey are extremely rare. The accent is on teaching the fundamentals of the game. A rule even exists that prohibits the checking of another player from behind. McCarthy, however, heard so many racial slurs on the ice that he made a deal with his mother, Doris—a deal that allowed him one fight per season to try and get the anger out of his system.

"People who are very confident about themselves don't have to use [racial slurs]," he said. "Those words come from a weak person with a weak mind and a weak upbringing. In the NHL, there's a lot of nasty language heard on the ice and people shouldn't have to hear it. But it's being said to try to get [an opponent] to do something stupid—take a penalty that could hurt your team, get yourself out of position, lose your concentration. Things are said to try to get an edge. The majority of the time, though, people respect each other enough not to cross that line."

McCarthy himself and teammate Darcy Tucker were accused of racially slurring black winger Peter Worrell in a 1998 exhibition game. Worrell, then of the Florida Panthers, said he didn't hear any slurs, but two Panthers employees claimed they had. A league investigation found no evidence. Nor was it ever proven that Philadelphia Flyers winger Chris Gratton had called Worrell "an ape" in a 1998 game, even though two Florida newspapers reported it as fact. Worrell helped exonerate Gratton by telling the NHL he had heard no such slur during the game.

When evidence of a racial slur has been uncovered in recent seasons, the NHL has taken punitive action. Washington Capitals winger Craig Berube was suspended one game without pay for calling Worrell "a monkey" in a 1998 game. Bryan Marchment of the San Jose Sharks got a one-game suspension without pay after he called black Vancouver Canucks winger Donald Brashear "a big monkey." Chris Simon, a

Capitals winger, incurred a three-game suspension without pay for calling Edmonton forward Mike Grier "nigger" after a November 8, 1997 game. Simon, a Native Canadian from the Ojibwa tribe in Wawa, Ontario, issued a face-to-face apology to Grier in a Toronto hotel three days later.

"He said 'I'm sorry' several times and I believed him," said Grier, the NHL's first black American star. "He had a very sincere look in his eye and his manner about him seemed very honest. It takes a stand-up person to come out here and handle the situation as quickly as he did. I accept his apology."

Coincidentally, Grier and Simon became teammates when Grier was traded to Washington before the 2002–03 season. But in December 2002, Washington traded Simon to the Chicago Blackhawks.

At least Grier got an apology from his tormentor and resolved the issue. Graeme Townshend, an NHL player for parts of five seasons (1989–90 to 1993–94), never got that satisfaction. The first NHL player from Jamaica, Townshend's most memorable moment in hockey's major league is one he would rather forget.

♦ ♦ ♦

Having been called up to the Boston Bruins from the minor-league Maine Mariners just three days earlier, Townshend stole the spotlight on February 3, 1990 in Boston's 2–1 loss to the New York Rangers at Madison Square Garden because of his visceral reaction to a racial slur. Townshend said he was called "nigger" by Rangers winger Kris King after a second-period collision along the sideboards. An enraged Townshend, who played at 6-foot-2 and 225 pounds, tackled King and punched him repeatedly until both linesmen pulled him away. Boston led 1–0 at the time, but with Townshend in the penalty box the Rangers tied the score and seized momentum. "It was a mistake on my part," he told reporters after the game. "I lost my discipline. It hurt my team. It won't happen again."

King had a reputation for verbally antagonizing opponents. Earlier in the season, he received a misconduct penalty in a game for provoking a fight with Dino Ciccarelli by taunting the Minnesota North Stars winger about an arrest on a charge of indecent exposure. Still, King denied dropping the N-bomb on Townshend. "I called him something I can't say, but which wasn't racial," he told reporters. "And I told him, 'Nice hit.' Of course, [the Bruins are] going to say what they're saying now. It was a dumb play by the guy."

A league investigation produced no corroborating evidence, so King was not punished. It is unlikely that a player in only his second NHL game would tackle and pound an opponent for no reason, subjecting the player to a penalty and his team to an on-ice disadvantage. However, that is what the league ruled in Townshend vs. King. Referee Bill McCreary told Bruins captain Ray Bourque during the game that he had not heard any slur.

Townshend would play only two more games for Boston that season before being sent back to the minors. His NHL career proved disappointing. He felt typecast as a fighter because of his size and aggressive style. Frustrating as it was to be stereotyped as a player, Townshend suffered more from being subjected to racial insults. As a collegian at Rensselaer Polytechnic Institute in Troy, New York, he saw coach Mike Addesa resign under fire after using a racial slur to criticize his play. As a minor leaguer in the New York Islanders system in February 1992, he went into the stands after a game to confront a player who had slurred him. The player (Gord Kruppke) later apologized, yet Townshend again regretted his outburst. "I didn't react in a professional or mature manner," he said. "I'm sure my mother would be ashamed of the way I reacted. I'm ashamed."

It is not likely his father would have been ashamed. Townshend, whose family moved to Toronto when he was two, remembered attending nursery school when he was called "nigger" for the first time. He asked his father what the word meant and was told, "Go back to school tomorrow and you beat up on him." Townshend followed orders while admitting he wasn't sure why he was issuing a beating.

Had he remained in Jamaica, he might have used his athletic talent on the cricket patch, soccer field or running track. However, being reared in Toronto gave Townshend immediate exposure to hockey. Exposure, but not easy access. The cost of skates, sticks, helmets, gloves, pads, skating lessons, hockey instruction and team fees proved prohibitive until he was ten, making him a veritable old-timer among hockey novices. But once he started in the sport, he caught on quickly and progressed rapidly. After a year of junior hockey, Townshend played four years in college and was named co-captain by the coach whose use of the N-bomb cost him his job.

Referring to his college experience as a black Canadian in the U.S., Townshend said, "It was very strange. The black [American] kids wouldn't talk to me because I was different, you know, not one of them. And the white guys didn't know what to make of me, a black hockey player." When the Bruins signed him as a free agent in May 1989, he did not enter pro hockey unaware of its potential pitfalls. He had heard about the McKegney incident in 1978 when the Birmingham Bulls of the WHA signed McKegney to a contract only to renege after white fans threatened to cancel their season tickets if the team added a black player. Still, Townshend's own handling of the King incident remains a regret.

"I got a letter from a young kid in New Hampshire. He was having a rough time with racial slurs [in school] and he asked me how I would handle it," Townshend said. "I wrote back and I told him I thought I was wrong in how I handled my situation." Had he not pummelled King on the ice at Madison Square Garden and precipitated a deluge of unwanted attention, he might have had a longer stay with the Bruins or in the NHL. Or perhaps he might have endured more games in what he considered an ill-fitting role as a fighter, a hired hand known more for his fists than his hockey skills.

Townshend has had a bigger impact on hockey as a coach, general manager and talent evaluator. Few black former players have had the opportunity to segue into such positions. Dirk Graham remains the only black coach in NHL history, compiling a record of sixteen wins, thirty-five losses and eight ties for the 1998–99 Chicago Blackhawks. When Townshend coached the Macon Whoopee of the Central League in 2000–01, he was the only black coach in any of the eight largest professional hockey leagues, including the NHL. The following season, he became coach and player personnel director of the Greensboro Generals of the East Coast Hockey League.

The coaching bug bit Townshend in 1997 when he played for the Houston Aeros of the International League. As he sat in the penalty box, he noticed for the first time that the Atlanta Knights coach, John Paris Jr., was black. "That was such a huge inspiration to me," he said about Paris, the first black coach in any of the top eight leagues. "That's when I said to myself, 'If he can do it, so can I.'"

That Townshend became coach of two professional franchises in the American South is particularly unusual because he had had such an aversion to the region, because of the McKegney incident and his own experience playing for the Lake Charles Ice Pirates of the Western Professional League from 1997–99. Although he excelled with the Ice Pirates, netting seventy-one goals and 144 points in 128 games, and receiving the league's "Man of the Year" award for his community involvement, he, wife Lori-Ann and son Seth encountered bigotry.

"Our neighbours wouldn't talk to us," he said. "My son's friends weren't allowed to play with him. It was pretty amazing."

◆ ◆ ◆

About as amazing as a nineteen-year-old team captain skating blissfully along a fast track to the NHL only to be derailed by a racial slur from his own coach and general manager. Trevor Daley now faces the challenge of putting himself back on track in Sault Ste. Marie and keeping his eyes on the prize. And the league in which Daley played in 2003 faces the challenge of ensuring that other black players are not stepping onto a racial minefield after they sign a contract.

"Player to player, we know [racism] is there," said Branch, the OHL commissioner. "We know it occurs much more than it should. Still, I'm of the opinion that young people today are better informed than any previous generations. I'm proud of the way the young people understand how hurtful it can be, and when it occurs we respond."

Perhaps Daley, a black defenseman, could someday play for a NHL team led by Townshend, a black coach. The notion may not be as farfetched as once thought. There's another man who would welcome a chance to coach Daley, the man who was the third black to suit up for an NHL game.

Bill Riley, a rugged right wing, was the National Hockey League's third black player when he joined the Washington Capitals in 1974.
O-Pee-Chee/Hockey Hall of Fame

The Jackie Robinson of Amherst

Not every black man would find humour in recounting a story such as this, but Bill Riley, the NHL's third black player, regards the following episode from the mid-1970s as a real knee-slapper.

"I played in the minors, with the Dayton Gems," he says, "with a guy named Larry Belanchuk. Great guy. He even named his son, Riley, after me. One night he and his wife wanted to go out. And you see, we were such a tight-knit team that guys who didn't have kids would sometimes babysit for the guys who did. My wife was in Canada at the time, so I was in Dayton, Ohio, by myself. So Larry said, 'Why don't you come over to our house for dinner and then babysit my kid so I can take my wife to a show?' I said, 'OK, no problem.' I came over and Oh, Lord, they must have had a steak there that was two pounds. And I love to eat. And they had all these baked potatoes and sour cream and salad. Jesus! They just loaded me up, man. Fattened me up as much as they could. And they had apple pie and ice cream for dessert. Man, I had to unfasten my pants afterward. So Larry said, 'Whatever you do, don't fall asleep. Sometimes the baby doesn't sleep too good and he tries to get out of the crib.' I said, 'OK. OK.' Well, the guy must have hypnotized me into going to sleep by constantly telling me not to go to sleep 'cause as soon as he went out the door I went right to the couch and fell asleep. The guys on the team all pretty much knew that soon after a big meal I liked to go to sleep. Anyway, after about two minutes on that couch I was out like a light, eh? So I'm sleeping when all of a sudden I hear this noise, eh? So I went to the window to look and there are guys coming into the house from the patio door and the front door, and these guys have got white pillowcases on their heads and white sheets on! They look like the Ku Klux Klan! And they've got guns in their hands, and they're yelling, 'Kill him! Kill him!' And, man, I'm scared to death. I'm yelling, 'Don't shoot! Don't shoot!' And I'm grabbing the couch hoping these guys don't try to pull me out of the house. And all of a sudden, the guys take off the pillowcases and they fall down laughing. It's my teammates, eh? The boys set me up. I said, 'Boys, you got me. You got me that time.' That's the kind of shit I had to put up with. But it was a fun deal. I didn't take any offense to it. Those guys had stuck up for me on numerous occasions over racist remarks made by [opposing] players and fans."

That Riley could find humour in a stupid prank that could have stopped his heart, or at the least offended him to the core of his being, underscores his easygoing demeanour and ability to get along with others. That there were in his words "numerous occasions" when teammates felt compelled to defend him from racial taunts and attacks on and off the ice indicates how difficult a road he travelled as a black professional hockey player more than a quarter-century ago. Blessed with more toughness, resiliency and perseverance than hockey talent, Riley nonetheless made himself an NHL player for 139 games, beginning in the 1974–75 season with the expansion Washington Capitals and ending in the 1979–80 season with the Winnipeg Jets. Nothing came easy to Riley, but he battled constantly for all he could get. Indeed, his pro career became a manifestation of a notable quote from Whitney M. Young, an American civil rights leader of the 1960s: "It is better to be prepared for an opportunity and not have one than to have an opportunity and not be prepared."

A burly right wing at 5-foot-11 and 195 pounds with the thick thighs and broad-sloped shoulders characteristic of a hockey man, Riley lacked the innate talent of a Mike Marson, the NHL's second black and his Capitals teammate on and off for parts of four seasons. Marson had been the nineteenth player taken in the 1974 NHL draft and a "bonus baby" armed with a five-year contract worth half-a-million dollars before even stepping onto the ice. Riley, neither smooth nor swift as a skater, went undrafted by the NHL. Never did he enjoy any semblance of job security in a league he forced his way into with grit, cunning and desire.

"I was the guy who wasn't supposed to make it," Riley said in a strong and resonant voice like a broadcaster's. "There were white boys in the town I grew up in who were supposedly better hockey players and more talented than me. To this day, if you go to Amherst and ask the people who was the best hockey player to come from this town they would not say Bill Riley."

But let the record show that the Amherst resident to play the longest in the NHL was Bill Riley. And let the record show that the first Amherst resident to follow Riley into the NHL is also black. Craig Martin, a right wing, played twenty games for the Jets in 1994–95 and one game for the Florida Panthers in 1996–97. And let the record further show that Alton White of Amherst, who played three seasons in the WHA, a professional rival of the NHL in the 1970s, is also black. White had thirty-eight goals and forty-six assists in 145 WHA games for the New York Raiders, Los Angeles Sharks and Michigan Stags/Baltimore Blades from 1972–75.

A hard-fisted player, Riley had thirty-one goals, thirty assists and 320 penalty minutes in five seasons in hockey's major league. He scored a career-high thirteen goals for the 1976–77 Capitals despite spending thirty games in the minors, and equalled his career-high the following season in just fifty-seven games before severing a tendon—an injury from which his career never recovered.

To understand how Riley succeeded against the odds, it is important to learn more about the small, blue-collar town in Nova Scotia that helped shape the man he would become.

◆ ◆ ◆

"The number one thing I did for Billy was encourage him to get out of Amherst as early as he could," Gladys Riley, his seventy-four-year-old mother, said from the home in which Riley was reared. "The only difference between Amherst and the Deep South was that in the Deep South they put up signs that said NO COLORED. Here, they're more discreet. I was born here. My husband was born here. We grew up here together and went to school together. I'm telling you, when Billy was growing up here, there were no blacks on the fire department or the police department. In fact, just recently [in 2002], we got our first black young man on the fire department. This town is something else, I'll tell you."

Visiting Amherst was like stepping into a time machine and travelling back to the early 1960s, said Al Williams, a former sports writer who covered Capitals games in the seventies. A decade later, he visited Amherst at Riley's request. "It was like a time warp; you leave the Washington, D.C. area and all of a sudden you're in Mayberry," Williams said, referring to the fictional North Carolina town from television's *Andy Griffith Show*. "The houses were half a mile apart and each house had what they called 'a drinking house' in the back—a shed with a table, a few chairs and a urinal. The men weren't allowed by their wives to drink and shoot the breeze with their buddies in the big house, so they would go do it in the drinking house. And to make a phone call, you would have to dial the operator and she would put your call through as soon as a line was free. While I was there, Bill had a plumbing problem. It was an emergency. So he called some guy, Joe the plumber. Then he had to wait for hours for Joe, the town plumber, to show up because Joe was out doing something else."

Bill Riley, born in 1950, is the oldest of Gladys and James Riley's five children. He was encouraged to learn a trade and become self-sufficient because finding a job in Amherst depended largely on who you knew, and no matter how many people a black in Amherst knew, he did not know enough of "the right people."

"I worked as a domestic outside the home," Gladys Riley said. "In later years, I got a job at the Department of Tourism and I worked there for fifteen years. That job was like striking gold because I finally got health benefits and retirement benefits. My husband owned a garbage business and before that he was in the Canadian armed forces. He's retired now. Billy saw from our example that he should be honest and work hard. But we let him know that he would have a hard time making it if he tried to do it in Amherst."

As a boy, Riley also heard from his parents the advice countless other black children have heard from theirs: "You have to be twice as good as a white person to get just as much." In this context, being twice as good did not mean twice as talented, but rather twice as diligent, twice as determined, twice as tenacious. And Riley took the advice to heart. He had no choice.

"I could move freely in my hometown until I wanted a job," he said. "There's prejudice in Canada, make no mistake about that. But it's hidden."

◆ ◆ ◆

Riley exposed some of the hidden racism after the 1976–77 NHL season, when he attempted to purchase a cottage in an area just outside Amherst, in what had been an all-white resort on the Northumberland Strait. Riley, married to his black childhood sweetheart, Joanne, wanted a place where he could relax in the off-season and where their young children could play. During his search for tranquility, he became the Jackie Robinson of Amherst.

"I couldn't understand why it was taking so long to have my loan approved," he said. "I had more money in the bank than what I was trying to borrow. Jesus, I found out the bank and a bunch of other people were in cahoots to try to prevent me from buying property in that neighbourhood. It became a national story in Canada when I sued the bank and the town. The courtroom was packed with black people and white people turning out in support of me. I grew up playing hockey with a lot of the whites, eh? The press was interviewing me and I guess I got a little excited one day and I said, 'I'm going to win this case and become the Jackie Robinson of Amherst. My family is going to integrate that neighbourhood!'

"Had this happened in the United States, I probably would have got the cottage for free and one million dollars in punitive damages. Basically, I got the place but I still had to pay the lawyers. When I should have been getting ready for training camp that summer, there I was in court fighting for the right to spend my own money to buy a cottage near my own hometown."

Getting into the NHL was another battle for Riley. No team drafted him despite back-to-back thirty-goal seasons from 1968–70 for the Amherst Ramblers in major-junior hockey. Riley became a welder in an aluminum plant in British Columbia, and in 1974 he was also playing semi-pro hockey in Kitimat, British Columbia when NHL scouts from the Capitals and Philadelphia Flyers became intrigued by his aggressive style of play. He accepted the Capitals' invitation to training camp because he thought better of his chances of making an expansion team.

Assigned to the Capitals' top farm club in Dayton, Riley racked up more than twenty times as many penalty minutes (279) as goals (twelve). The man with the four-inch Afro compressed into a hockey helmet, bushy black mustache and deep-set brown eyes let his fists respond to a racist taunt or a cheap shot on the ice, and he received many.

"I never worried about dropping my gloves and fighting on the ice," he said with a chuckle. "I knew I didn't have to worry about 'The Man' putting me in jail. In the NHL I fought Dave Schultz, Tiger Williams. I fought all the tough guys of that era [the 1970s]. I didn't go looking for the little guys. I fought to get back at somebody who had done something to me, or said something racist to me, or I fought to stick up for one of my teammates who couldn't fight. I kept myself in such good physical condition that I honestly felt I would have had a chance against Muhammad Ali. He was such an incredible athlete, but I would've taken my chances with him, eh?"

In the minors, Riley received an introduction to racism south of the border. Spectators in Toledo who rooted for Dayton's intrastate rival in the International League, routinely asked Riley if he sat in the back of the team bus or sharpened the skates and shined the boots of his teammates. He also remembers the Toledo arena's organist providing spectators with musical cues for this offensive rendition:

"Riley's little baby loves shortnin', shortnin'...
Riley's little baby loves shortnin' bread..."

"I stopped going to Billy's games in Ohio, the people were so bad," Gladys Riley said. "My God, they called him names that he didn't even know because he had never heard those names up here in Canada. There would be all these people at the games making sounds like monkeys, taunting Billy. And they used to throw chicken at him! Chicken bones, pieces of chicken. So he asked an American guy, a black guy, why those people were doing that. And the guy said, 'Well, they say we all like to eat chicken.'"

"I felt so sorry that black families that came to the games to support me had to hear those ugly things from cowards in the stands," Bill Riley said. "I'll tell you what, though, it used to energize me. I think you had to look at it that way. You couldn't let those cowards beat you."

◆ ◆ ◆

Prior to the 1976–77 season, Riley had played only one game for the Capitals and 162 minor-league games for the Dayton Gems. A perturbed Riley vowed to Gems' and Capitals' management that if he didn't get an in-season tryout with the NHL club by New Year's Day he would return to Amherst and forget all about hockey. He actually had no intention of quitting, but his pleas to Gems coaches for a call-up had not worked, and the sight of one Gems teammate after another becoming an NHL player while he remained stuck in Dayton compelled him to call the Capitals' bluff.

The ruse worked. Washington gave Riley a ten-game tryout that began on New Year's Day 1977 in Toronto. He seized the opportunity, bringing aggressive checking, sound defense, a bullish tenacity and flashes of playmaking ability to a last-place team severely lacking in each area.

"I didn't want to do anything stupid," he said. "I wanted to show them that I could play hockey and I didn't want to do anything to hurt the team. All the guys helped a lot. They were really pulling for me." The Capitals signed Riley for the rest of the season, but only after some hardball negotiating with general manager Max McNab.

"He said to me, 'I've got a one-way ticket to Dayton [back to the minors] and a one-way ticket to Buffalo [site of the Capitals' next game],'" Riley said. "'If you sign the contract, you go to Buffalo. If you don't sign it, you go back to Dayton.' I didn't want to go back to the minors. I had proven I could play in the National Hockey League. So I signed the contract, went to Buffalo and set up three goals in the game. But I was ticked off, too. I never got a decent signing bonus from that team. With that contract I was forced to sign, the signing bonus was only $1,500. I told McNab, 'I worked all my life for this. All I want is a car.' I really wanted to buy a Blazer, a four-wheel drive because I like to hunt and fish. I told McNab all I wanted was enough money to get a decent vehicle. He wouldn't give it to me."

Riley's peers voted him the Capitals' outstanding rookie in 1976–77, and he established himself as the team's toughest battler for pucks in the corners and along the boards. His reward: a two-year contract worth

$50,000 a year, the most money he ever made as a player. However, the deal left him embittered.

"The Capitals never gave me a decent contract," he said. "I was grateful to the Capitals for giving me an opportunity to play against the best players in the world in the National Hockey League and I was proud to be the third black, but the Capitals took advantage of that. I was a bit naïve. That $100,000 contract was peanuts compared to what other guys were getting who weren't contributing anywhere near as much as I was. But I always knew that if I didn't sign the contract they gave me, I was gone."

When Riley and Mike Marson suited up on December 26, 1974 against Philadelphia, it marked the first time two blacks had appeared in an NHL game. Riley was sent down to Dayton right after the game, but he and Marson teamed up again in the 1976–77 season. Riley, a right wing, and Marson, a left wing, occasionally skated on the same line with centre Gerry Meehan. Teammates called it "the Oreo cookie line."

"Billy was a great teammate; he and I got along great," Marson said. "I thought we really clicked on the ice when we had a chance to play together. But that didn't happen often enough."

In one game in Detroit, Riley and Marson set up a trap to punish Red Wings skaters. Riley said, "I'd chase a guy with the puck behind the net and Mike would pop him when he skated to the other side. I mean, Mike really belted a couple of guys, eh? All clean checks. And of course, we both could fight. So we were just rockin' guys and we knew the Wings weren't going to run us out of the building. The next day in the newspaper the article quoted the Detroit coach Bobby Kromm calling us 'those two roundball players out there.' That was out of line. Totally out of line."

Riley said he often tried to be a big brother to the introspective Marson, who is five years younger. As the NHL's only blacks at the time, both were subjected to racial slurs, cheap shots on the ice and an air of indifference from Capitals' management. Marson, thoroughly fed up with life in a hockey fishbowl, retired at twenty-five. Riley said he often tried to get Marson to relax, but to no avail.

"Guys on the team really liked Mike, but they found that he couldn't take a joke," Riley said. "They would just keep teasing him, about his weight or whatever, and he would take a lot of those things to heart because he was just a kid. Management never knew the kind of hardships Mike and I went through. We got taunted, high-sticked, slashed. He got a death threat. But management expected us to just keep our mouths shut and play. That's basically what we did. We didn't want to rock the boat."

Riley said the last thing he and Marson wanted was to be considered troublemakers. "We both felt that if the team thought we were problems, they would do what anybody does with a problem: they get rid of it, eh? They could have sent us down to the minors. They did send us down. I only got to play one season without getting sent down by the Capitals [1977–78]. Mike only got to play one season without getting sent down by the Capitals [1974–75]. They could have sent us down if we complained about anything and then said to the press, 'Oh, no, it had nothing to do with race.' The league had no support system for us blacks then, and Mike got more upset about things than I did. I guess it was because I was used to so many drawbacks in my life. I know Mike got very angry when somebody called him 'Uncle Ben.' But what was he going to do, beat 'em all up?"

◆ ◆ ◆

Support for the Capitals' two black players hardly existed in Washington's black community, which in the mid-1970s comprised about 70% of the District of Columbia's population. Support was scarce in part because the Capitals played in suburban Landover not in Washington, D.C. proper, and blacks showed little inclination to drive to suburbia to watch a sport with which they were unfamiliar. Furthermore, the Capitals did not aggressively market themselves in the black community, said Al Williams, who covered the team for the *Afro-American*, a chain of weekly newspapers in predominantly black areas like Washington and Baltimore.

"Whatever level of interest blacks had in the Capitals was generated by Bill Riley himself," Williams said. "He's a gregarious, outgoing guy. He was interested in learning about Washington's history, the people, the culture. I'd show him where he could get an Afro haircut in Washington, because his teammates couldn't help him with that. I'd take him to black restaurants and other black-owned businesses and the people would be so surprised. They had never met a black hockey player. A lot of them didn't know there were any black hockey players."

Williams also worked as a Washington, D.C. police officer on the overnight shift, and Riley sometimes accompanied him in the back seat. "He really shows a genuine interest in getting to know people," Williams said. "It's unfortunate that his place on the team wasn't always secure and he was making a minimum salary, as hockey players go. Otherwise, he could have become very well-known in Washington."

Like his teammates, Riley did not live in Washington, D.C., but in suburban Maryland, minutes from the team's home rink, the Capital Centre. Unlike Marson, who felt alienated from his teammates, Riley socialized with them, to a point. "One time on a day off, a guy invited the whole team out to his establishment in Maryland, a place with pool tables and a big bar," Riley said. "When I was about to go in, I saw a bunch of black guys drinking their stuff out of brown paper bags outside. I said, 'How come you guys aren't in there drinking?' And they said, 'We can't go in there. They let us buy the stuff, but they don't let us sit in the place.' So I didn't go in there, either. I stayed and talked with the fellas for a while and then I went home. I'm telling you, man, racism is just sick."

In the 1977–78 season Riley played superbly, skating on the Capitals' top line with centre Guy Charron and left wing Bob Sirois. He established himself as a fierce checker, a disruptive force in front of the net, a reliable player with the puck and a dynamic fighter. But fifty-seven games into the season, adversity arrived. The skate of Buffalo defenseman Jim Schoenfeld inadvertently severed a tendon in Riley's left leg. Although the injury occurred early in the second period, Riley, not knowing the severity, completed the period with blood nearly filling his left boot.

"It was almost a career-ending injury and my leg bothers me to this day," he said. "I had thirteen goals at the time and if I don't get hurt, I get to play the full season and that translates into twenty to twenty-five goals. Man, that injury was frustrating. I never was a fluid skater. I had to work hard to skate. I had those choppy strides. The Capitals sent me to power skating school after my second year in the organization. But I improved my skating a lot. Then this happened. I was never as strong in the legs after that."

With a gimpy left leg, Riley recorded just four points in twenty-four games in 1978–79, his final season with the Capitals. Four years into the expansion team's existence, Washington had few players other teams would covet. The Capitals finished last in the Norris Division three times and next-to-last once with a combined record of sixty wins, 217 losses and forty-three ties. Yet in 1979, every NHL team had to expose a few players to an expansion draft that would supplement the rosters of four teams from the defunct WHA that would be joining the NHL (Edmonton Oilers, Winnipeg Jets, Quebec Nordiques and Hartford Whalers). Washington left Riley unprotected and Winnipeg claimed him. He began the 1979–80 season in the minors before joining the Jets and being reunited with former Capitals coach Tom McVie. Not long after McVie put Riley on the Jets' top line, Riley became expendable. Winnipeg general manager John Ferguson, who had been a hard-nosed winger on five Montreal Canadiens' Stanley Cup winners in the 1960s and '70s, had another player in mind for Riley's spot.

"Ferguson had drafted a guy in his own image named Jimmy Mann," Riley said. "Jimmy had been a big tough guy in the Quebec League and he was a first-round draft pick [nineteenth overall], which put extra pressure on the kid because the consensus was this kid was not good enough to be a first-round pick. So the situation was this: if I played, Jimmy Mann didn't play. So to make room for Jimmy Mann, I got sent down. And Jimmy Mann never became the player Winnipeg thought he would be."

Mann used his fists to hang onto an NHL job for nine seasons, amassing ten goals, thirty points and 895 penalty minutes. He never became another John Ferguson. He never became as good a player as Riley.

◆ ◆ ◆

Riley has been trying to get back to the NHL ever since. From 1980–90 he spent seven seasons playing for Canadian-based minor-league teams and three seasons coaching them. Since 1990 his resourcefulness, affability and hockey knowledge have enabled him to segue into positions of management in the sport, but not at the level to which he considers himself suited.

In the 2002–03 season, he served as general manager of the Moncton Gagnon Beavers of the Maritime Junior League. Players range in age from sixteen to twenty-one, and the level of play is below that of major-junior hockey associations such as the Ontario League. Riley has been a team builder in junior hockey for more than a decade, but he yearns for an opportunity to be a general manager or coach or talent evaluator for an NHL team or a professional minor-league team in a league such as the AHL or East Coast Hockey League.

No black has been a general manager or assistant general manager for an NHL team. A black GM for a professional minor-league team is exceedingly rare, as rare as a black NHL player used to be. Dirk Graham is the only black to coach an NHL team, for fifty-nine games with the 1998–99 Chicago Blackhawks. In the first decade of the twenty-first century, when blacks are increasingly making their mark in every position on the ice, the efforts of former black players like Riley to secure positions of authority and influence off the ice is the next important struggle.

"I've had numerous calls from hockey people who say I've been highly recommended and they'd like to hire me as coach and I've gotten half-excited about it and then with the Internet now I guess they go on-line and take a look at me and I'm not what they want," Riley said sarcastically. "There's no question in my mind that race is a factor. Let me tell you something: I was a captain or an alternate captain on virtually every team I ever played on in professional hockey. I've always gotten along well with people, always gotten along well with my teammates. I can't think of one person I ever played with that I didn't get along with. I coached people who are coaching now in the professional ranks and the major junior ranks. But I could never get through the door. I can't even get a job as a scout."

Said Williams, the former Washington sports writer: "Reality has smacked Bill in the face. It's painful to hear him talk about the way he's been passed over for jobs with NHL teams by people he played with and against. Guys he thought he had great relationships with, guys he considered old friends. I'm sure he never expected this to happen almost thirty years after he played hockey with those guys."

Craig Patrick, the general manager of the Pittsburgh Penguins and the U.S. Olympic team, is a former teammate of Riley's. So is Ron Low, the former coach of the Edmonton Oilers and New York Rangers who scouted for the Rangers in 2002–03. Garnet "Ace" Bailey, another former teammate, was the chief scout for the Los Angeles Kings when his plane was hijacked by terrorists and flown into the World Trade Center on September 11, 2001. Schoenfeld, the former Buffalo defenseman whose skate accidentally severed Riley's tendon in 1977, has coached several NHL teams and served as a Rangers assistant coach in 2002–03. Riley knows or has known many men of influence at the highest levels of hockey. But the thickness of his Rolodex has not helped yet.

"I've talked to people who give me a tremendous amount of credibility as far as being a knowledgeable hockey guy," he said. "I have basically helped scouts prepare their lists of players for the NHL draft. But I still can't get my foot in the door. The story they used to give me was, 'There are no major junior-league hockey clubs in the Maritimes.' Well, guess what? Now we have four major junior-league hockey clubs in the Maritimes, and I still can't get a job."

Riley said he has written letters to inquire about jobs to Patrick, Detroit Red Wings general manager Ken Holland and Columbus Blue Jackets coach, president and general manager Doug McLean, among others. So far, no good.

"I could show you the letters they send back," Riley said. "They say, 'I know how good you are. You don't have to explain yourself to me. I know you can do the job. But I just don't have anything.' Patrick, Holland, McLean. I outcoached, outmanaged and outrecruited those guys in the minor leagues. Now they're in the NHL and I can't get in. I wrote McLean a letter asking for a job in the minors as a coach or a scout. Man, they always tell me where I could get a job somewhere else, but not with them."

As an experienced general manager on the junior-league level, Riley is used to acquiring players, coaches and other team personnel as well as negotiating contracts and conceptualizing and articulating a vision of what his team should look like on the ice and how he expects his team to perform. An NHL general manager handles the same tasks, but with an operating budget in the tens of millions of dollars and with high-powered agents representing coaches and the world's finest players while under the daily scrutiny of media, rabid fans and, in most instances, a corporate board all demanding victories or a new man in the GM's chair. Riley's quest to be hired as a team builder at the highest level of hockey is an effort to break through a glass ceiling and overcome the stereotypical negative assumptions that are likely still held about the capabilities of blacks to handle such a position—stereotypes that were given a public voice in 1987 by then-Los Angeles Dodgers general manager Al Campanis who, in explaining why there were no black men with his title in Major League Baseball, said that blacks "lacked the necessities" to handle the job. Team executives and franchise owners may no longer be as publicly maladroit as Campanis, but given the paucity of black team builders in major professional sports, there is no reason to believe such negative assumptions about the capabilities of blacks do not still exist.

In a lifetime of challenges, Riley's struggle to become the Jackie Robinson of professional hockey team builders figures to be his toughest yet.

Peter Worrell, a hard-fisted left wing, is one of several Caribbean Canadians in the National Hockey League. His familial roots extend to the island of Barbados. Shown here as a Florida Panther, he was traded in June 2003 to the Colorado Avalanche.
Dave Sandford/Hockey Hall of Fame

Hired Hands

His familial roots extend to the Caribbean island of Barbados, hardly a hotbed of hockey. Still, there seemed little doubt once Peter Worrell took up hockey as a boy in Canada that he would develop into the kind of player no opponent dared to cross. He grew to the size of a super-heavyweight boxer, the size of a Lennox Lewis, another man of Caribbean origin and reared in Canada. Worrell stands 6-foot-6, weighs 235 pounds and plays with a nasty streak forged in the crucible of junior-league hockey.

Not every NHL player can draw upon teenage hockey memories like these: a spectator at a Quebec Major Junior League game once grabbed a bullhorn and shouted at Worrell, "Go back to Africa!" As if the offending voice had not captured Worrell's attention, other spectators at the rink threw bananas at him as he sat in the penalty box. At another game, he remembers seeing a sign that read, "6-FOOT-6 OF PURE SHIT. GO BACK TO HELL." Being a black teenage player on the ice made him stand out. Being a black teenage player who could physically dominate an opponent made him an object of fear, scorn and vilification from opponents and spectators. Ultimately, it made him more determined to graduate to hockey's premier league. No way would racial hostility make him quit the game.

"If anything, I take it as motivation," Worrell said in a television documentary, "Too Colourful For the League," that aired on CBC in 2000. "If somebody is going to say, 'You're a monkey. Go back to the jungle. Stop playing our game. Go play basketball,' well, I'm going to say to them, 'I could probably be on the basketball court, but I'm going to prove something to you. I'm going to be out here and I'm going to beat you here, too. If you let them use words to take you out, you're making their job so much easier."

Taunts he endured as a teenager on rinks in and around his Canadian hometown of Pierrefonds, Quebec and taunts he hears to this day in some NHL arenas provide the fuel that powers Worrell around the rink like a heat-seeking missile. He hits everything that moves in a different colour sweater, and if gloves are dropped and punches thrown he nearly always gets the upper hand. Just as raising the stick aloft is the celebratory gesture of a goal scorer, Worrell has his own after winning a fight. While skating to the penalty box, he often wipes his hands as though ridding them of the germs and blood of an unworthy opponent. It is a gesture Florida Panthers fans loved and opponents reviled.

Now, Colorado Avalanche fans will have a chance to embrace Worrell. The Avs acquired him in a July 19, 2003 trade, adding toughness to a roster of highly skilled players that includes Joe Sakic, Peter Forsberg, Rob Blake, Paul Kariya and Teemu Selanne.

Because of Worrell's physical presence, he generally has no trouble finding skating room when he has the puck in the offensive zone. Were he a more skilled offensive player, he could make better use of that room. But Worrell is more of a hired hand, a man who does more on the ice with his fists than his stick, a man whose physical prowess overshadows his hockey prowess. Defensemen bent on knocking him off the puck often are repelled like bullets against Superman's chest. His punishing hits delighted fans of the Panthers while making him public enemy number one on the road. "Worrell Sucks!" a chant heard during a March 1, 2003 Panthers-New York Rangers game at Madison Square Garden, is among the more benign things he hears in an opposing team's arena.

Routinely, Worrell is cast as the heavy in an NHL production and he looks the part. With a clean-shaven pate the colour of dark chocolate, piercing brown eyes and a black goatee, he is a cross between the actor Ving Rhames in his mid-twenties and the 1970s heavyweight fighter Earnie Shavers, whom Muhammad Ali once dubbed "The Acorn." Worrell, too, is tough to crack. He is the rare player who can change the tenor of a hockey game without even touching the puck, so forceful is his hitting, or the threat of being hit by him.

Worrell made $600,000 in 2002–03, his fifth NHL season, all with the Panthers. Not bad for a player who has never scored more than four goals in a season. His yearly statistics since the 1994–95 season show how overwhelmingly his penalty minutes (PIM) surpass his total points (TP), a true measure of a hired hand:

Season	Team, League	TP	PIM
1994–95	Hull, QMJHL	9	243
1995–96	Hull, QMJHL	59	464
1996–97	Hull, QMJHL	63	437
1997–98	New Haven, AHL	27	309
1997–98	Florida, NHL	0	153
1998–99	New Haven, AHL	4	65
1998–99	Florida, NHL	9	258
1999–00	Florida, NHL	9	169
2000–01	Florida, NHL	10	248

| 2001–02 | Florida, NHL | 9 | 354 |
| 2002–03 | Florida, NHL | 5 | 193 |

QMJHL—Quebec Major Junior Hockey League
AHL—American Hockey League
NHL—National Hockey League

Worrell, born in 1977, is among a group of fighting men that includes but is definitely not limited to other black players such as Georges Laraque, Donald Brashear and Sandy McCarthy. "I think maybe I fight so much now because I had to fight so much when I was a kid," said Laraque, who as a boy fought against racial antagonism in his Montreal neighbourhood. "But I don't like for people to think that the black players are just fighters. That's not so. It's not like we're just animals who go out on the ice and fight all the time. We have skills. We can play hockey. But the thing is a lot of us are big men, physical players. Being physical is a big part of our game. We fight. But that's not all we do."

The NHL's fighting men prefer to be called "tough guys." That term, however, is a misnomer. There are plenty of tough guys in the NHL who are not fighters; indeed, the vast majority of players who don the equipment and step onto an NHL rink can be accurately described as tough. Yet only hired hands express themselves with their fists as often as Worrell, Laraque, Brashear and McCarthy and their white counterparts such as Jody Shelley, P.J. Stock, Eric Cairns and Rob Ray.

However, the role of the hired hand has diminished considerably in recent years as the league seeks a more telegenic image that it hopes will broaden its appeal to advertisers, U.S. television networks and potential customers desiring a family night out. Because of stiffer penalties handed down by game officials and hefty fines and suspensions meted out by league officials, the bench-clearing brawl—so familiar during the reign of Boston's "Big Bad Bruins" and Philadelphia's "Broad Street Bullies" in the 1970s—has become an anachronism. Hockey fans nostalgic for the days of full-scale donnybrooks with the gloves, sticks and helmets of every player on each team littering the ice along with splotches of blood as beer-guzzling fans pound the Plexiglas with glee, now must visit the lowest levels of minor-league hockey, where such incidents are still considered part of the "entertainment" experience, or watch the 1977 cinematic farce, *Slap Shot*.

In the mid-1980s, an average of 2.1 fights occurred in an NHL game. In the 2002–03 season, the per-game fight average dropped to 1.0. In more than 60% of NHL games in 2002–03, no fighting occurred. This significant decline is owed to rule changes such as a fine and suspension for coaches who put hired hands on the ice leading to a fight in the waning seconds of a one-sided game; the implementation of an extra two-minute minor penalty for the player who instigates a fight, which gives the other team a power play (a manpower skating advantage); faster faceoffs, which prevent eager fighters from lingering on the ice and provoking opponents; more minor penalties being called for obstruction and interference, which if uncalled could lead to frayed tempers and fights; and quicker line changes by coaches, from nearly fifty seconds down to about thirty seconds, which also limited the ice time of hired hands. The calling of more minor penalties leads to more power plays, which puts more highly skilled offensive players and penalty-killing specialists on the ice. Since hired hands are neither highly skilled offensive players nor penalty-killers, they spend more time watching from the bench and less time fighting on the ice.

Yet fights still occur in the NHL. However, fights today tend to be mano-a-mano scraps between hired hands, not the hockey equivalent of a Jets vs. Sharks rumble from *West Side Story*. Fights still occur because physical contact cannot be legislated out of pro hockey and the major professional leagues lack Olympics-style rules that would suspend fighters for the duration of the Games. Hence, Worrell and other hired hands still have a role, albeit a significantly reduced one.

How to identify a hired hand? If he's a centre or winger, the ratio of penalty minutes to total points is the best indicator. A five-to-one ratio, that is five times as many penalty minutes as total points, often identifies a hired hand. Teams nowadays still look for an enforcer-type to protect non-combative teammates, avenge cheap shots by an opponent, intimidate an opponent or change the momentum of a game. However, teams also expect such a player to be talented enough to skate regular shifts on one of the top three lines. Still, the hired hand is more often than not an infrequently used fourth-line player kept on the bench until his team needs a jolt of physical energy.

◆ ◆ ◆

For an inordinate number of black players, the role of hired hand is what got them into the NHL. Take Steve Fletcher. He made his NHL debut in the Stanley Cup playoffs, but not because of his hockey prowess. The Montreal Canadiens had been consistently outhit by the Boston Bruins in the first four games of the 1988 Adams Division finals. So Canadiens coach Pat Burns promoted Fletcher, the top fighter in Montreal's minor-league system. That season, he had 338 penalty minutes and twenty-nine points for the Sherbrooke Canadiens. A part-time left wing, part-time defenseman and full-time hired hand, Fletcher suited up for Game 5 of the series and promptly got a five-minute penalty for fighting. Montreal lost the game anyway, and the series four games to one. Fletcher then signed as a free agent with the Winnipeg Jets, for whom he played his only three regular-season games. Thereafter, he bounced around the minors and retired in 1996.

Fletcher, the twelfth black in NHL history, played the same number of regular season games as Brian Johnson, the league's ninth black. Twice in the Quebec Major Junior League, Johnson scored thirty goals in a season. Three times he had more than one hundred penalty minutes. The Detroit Red Wings, who signed him as a free agent in 1979, accentuated the fistic side of his game. His three scoreless games with five penalty minutes for the Wings interrupted three minor-league seasons in which he compiled 706 penalty minutes and 107 points. By 1986, Johnson's hockey career had ended.

Darren Banks, a left wing, went undrafted by the NHL but not unnoticed. The Calgary Flames signed him as a free agent in December 1990 in the midst of a season when he amassed sixteen points and 286 penalty minutes for the minor-league Salt Lake Golden Eagles. The next season, the feisty Banks recorded ten points and 303 penalty minutes. Boston then signed the free agent and he played twenty NHL games from 1992–94. His career totals: two goals, four points, seventy-three penalty minutes. He wore nine different minor-league uniforms throughout North America from 1994–99 before joining the London Knights of the British League. A penchant for pugilism followed him across the pond. His British statistics were twenty-six games, eight goals, twelve points, 117 penalty minutes. He retired in 2000.

Valmore James, the eighth black in the NHL, lasted only eleven games but made a lasting impression on Tony McKegney, a former teammate on the 1981–82 Buffalo Sabres. "Val had been called up to the team before we went into Philadelphia and Boston for games," McKegney said. "Philly and Boston were physically tough teams, and everybody on our team knew Val had a reputation in the minors for being as tough as nails. You couldn't hurt the guy. He was nothing but a mass of muscle. No body fat on him whatsoever. So we went into Boston and Val basically beat up Terry O'Reilly twice. One of the toughest guys in the league and Val beat him twice! Val went back to the minors after that, but the next year when we went into Boston the arena attendant said to me, 'Hey, you played pretty well when you were here last time.' The guy mistook me for Val. All he must have remembered was that a black guy on Buffalo had beaten up O'Reilly twice."

James achieved something of more significance in hockey, although it has gone largely unnoticed: he was the first black American to reach the

NHL. Mike Grier, a Detroit native, has been widely recognized as the first. But Grier, a Washington Capitals right wing, debuted in the 1996–97 season, fifteen seasons after James. A left wing, James hails from Ocala, Florida., and grew up on Long Island, New York, where his father drove the ice-smoothing Zamboni machine for the minor-league Long Island Ducks. Watching Dad maneuver the old Zamboni around the rink was James' introduction to hockey. A sturdy 6-foot-2 and 205 pounds, James went undrafted by the NHL. But in the season before he became a Sabre, he compiled 179 penalty minutes and twenty-one points for the Eastern League's Erie Blades. He literally fought his way back to the NHL with the 1986–87 Toronto Maple Leafs. He went scoreless with thirty penalty minutes in eleven career games and retired in 1988.

While there's no doubt Fletcher, Johnson, Banks and James did little more than fight for their cups of coffee in the NHL, one question persists: were they just hired hands or had they been typecast as such by coaches?

Johnson, in particular, had a pair of thirty-goal seasons in major-junior hockey. Clearly, he had offensive skills that were never developed in professional hockey. The career of Johnson, who played at 6-foot-1 and 185 pounds, strongly suggests he had been seen strictly as a fighter and, consequently, assumed a role that may have been too constricting. Perhaps in better circumstances Johnson could have had an NHL career similar to that of Terry O'Reilly, a Bruins star for fourteen seasons who combined physical toughness and tenacity with more than an occasional jolt of offensive energy. Four times he scored at least twenty goals in a season. Five times he accumulated more than two hundred penalty minutes in a season. Twice he appeared in the NHL All-Star Game. Once he got a ten-game suspension for assaulting a referee. O'Reilly had an opportunity to cultivate his unique skills and became someone tough enough to fight anyone on the ice yet talented enough to play and produce a game-winning goal. His NHL potential as a hard-fisted right wing with offensive ability was realized the season after he racked up sixty-five points and 151 penalty minutes in his final year in junior hockey. A black right wing named Brian Johnson appeared to have the same potential as O'Reilly. Whether Johnson was unable to bring it to fruition or was never encouraged to do so by his coaches, the result was a once-promising hockey player virtually lost to history.

◆ ◆ ◆

Throughout a nomadic ten-year career, the feeling of being typecast as a hired hand has dogged McCarthy, a right wing who signed a one-year, free-agent contract with the Boston Bruins on August 12, 2003. A player of black and Irish ancestry, McCarthy had felt restricted as a hired hand for four-and-a-half seasons with the Calgary Flames. Thus, he welcomed a trade to the Tampa Bay Lightning in March 1998. However, that was the first of four trades in a three-year span. McCarthy's other NHL pit stops were in Philadelphia and Carolina before he joined the New York Rangers in August 2000. McCarthy thought he had broken free of typecasting with the Rangers. But by the end of the 2002–03 season, general manager and coach Glen Sather had relegated him to fourth-line status. And as the Rangers floundered to their sixth straight non-playoff season, McCarthy's ice time became sporadic, dictated more by the physical capabilities of the opposing team than his coach's perception of what McCarthy could bring to the ice.

"It's been difficult for my whole career to establish myself as more than just a fighter," said McCarthy, who made $1.3 million in 2002–03. "It's something I'm going to have to work on every day. You get disappointed about it, but you don't let it affect your life, your family, your play. I'm just going to keep working to improve myself."

In 2000–01, Rangers fans voted McCarthy the recipient of the Steven McDonald Extra Effort Award, named for a New York City police officer paralyzed in the line of duty. McCarthy moved up that season from the dreaded fourth line and became one of New York's top nine forwards because of aggressive and high-impact play on defense and offense while still using his fists.

"Either I'm sticking up for a teammate who took a cheap shot or I'm defending myself," McCarthy said in explaining why he fights. His is a soft and friendly voice that belies the hard-charging style in which he plays. His skin is light enough so that he could be mistaken for white if not for the broad nose and full lips characteristic of a person of African origin. In past seasons, McCarthy's hairstyle made a statement of his ethnicity, as he favoured a three-inch Afro or cornrows of braids. But in 2002–03, he opted for an aerodynamic cut, his brown hair sheared to the almost imperceptible length of fuzz on a peach. Although he has worked hard to improve his conditioning by losing twenty-five pounds and cutting his percentage of body fat in half before the 2000–01 season, he is best known for his fistic skills. But whatever you do, do not call him a goon. That's a fighting word to any hired hand.

"A goon doesn't have any skill. All he does is fight," McCarthy said. "A goon can't score. He can't play the game. I'm a tough guy. I can play the game. I've got hockey skills. When I fight I'm usually fighting another tough guy to see who's tougher."

When hired hands on opposing teams hit the ice together, a game within a game begins. Sometimes the inside game is triggered by a series of verbal challenges. When the final challenge is accepted, hockey fans immediately turn into fight judges at rinkside. Said McCarthy: "Sometimes it's as simple as saying to another guy, 'I know you're tough. You know I'm tough. Let's go.' That's all it takes a lot of times. You definitely know who all the tough guys are. The majority of the time you don't know in advance that there's going to be a fight. But you know who you're playing against and if it's a physical team chances are there's going to be a fight or fights."

If one hired hand punches out another one early in a game, the loser is going to spend the rest of the game trying to promote a rematch. And if the loser is beaten again in the same game, he will do whatever he can to promote a third round. An extreme example of this occurred February 21, 2000 in Vancouver in an appallingly ugly incident that gave hockey the kind of front-page newspaper attention it could do without.

◆ ◆ ◆

In the first period of a game between the Boston Bruins and Vancouver Canucks, Donald Brashear, then a Canucks hired hand, outslugged Bruins pugilist Marty McSorley to the delight of fans at Vancouver's General Motors Place. The inevitable rematch occurred in the second period, and again Brashear pounded out a unanimous decision, punctuating matters with a fist pump to the cheering crowd. Since Boston and Vancouver play in different conferences, the teams were meeting for the second and final time of the season. McSorley, then thirty-six and in the twilight of a fight-filled career, had only one period left to try to save face. A third round of Brashear vs. McSorley could have been avoided if game officials had banished both men after the second fight, or if Bruins coach Pat Burns or Canucks coach Marc Crawford (who had the final say in on-ice matchups as the home team's coach) had made sure the hired hands were not on the ice simultaneously.

Yet during what should have been a routine faceoff in the final minute of play with Vancouver leading 5–2, McSorley and Brashear were on the ice together. McSorley did his utmost to verbally provoke Brashear who ignored him, perhaps the cruellest response to a twice-vanquished hired hand. As the game's final seconds ticked away, Brashear turned his back to McSorley and skated up the ice. McSorley slashed him once and again on his right side, which Brashear tried to ignore. Neither of the two on-ice referees blew a whistle to call a slashing penalty, which would have got McSorley off the ice. As Brashear skated away with his back turned, McSorley raised his stick and swung it, lumberjack-style, against the helmet and right temple of Brashear. The force of the blow dislodged the helmet and disoriented Brashear who fell backward, his bald head bouncing off the cold hard ice where he would lay unconscious.

If hockey thought it had an image problem because of violence before, now it had to deal with a television universe of twenty-four hour news networks providing hourly slow-motion replays of a white man hitting a black man in the head with a hockey stick, rendering the black man unconscious.

The NHL fined McSorley $72,000 (U.S.) and suspended him for one year, the largest fine and longest suspension in NHL history, one that effectively ended the seventeen-year veteran's playing career. A British Columbia judge found McSorley guilty of assault with a weapon. The judge said McSorley "slashed for the head. A child swinging as at a T-ball, would not miss. A housekeeper swinging a carpet-beater would not miss. An NHL player would never, ever miss. Brashear was struck as intended." McSorley, who apologized publicly to Brashear, got no jail time, only a conditional discharge meaning no charge appeared on his record after eighteen months of community service.

"The court in Vancouver has made its decision and it's time to move on," said Brashear, who missed twenty games with a concussion and returned to action April 5. McSorley now coaches the Boston Bruins' top farm club in Springfield, Massachusetts, which makes a retired black player like Bill Riley wonder what he has to do to get a coaching job one level below the NHL. Although McSorley's assault made for a chilling visual image, it had no apparent impact on at least one other NHL player. Less than a month later, on March 19, 2000, New Jersey Devils defenseman Scott Niedermayer got a ten-game suspension for hitting Worrell on the head with his stick. More than a few followers of current events were moved to ask, "Another white player hitting another black player on the head with a hockey stick?" Well, at least Worrell's helmet absorbed the blow this time, leaving Worrell with enough mental clarity to give three throat-slashing gestures to the Devils' bench—gestures he has not acted upon in subsequent games against New Jersey.

Prior to Brashear's brush with tragedy, he had been unknown to those who don't follow hockey and known as a fighter by those who do. His penalty minutes annually dwarf his total points. In 1997–98, he had eighteen points for the Canucks and a league-leading 372 penalty minutes. In his star-crossed 1999–2000 season, he had a career-high eleven goals along with two assists and 136 penalty minutes. A 6-foot-2 and 225-pound brown-skinned left wing, Brashear has continued his rugged play since being traded to the Philadelphia Flyers in the 2001–02 season, but without any other front-page incidents. Someday, though, his name could appear in the entertainment section of the newspaper. The man who uses his hands to leave welts on people's faces is also a composer and classically trained pianist.

Born in 1972 in Bedford, Indiana, he was adopted by a white family as a boy and moved to Montreal. "I didn't have anything racial happen to me when I was growing up," he said in a low, deep voice. And the McSorley assault, despite its superficial racial overtones, was not racial either. Rather, it was the tragic outgrowth of a dispute between hired hands that can occur in any game, whether the combatants are black or white. Hired hands routinely challenge each other to fight. It is up to the coaches and on-ice officials to prevent it by keeping such players apart or off the ice. Still, such misplaced machismo from hockey's hired hands is not supposed to lead to stick swinging. That is where McSorley, to his everlasting shame, skated way over the line—like a goon.

◆ ◆ ◆

The NHL understands that if it wants to continue its U.S. television partnership with Disney-owned ABC, ESPN and ESPN2 beyond 2004 when the five-year, $600 million deal expires, McSorley-type assaults cannot be repeated and bench-clearing brawls cannot be revived. Ratings for hockey on NBC during the 2002 Olympics indicated viewers enjoy the sport without goonish tactics. Olympic rules ban any player who fights, which is why nobody does. And the gold-medal game, between Canada and the U.S., on Sunday, February 24, drew a 10.7 rating and a 23 share, the best numbers ever for a hockey telecast in the U.S. (One ratings point equalled 1.05 million homes. The share represented the percentage of televisions in use and tuned in to a particular program at the time.)

For many fans, the speed and grace, teamwork and precision, passing and shooting, defense and strategy, remarkable saves and hard but clean hitting are more than enough to sell hockey. Fighting, to many fans, is not only unnecessary but an odious stain upon the game. Hired hands, however, see things differently. They believe fighting is absolutely necessary because it helps police the game in a manner that on-ice officials cannot.

"There would definitely be less cheap shots with the stick if guys were allowed to settle things for themselves on the ice," McCarthy said. "It's not only the cheap stick work that would be taken out of the game if we could fight. You wouldn't have the guys who play a tough game [hitting players with sticks or elbows] and don't have to back it up [by fighting]. They run around and hit guys from behind, they slash guys, they butt-end guys, they run over your goalie, they hit after the whistle and they don't have to worry about paying the consequences because the league has got the instigator rules and other rules like throwing the third man [into a fight] out of the game that protect the cheap-shot guys. I've been complaining to the league about this for years. I think you take away a lot of the edge from hockey when you don't let guys fight, because you've got guys playing now that aren't as tough as they appear."

McCarthy seems to be advocating a lost cause with the position that fighting could make hockey a cleaner and safer game by eliminating the cheap-shot artists. In an era when boxing is under siege from powerful and influential medical associations, fighting in hockey has never been harder to justify since it is not, and has never been, an *essential* part of the game. Fans who found the 1970s reign of the "Big Bad Bruins" and "Broad Street Bullies" endearing would have trouble recognizing the game today. Collectors of "greatest hockey fights" videos are finding few new scraps to add to their library. Hired hands, while not yet an endangered species, have been reduced to bit-player, sideshow status. And as hockey continues on a path toward change, the players of the future are not likely to bear any resemblance at all to the McSorley of February 21, 2000.

Mike Grier, one of the NHL's premier power forwards, was among a league-record four blacks to play for the Edmonton Oilers in the 2001–02 season. Grier along with then-teammates Sean Brown, Anson Carter and Georges Laraque skated with children in New York's Ice Hockey In Harlem program in December 2001. Grier was traded to the Washington Capitals in 2002.
Dave Sandford/Hockey Hall of Fame

Tiger Hunting

It would be easy to mistake the group's name for a dreadful situation comedy on the television network, UPN. But Ice Hockey In Harlem only sounds like a program that could follow "Homeboys In Outer Space" on a fledgling network's prime-time schedule. Fortunately, though, Ice Hockey In Harlem is a program worthy of attention. Since 1987, IHIH has made education its major goal while building an interest in hockey and improving the self-esteem of the thousands of boys and girls who have participated. That's right, thousands. In 1999 alone, there were 275 children, ages five to seventeen, including fifty girls, in the IHIH program. In 2003, the number of participants was 175, ages three to seventeen, including eleven girls. But having fewer children involved should not be seen as evidence of a declining interest in the program.

"Ice Hockey In Harlem got to the point where the program was too big and there were too many kids, so we had to bring it down to a more manageable number," IHIH director Jack Abramson said. "At 175 kids, we can make sure every kid gets the attention he or she deserves, on the ice and in the classroom."

Public School 101 on East 111th Street in Harlem is the program's home base. From the 1920s through the 1960s, Harlem stood proud as a cultural and entertainment mecca in the Manhattan borough of New York City. Among Harlem's jewels were the Apollo Theatre, Small's Paradise, the Renaissance Ballroom and The Cotton Club. While the famed Ballroom no longer exists, the other three venues do, but only as shells of their once majestic selves. Although Harlem is no longer the showplace it once was, it is an area in the midst of an economic revitalization, with major retail chains such as HMV, The Body Shop, Seaman's Furniture and Starbucks Coffee taking up residence in what had been since the 1970s decrepit, boarded-up buildings.

The NHL is hoping this neighbourhood of renewed hope could have a significant role in its effort to expand hockey to a new audience, an audience more accustomed to cheering basketball players at the Rucker Playground, amateur boxers in search of Golden Gloves championships and professional glory, and pint-sized baseball players en route to the Little League World Series. The NHL knows The Next Big Thing in hockey, a player with an irresistible combination of talent, grace, poise and charisma, is out there somewhere. The player who can be hockey's answer to tennis' Williams sisters or golf's Tiger Woods is out there, and the NHL would love nothing better than to have him skate into its warm embrace through a program such as Ice Hockey In Harlem. And does hockey ever need such a player.

With Wayne Gretzky in retirement since 2000 and Mario Lemieux contemplating retirement in 2003, hockey has a glaring hole to be filled by an iconic star, one who could captivate sports fans with extraordinary ability on the ice and a dignified demeanour off the ice. Hockey doesn't lack star power, but once Lemieux hangs up the skates it will lack a transcendent player. Even with Lemieux competing in Pittsburgh, hockey's appeal as a televised sport in the U.S.—where twenty-four of the league's thirty franchises reside—is lagging. The number of nationally televised NHL games on U.S. cable networks ESPN and ESPN2 fell from 102 in the 2001–02 season to seventy-one in 2002–03, largely because of the networks' acquisition of higher-rated NBA games. While ESPN and ESPN2 put pro basketball games on each Wednesday and Friday night in 2002–03 to make them easily accessible to viewers, the NHL games were scattered about the networks' prime-time schedule making them harder than ever to find. As a result, ratings for regular-season NHL games on ESPN and ESPN2 dropped nearly 8% in 2002–03.

Clearly, hockey must find a way to expand its U.S. audience to reach more black households, who on average spend more hours watching television each week than any other ethnic group, according to Nielsen Media Research. In 2002, for example, blacks spent five hours and thirty-eight minutes each week watching television during prime-time viewing hours (8pm-11pm, Monday-Saturday, 7pm-11pm Sunday), compared to four hours and nine minutes of weekly prime-time viewing by all households. Having a black MVP in Jarome Iginla in the 2001–02 season has not led to an increase in NHL ratings on American television, because U.S. hockey fans rarely get to see Iginla as he plays for a Canadian franchise, the Calgary Flames.

"The networks go where ratings are generated," said John Saunders, the studio host for ABC's and ESPN's hockey telecasts and the brother of Bernie Saunders, the NHL's fifth black player. "The problem is, if you put a Canadian team on [ABC or ESPN], you lose half your audience. If you've got New York playing Boston, the New York audience is interested and the Boston audience is interested. But if New York is playing Calgary, [ESPN or ABC is] not seen in Calgary. There goes half your audience."

Breaking the Ice

The ABC network's five Saturday afternoon regular-season hockey telecasts in 2002–03 did not feature one Canadian team. Hence, fans in the U.S. did not see Iginla on ABC and did not see Anson Carter, another gifted black player, until mid-March, when the Edmonton Oilers traded the forward to the New York Rangers. The Rangers failed to make the 2003 Stanley Cup playoffs, and thus were not part of the network's weekly playoff coverage from mid-April until mid-June.

Hockey will always be a staple of Canadian television. But it could become harder to find on U.S. television if ratings do not improve before the NHL's contract with Disney-owned networks expires after the 2003–04 season. Hockey remains a distant fourth in televised team sports in the U.S., behind football, basketball and baseball. For the NHL, then, finding a black superstar—preferably an American-born player on an American-based team—is the best way to elevate hockey's profile in the crucial U.S. market. That is why the NHL's investment of time, money and its most valuable commodity—players—in national programs like the NHL/USA Hockey Diversity Task Force and local programs like Ice Hockey In Harlem is an economic imperative.

Ice Hockey In Harlem has an annual operating budget of $800,000, which includes financial donations from the NHL and other corporate entities such as American Airlines. The air carrier provides free transportation for promising IHIH participants to attend hockey camps outside New York City.

Program graduates who once didn't know a puck from a paperweight often come back as volunteer coaches and teachers. "The program showed me there's much more to life than what I saw on the streets," said IHIH graduate Marc Verdejo who later graduated from college with a degree in business. "In my third year in the program, I was sent to a hockey camp in Toronto. I'd never been on a plane before. It opened up a whole new world for me."

Hockey is the hook that draws the youngsters into the not-for-profit, after-school program. IHIH provides educational and social services along with instruction in skating and hockey rules and fundamentals. The notion that Harlem youngsters would have more than a passing fancy for hockey might, at first thought, seem far-fetched. Until you meet the youngsters themselves.

Jonathan Dry, a fourteen-year-old high school freshman, is a hockey player of promise. In five years with IHIH, he has spent summers at hockey camps in Toronto and Calgary. A strapping six-foot defenseman, he also plays for the Harlem Rangers youth team, which is sponsored by the New York Rangers. "I used to play basketball and didn't really like it," said Jonathan, a Harlem resident of black and Latino heritage. "And

I tried soccer and baseball, but I didn't really feel comfortable. I told my mom I wanted to try hockey because I saw it on TV and it looked like fun. And she found Ice Hockey In Harlem."

IHIH provided Jonathan with a scholarship to attend St. Raymond's High School, a private school with a hockey team in the borough of The Bronx. He was the only black or Latino on the team in 2002–03, and he said he didn't experience any problems with his teammates. "If I have an opportunity to play hockey as a professional, I would definitely take it," he said. "But first I want to stay with the [IHIH] program until I finish high school and then play college hockey."

Participants in programs like Ice Hockey In Harlem pay for absolutely nothing. Everything—the skates, sticks, gloves, socks, pads, helmets, jerseys, ice time and tutelage—is provided free. "I'm a single parent and there's no way I could have my two boys in a program like this if I had to pay for the hockey equipment," said Monique Gueits of Harlem. Added Jonathan Dry: "Until I started buying my own equipment, I had no idea how expensive this sport was. A helmet cost me $100."

Jabari Scutchins, Jonathan's IHIH classmate and Harlem Rangers teammate, said that before he joined the program in 2000, "All I knew about hockey was there was a whole bunch of people skating around chasing a black puck." Now fourteen, Jabari has put his baseball gear in the back of the closet. The hockey equipment sits right up front. The left wing looks forward to chasing pucks in high school and beyond. He has attended camps for hockey and power-skating in Canada.

Who is to say both Jonathan and Jabari cannot someday advance from Ice Hockey In Harlem to the NHL? The program rents ice time each week during the winter for games and instruction at Riverbank State Park near the Hudson River and Lasker Rink in Central Park. The latter venue is where IHIH kids met Anson Carter, Georges Laraque, Mike Grier and Sean Brown, then Edmonton teammates, in December 2001.

"It was really great to see so many kids from Harlem having fun playing hockey," Brown said. "The important thing is getting an opportunity to learn the game and play it on a regular basis. A lot of black kids don't get to do that. Programs like that are very important. There's talent out there. The kids just need a chance."

◆ ◆ ◆

Brown made the most of his chance to play while growing up in Oshawa, Ontario. The youngest of three sons born to a black man and a white woman, Brown first took to the ice at age six, "because Dad wanted us to have something to do. There was never any talk about any of us getting to the NHL." For Sean, having two older brothers meant playing with hand-me-down hockey equipment to save money. "I wish I could have been in a program where all the equipment was free," he said. "I can't even remember how old I was when I first got new equipment."

Certainly it occurred by the time Sean joined the Belleville Bulls of the Ontario League as a seventeen-year-old in 1993. By that time, he had eclipsed brothers Lamont Jr. and Ryan in hockey ability and, he said, good fortune. "My brothers have diabetes and I'm just lucky not to have it," he said. "I guess I was the one chosen to represent the family in the NHL."

Brown, at 6-3 and 205 pounds, is considerably bigger and stronger than either of his brothers. The Boston Bruins, his current team, drafted the defenseman with the twenty-first overall pick in 1995. A year later, he was traded to Edmonton, where he made his major-league debut in 1996–97. Physical play is his bent. From 1998–2000, his first two full seasons with the Oilers, he racked up 188 and 192 penalty minutes respectively. When the Bruins reacquired him before the 2002–03 season, Coach Robbie Ftorek moved him to wing, believing his hard-hitting style would help the team more as a forward. But despite a *Boston Globe* article dubbing him "The Brown Bomber," he saw himself as neither a hired hand nor a forward.

"I prefer defense. I've played it pretty much my whole life," he said. "I definitely don't see myself as somebody who's just going to go out there and fight. You have to have skills to play the game now."

After Ftorek was fired with a month left in the season, Brown moved back to defense—the position where he believes he'll have the most impact on the ice. Brown, who made $687,500 in 2002–03, has found being one of the NHL's fourteen blacks in 2002–03 to be a position of influence off the ice.

"You're definitely a role model and I'm all right with that because I had role models growing up myself," said Brown, whose father once gave him an autographed picture of Willie O'Ree, the NHL's first black player. "Willie didn't let race be a barrier to his making it to the NHL, and I was fortunate that race wasn't a barrier for me. I come from an interracial family, and it was always open in our house to talk about race and not be embarrassed about it. I grew up knowing that if somebody said something [racist] to me, they were just exposing themselves as ignorant. To me, who makes it in pro hockey isn't about race. It's about who gets the opportunity and takes advantage of it."

◆ ◆ ◆

Programs like Ice Hockey In Harlem and Art Dorrington Ice Hockey are about providing opportunities in hockey to kids who might never have been exposed to the sport. The Canadian-born Dorrington became a U.S. citizen in the 1950s. While playing in the minor-league East Coast Hockey League, he became the first black American to play pro hockey. He started his program after watching a group of boys involved in a spirited game at a rink in his adopted hometown of Atlantic City. "The rink manager told me black kids don't skate there because it's too expensive for them," he said. "I had to do something about that."

Dorrington's program, which began in 1999, follows the same model as Ice Hockey In Harlem—a volunteer-driven effort supported by corporate donations and funding from the NHL that provides free instruction in hockey, academics and life skills to youth. However, his program, which serves up to fifty kids a year, is open to Caucasians as well as African-Americans, Latinos, Asians, Indians, Native Americans, et al. As with IHIH, his program provides the financial wherewithal for a promising youngster to attend hockey camps and play on the high school level.

Nevertheless, Bill Riley, the NHL's third black, said the league is not doing enough to provide opportunities for blacks in hockey *on any level*. He argues that position despite the presence of O'Ree as director of youth hockey development for the NHL/USA Hockey program.

"The league has this diversity thing going with Willie O'Ree, right? Well, they've got myself and all of us other retired players. Why aren't they taking us into the inner cities to work with these kids and be role models to these kids?" asked Riley, the general manager of a junior-league team in Moncton. "I mean, the NHL won't hire us to coach. They won't hire us to be assistant coaches. They won't hire us to [be general managers]. They won't hire us to scout. At least give us some type of employment to go and work with these black kids. And I don't think the NHL wants to because if you look at baseball, if you look at basketball, if you look at football, who's dominating it? Black players. If you get down there to the inner cities and you get some of those kids who are 6-foot-6 or seven feet tall and you teach them how to skate and how to handle the biscuit, hey, look out!"

Programs like Ice Hockey In Harlem are not owned or operated by the NHL, however. But the programs receive some of their funding from the NHL. Businessman Dave Wilk founded IHIH in 1987 with an assist from former New York Rangers winger Pat Hickey. The program began with forty kids ages seven to seventeen. Throughout its existence, volunteers like Teresa Genaro have been the backbone of the program.

A full-time educator and dean at a Brooklyn high school, Genaro first heard about IHIH at a Rangers game and then saw an article about it in *The New York Times*. She has volunteered her time since 2000. "I have season tickets for the Rangers, and I've never missed a game because of

Ice Hockey In Harlem and I've never had to miss a class because of a Rangers game," she said. "It's really fun to use hockey as a way to teach academic skills to kids. I get to do two things I really love, teach and talk hockey."

Part of what keeps corporate dollars flowing into IHIH is the educational component. IHIH has never been about hockey alone. Teachers like Genaro use hockey to instruct youngsters in reading, writing, arithmetic, history and geography. In a March 31, 2003 class, the NHL standings were used to subtly teach multiplication and addition. Kids were told the Rangers' record of thirty-two wins, thirty-four losses, nine ties and four overtime losses and asked to figure out their point total. (Answer: 77. Each student had already learned in class that a win is worth two points, a loss no points, a tie one point and an overtime loss one point. Each student then multiplied 32 x 2 to get 64, then added 64 and 9 and 4 to get 77.) Then came a general interest/geography question: how many NHL teams are based in Canada? Students were not only expected to know the answer is six, but also were expected to identify Toronto, Montreal, Ottawa, Vancouver, Edmonton and Calgary.

◆ ◆ ◆

In 2003, more than thirty volunteer-driven programs received some funding from the NHL/USA Hockey Diversity Task Force. A partial list included IHIH; Art Dorrington Ice Hockey; Mariucci Inner City Hockey in St. Paul; Clark Park Coalition Hockey in Detroit; Cobbs Creek Hockey Program in Philadelphia; S.C.O.R.E. Boston; Hockey Kids in Dire Straits in Cincinnati; Coconut Grove Kings Hockey Program in Miami; Columbus Ice Hockey Club in Columbus; Dominik Hasek/Variety Club of Buffalo Youth Hockey; Positive Upliftment of Chicago's Kids (PUCK); Shaka Ice-Shaka Franklin Foundation in Denver; Youth Indianapolis; Disney GOALS in Anaheim, California; Fort Dupont Ice Hockey Program in Washington, D.C.; Creative Concepts Ice Project in Bellingham, Washington; Mount Vernon Ice Hockey Club in Westchester County, New York; and Hockey on the Hill in Albany.

The objectives of each program are the same: plant the seeds of interest in hockey among young racial minorities by making the sport affordable and giving them access to skilled coaches, teachers and the occasional hockey celebrity because there is no telling how much fruit those seeds could bear.

Not even the most avid follower of sports saw Tiger Woods on the horizon more than a decade ago. Now he is the most dominant player in golf, and he is black and Asian. Devotees of sports did not see Serena and Venus

Williams on the horizon ten years ago. Now they are the dominant players in women's tennis, and they are black. The most rabid football fan could not have known about Michael Vick a decade ago. Now the Atlanta Falcons left-hander is the dominant player at the position of quarterback, a position that had been filled only by white players for decades, and he is black. There is no reason to believe, then, that inner-city programs that are making hockey more available than ever to racial minorities will not eventually produce professionals—if not All-Stars and superstars—who are black.

Youngsters involved in such programs also are likely to become life-long hockey fans that share their pastime with future generations.

Consider this: what got the Williams sisters interested in a stuffy, country-club sport like tennis, a sport in which Harlem-bred champion Althea Gibson had to struggle to gain entry into tournaments in the 1940s and '50s? It took a father who believed it possible to teach his daughters to play the game well enough to someday rule it. And what got Eldrick Tiger Woods interested in an exclusionary, upper-crust sport like golf, a sport in which many privately owned venues still routinely bar blacks and women from becoming club members? It took a father who believed it possible to teach his son to master the game and become its signature talent.

Hockey has no such country club pretenses. If ever there was a sport that should be open to anyone with the ability and desire to play, hockey is the one. But for hockey to find its Tiger, the sport needs to increase its accessibility to those that had long been excluded because of economics, geography, culture or race.

◆ ◆ ◆

In August 2002, the annual Ice Hockey In Harlem fundraiser at Winged Foot Golf Club in Mamaroneck, site of the 1997 Professional Golfer's Association of America Championship, brought local business and civic leaders together with current and former black NHL players such as O'Ree, Jamal Mayers, Jason Doig and Jean-Luc Grand-Pierre. "If you can get a kid hooked on hockey early, he's going to stay hooked; I know because it was that way for me," said Grand-Pierre, a Columbus Blue Jackets defenseman of Haitian descent who learned hockey while growing up in Montreal. "I know it's different in Canada because there are so many places to play hockey. There's so much more ice. You can go play on a pond. But in a lot of places in the States, you don't have the ice. But you can still teach kids the game."

Particularly kids who are in-line skaters, an activity that grew exponentially from two hundred thousand participants in 1989 to thirty-two million in 1999. Street hockey would seem an ideal fit for such youngsters.

Carter, the New York Rangers winger, grew up in the Toronto suburb of Scarborough where "foot hockey" was his introduction to the sport. Neither he nor his boyhood friends owned sticks, skates, gloves or any other piece of hockey equipment. "But as long as kids are playing some form of hockey and learning the rules and getting accustomed to playing the game and being part of a team, that's the important thing," he said. "Once you get the basic skills down, then those skills can eventually be transferred to the ice."

Because Ice Hockey In Harlem exists in the world's media capital, New York City, it garners more attention than other youth hockey programs geared toward racial minorities. But in the U.S., Mariucci Inner City Hockey in Minnesota came first. The program bears the name of John Mariucci, a member of the Hockey Hall of Fame, who died in 1987. Known as "the godfather of hockey in Minnesota," he was the NHL's first American-born player when he debuted with the Chicago Blackhawks in 1940–41. Mariucci later fought in World War II and then coached at the University of Minnesota for fourteen seasons. The Mariucci hockey program began in 1984, the year black NHL player Tony McKegney joined the Minnesota North Stars.

"When I played in Minnesota, high school hockey was bigger there than the NHL, so there was always a lot of hockey interest among the youth, but it had not reached the inner city," he said. "It was really interesting to see the way the program progressed. We started out with kids on the ice using chairs as walkers. They would skate with the chairs to maintain balance, but by the next year the kids were skating so well we would have regular scrimmages. I would say 80% of the kids were black. We had good corporate support and the hockey equipment was donated through certain agencies. On our off days, I would bring some of my teammates to the practices to help out. You could see the confidence of those kids grow as their skills improved. That's the great thing about the diversity youth programs popping up around the country. But getting ice time is still the most important thing."

Tiger hunting is particularly challenging in parts of the U.S. where ice is scarce, particularly urban areas as well as the southern, mountain and western venues where many NHL franchises now reside—Carolina, Florida, Tampa Bay, Atlanta, Nashville, Dallas, Phoenix, Los Angeles, Anaheim and San Jose. In such areas dedicated parents rise before the sun to make sure their children get ice time for hockey instruction and games before school. McKegney believes that hidden somewhere in one of these relatively new hockey markets, amid the darkness of 5 a.m. face-offs or the obscurity of foot hockey games during recess, is a black boy whose ascension will profoundly change the sport.

"I'm thinking someday there's going to be a Michael Jordan-type athlete who's going to pass on basketball and baseball and football and boxing and track and field and he's going to be a hockey player," he said. "He's going to be the perfect size for hockey—let's say, 6-foot-2 and 220 pounds—and he's going to have the perfect dedication. He's going to have all the qualities Jordan has and Tiger Woods has only he's going to be on skates. It could happen in a big city like Chicago where they're building nice rinks in the city. There's really a nice double-rink facility where the Blackhawks practice, near the United Center (the Blackhawks' home arena). At least the inner-city kids in Chicago are close to the NHL: they can see it, feel it, touch it, smell it. It's much better than having to drive thirty miles to some suburb to play hockey and trying to fit in on a team with nineteen white kids who live out there. In a situation like that, it's tough for a black kid to survive.

"The situation of the lone black kid on a team is still prevalent, and the black kid is getting yelled at from the stands or from the opposing bench, and he's having a tough time fitting in with his teammates, and he's possibly having his ice time unfairly limited because of race. Those situations are prevalent, even in Canada."

Tom Kane could vouch for that. In the 1980s, Kane was a gifted and versatile star in youth sports in Montreal. Indeed, the great Lemieux was one of his hockey teammates. Just name the sport and Kane played it: hockey, basketball, baseball, track and field. Although he loved hockey, he abandoned the sport before reaching his teens because white spectators hurled empty Coca-Cola bottles at him after a game and his white teammates made jokes about the incident in the dressing room. Kane went on to play major college football at Syracuse University and became a wide receiver for the NFL's Seattle Seahawks.

But what of the young black athletes who don't have other options because they're not as versatile as Kane? Do they continue to endure the hostility and racial antagonism in youth hockey, as Laraque did in Quebec, or do they abandon the sport altogether, their chances of earning fame and fortune as a professional forever lost?

"Kids are still being yelled at in youth hockey because they're black," McKegney said. "It's got to affect you, absolutely. As a kid, it always drove me to be the best player on the ice. That was my way of basically saying to those people, 'F—you!' The better I was as a player, the more the racial part got pushed into the background and my ability got put into the forefront. That was my way of combatting racism."

Fortunately, a child doesn't have to fight racism on the ice if the other players are of similar background. His athletic self-expression is not stunted. Self-consciousness does not get the better of him. He can learn the basics and nuances of the sport at his own pace. He can make his mistakes, show flashes of excellence, cultivate an affinity for the sport and eventually find his level of ability, if not proficiency. And the processes of learning and growing take place in a nurturing environment, rather than one of antagonism and hostility. Out of such a nurturing environment sprang Serena and Venus Williams and Tiger Woods. The likelihood, then, of finding a Tiger of hockey seems dependent upon the continuance of inner-city programs like Ice Hockey In Harlem.

As part of their life-history lessons, IHIH students have met O'Ree and have been encouraged to learn about other Canadian black players who preceded him: Herb Carnegie, a star in various minor leagues in the 1930s, '40s and '50s and the best black player of the pre-expansion era (before 1967); Bud Kelly, a 1920s star whom Hall of Fame coach Frank Selke Sr. called "the best Negro player I ever saw"; Charley Lightfoot of Stratford, Ontario, and Hipple Galloway of Dunnville, Ontario, among the first black players at the turn of the twentieth century; and the Coloured Hockey League of the Maritimes, a largely but not exclusively black association that existed from 1903 until the 1920s. The Coloured Hockey League combined serious hockey with Harlem Globetrotters-style theatrics, but it was also a trend-setting league in one respect: CHL goaltenders were the first to fall on the ice to stop the puck, which eventually became a routine part of the game. Franchises in the Coloured Hockey League included the Truro Victorias, Amherst Royals, Halifax Eurekas, Dartmouth Jubilees and Africville Seasides.

IHIH students have found that the opportunity to enhance their learning and gain self-confidence through a hockey program has made a profound difference in their lives, and hockey professionals have noticed.

"I saw kids in the program five years ago who are just starting college now," former NHL defenseman Jeff Beukeboom said. "These are great kids who just needed opportunities. If it wasn't for the discipline they got from the program, maybe these kids wouldn't be in college now."

On her way to college and, quite likely, a women's hockey program is Natasha Underwood, a sixteen-year-old from IHIH who played centre with the boys on the 2003 Harlem Rangers because there weren't enough girls to field a team. If that put anyone at a disadvantage, she said, it was the boys. "They're no competition," she added with a wink. A swift skater with impressive skills, Natasha has travelled to girls' hockey camps in the U.S. and Canada, although she sometimes forgets the no-checking rule in the women's game and knocks other campers to the ice. Considered the most promising female talent in the sixteen years of IHIH, she could someday make a name for herself in hockey, while also pursuing her other passion: music.

♦ ♦ ♦

One could graduate from a program like IHIH and eventually become a hockey player, or perhaps the owner of a professional hockey team. Roy Rodney, a New Orleans-based attorney, could tell students what the latter experience has been like, warts and all.

Since 1997, Rodney has been a co-owner of the minor-league New Orleans Brass, a team in the East Coast Hockey League. Rodney's group, which had included New Orleans mayor Ray Nagin, was the first black ownership group of a professional hockey franchise. But pride turned to disillusionment in the autumn of 2002, when the Brass became a team with no place to play.

The Brass suspended operations for the 2002–03 season after being unable to secure a deal to play at the New Orleans Arena, its home rink since 1999, or the Municipal Auditorium, its home rink from 1997–99. Nagin, elected New Orleans mayor in November 2002, has gone out of his way to not appear preferential toward the Brass owners, Rodney said. But such neutrality has not helped the Brass' cause.

The Brass averaged less than 3,000 fans a game at the 17,000-seat Arena, and the team struggled to pay its rent there. Once New Orleans lured a NBA franchise, the former Charlotte Hornets, in the summer of 2002, the NBA team was given first call on available Arena dates. The city also told the Brass it did not want to incur the expenses of converting the Arena from a basketball court to a hockey rink dozens of times between Autumn 2002 and Spring 2003. But going back to the Auditorium was no longer an option for the Brass because it had removed the ice rink and ice-making equipment. And the city also hired a company to manage the Auditorium with whom Brass management was already in a dispute over the team's lease at the Arena. And that's how the Brass became homeless.

What's more, the arrival of the Hornets gave New Orleans a second major professional sports franchise (along with the NFL's New Orleans Saints), which gave some residents reason to believe the city had outgrown minor-league hockey. While Rodney maintains the Brass franchise should be saved for the fans, one letter-writer to the city's largest newspaper opined: "Exactly what hockey fans are you talking about? Would that be all 2,000 that showed up for the Brass at the Arena?...Please get NHL League Pass (a cable television pay-per-view package) and watch real hockey, or catch a flight to Dallas (home of the NHL's Stars) and watch real players play. The Brass is dead. It was dead even when they were alive."

The homeless hockey team had until April 1, 2003 to tell the East Coast League if it would play in 2003–04. Rodney decided the Brass would suspend operations for yet another season. He said the team, which had been a source of civic pride in New Orleans' black community, should resume play at the Municipal Auditorium in Autumn 2004. Black Canadians Jason Downey and Ted Laviolette played for the Brass during the franchise's first five seasons. Downey grew up with hockey after being adopted by a white family in Hull, Quebec. Laviolette was prodded to play by his Haitian-born mother, who wanted to disprove the crackpot theory of her white co-workers that blacks could not play hockey because of "weak ankles."

Compared to the political imbroglio in which the Brass owners found themselves, a black in hockey that gets hip-checked into the boards might just be better off.

◆ ◆ ◆

Rodney is not the only non-playing black trailblazer in professional hockey. Jay Sharrers, who worked 642 NHL games as a linesman, became the first black referee of an NHL game on April 3, 2001. And Chicago-born, Canada-reared, Harvard-educated Bryant McBride became the NHL's first black executive in 1994. That year, McBride, as the league's vice president in charge of business development, started the NHL/USA Hockey Diversity Task Force. In 1997, he created the Willie O'Ree All-Star Weekend, which invites youngsters from hockey programs that serve racial minorities to a different NHL city each February for a game, on-ice instruction and festivities.

"Tiger Woods is who he is because he had access. When he was a little boy, his father put a golf club in his hand," McBride said. "Arthur Ashe was who he was because he had access to tennis. We want to give as many minority youngsters as possible access to hockey. There's a kid out there right now who's got hockey on his radar. He's going to grow up to be 6-foot-3 and 220 pounds and a super athlete. And he's not going to want to play football at Florida State. He's going to want to play hockey at Notre Dame. And that kid is going to make it to the NHL and change the game of hockey."

McBride played college hockey at West Point and Trinity before earning a Master's degree in public administration at Harvard. He left the NHL in 2001 and became the only black certified player agent. His clients include Los Angeles Kings centre Jason Allison and Atlanta Thrashers goaltender Byron Dafoe. But under the heading of "Came So Far But Still A Long Way To Go," McBride's headshot is the only one that does not appear among the more than one hundred agents advertising for clients on the NHL Players Association Web site (www.nhlpa.com). Apparently, McBride has become convinced that showing his light-brown face to potential customers in the world of hockey in 2003 could be bad for business.

Darren Lowe has made a successful transition from NHL player to collegiate coach. Entering his ninth season at the University of Toronto, he was named the Ontario University Athletics East Division Coach of the Year in 2001 and 2003. The former Pittsburgh Penguins right wing starred on the 1984 Canadian Olympic team.
University of Toronto

Tomorrow's Game

That a Harvard-educated, former NHL vice president would still have reservations about showing his brown face on a hockey agents' Web page indicates that blacks in hockey have not completely shed their outsider status. Nevertheless, things are improving. The number of black players in hockey's premier league can no longer be counted on two hands. After the 2002–03 season, the number was fourteen and rising, considering that OHL standouts such as defenseman Trevor Daley and forward Anthony Stewart appear close to joining the elite. Today, an increasing number of blacks are taking up the game, invariably citing a reason as undeniably hopeful as one voiced decades ago by former Pittsburgh Penguins right wing Darren Lowe: "I always thought about hockey as something I just wanted to do. Race didn't have to enter into it."

As racial differences gradually fade in hockey, Lowe's status as a *second-generation* black player eventually won't seem so unusual. Neither will his current status as a head coach. He's entering his ninth season behind the bench for the University of Toronto Varsity Blues.

Lowe, a forty-three-year-old Toronto native, traced the skate marks of his father, Art, who played semi-pro hockey in the Ontario Senior Hockey League. Indeed, Art Lowe was part of an all-black line in 1951 that included Howard Sheffield and Gary Smith. For Darren, then, playing hockey became as conventional as attending school and dating girls.

While playing for the North York Rangers in the Ontario Junior Hockey League, Lowe's teammates included future NHL stars Paul Coffey and Bernie Nicholls. He turned down a scholarship to Dartmouth University, opting to play college hockey at obscure United States International University in San Diego, where he knew one of the coaches. Yet his California experiment lasted only one year. He transferred to the University of Toronto and became a goal-scoring machine, netting twenty-eight in 1980–81, thirty-six in 1981–82 and twenty-three in 1982–83 before becoming captain of the Canadian national team. He had two goals and an assist in seven games for Team Canada at the 1984 Olympics. Then the NHL beckoned.

"The New Jersey Devils made me an offer, but I would've had to go to the minor leagues," he said. "I signed as a free agent with the Penguins because I had an opportunity to play in the NHL right away. I was twenty-three and I didn't know if that chance would ever come again."

Days after the Olympics, Lowe donned number 35 for the Penguins and notched a goal and two assists in eight games. Not blessed with great size (5-foot-10 and 185 pounds) or extraordinary skills, Lowe was unable to stick with the Penguins or the NHL. But he facetiously takes credit in helping to transform Pittsburgh into a league powerhouse. His team finished with sixteen wins, fifty-eight losses and six ties—bad enough to earn the number one pick in the 1984 amateur draft, with which the Penguins selected Mario Lemieux. Seven years later, Pittsburgh celebrated the first of its two consecutive Stanley Cup championships.

Lowe played minor-league hockey in North America, Austria and Finland before returning to Toronto in the early 1990s to attempt to segue into an area of hockey where even fewer blacks resided: coaching.

"I'd always been interested in teaching," said Lowe, who used to teach academics at Toronto schools in between hockey seasons. "I thought coaching would be the best way to incorporate teaching and hockey."

Lowe served as an assistant at Ryerson College in 1991–92, then returned to U of T to assist his former coach, Paul Titanic. When Titanic stepped down in 1995, Lowe became the head man, following a Blues coaching tradition that includes Conn Smythe, Mike Keenan, Tom Watt and former Canadian Prime Minister Lester Pearson.

"I'd never been a head coach at any level, so it was really a trial by fire," Lowe said with a laugh. "Not until I was four years into it did I have a team that consisted totally of players I recruited."

Under Lowe, U of T has finished first in the Ontario University Athletics East Division and been ranked in the top ten in Canada in each of the past three seasons. In 2000–01 and 2002–03, he was named East Division Coach of the Year. Now, he's contemplating a new challenge.

"I'd like to go to the next level of coaching," he said, referring to an assistant's role or a head job in the NHL or a top-rated minor league like the AHL or IHL. "Our school is academically demanding, the Harvard of Canadian universities. I'd like the chance to work with players that, you could say, have a more realistic chance to reach the highest level of hockey."

Lowe said he has not begun to put out feelers yet, but as a former NHL player and a respected college coach who has also served as a director or instructor at numerous hockey schools in North America, he has no shortage of contacts. Whether those contacts will open the right doors is a question Lowe hopes he can answer affirmatively, unlike many of his black predecessors.

"In all my years of coaching, I have not coached one black player," he said. "But I can say I've taught one. Years ago, when I was playing pro hockey and teaching in Toronto at the end of the school year, I had a senior in one of my classes at Agincourt Collegiate High School. I was giving an assignment and I noticed he had a hockey magazine on his desk. I told him, 'Let me look at that magazine while you do the assignment.' That young man was Anson Carter.

"When I look at what Anson has accomplished in the NHL, and a guy like Jamal Mayers—whose family lived across the street from me and whose mother used to babysit me—and guys like Kevin Weekes and Freddie Brathwaite, it's just tremendous. Blacks that get into hockey now have so many role models, and they're going to have more as blacks continue coming up through the juniors and the high schools and colleges in Canada and the States. It's going to keep growing. There are so many tremendous black athletes and they're seeing that they have other options besides basketball, football and track. It's just going to be exciting to watch the progress."

Grant Fuhr ended his stellar nineteen-year career as an NHL goalie with the Calgary Flames in 2000. He won five Stanley Cups with the Edmonton Oilers between 1984 and '90 and became the first black elected to the Hockey Hall of Fame in 2003.
Dave Sandford/Hockey Hall of Fame

Afterword

The call came on June 11 while I was driving home from a mall here in Edmonton. I knew the call could be coming that day, but I went to get a haircut and to have my golf clubs altered. I just went about my normal routine. The call came from Jim Gregory, the chairman of the Hockey Hall of Fame selection committee. He said he had some good news. I knew right away what that meant: I was in the Hall of Fame.

Making the Hall of Fame was not something I thought about while I was playing. I was too busy trying for nineteen NHL seasons to help my team win games and be the best goalie I could be. But it's something you dream about when you're a kid. My wife (Candice) is excited. And my kids (Janine, Rochelle, Robert John and Kendyl) all think it's pretty cool.

I'm looking forward to the Hall of Fame induction in November. I've only been there once. I was really interested in seeing the goalies in the Hall. I always liked goalies, not just the great ones like Glenn Hall, Ken Dryden, Terry Sawchuk, Tony Esposito and Johnny Bower, but all goalies. To have my name mentioned now alongside the other Hall of Fame goalies is special.

And to be the first black member of the Hall of Fame is special. If you look at some of the great black men who've played the game—Willie O'Ree, Mike Marson, Tony McKegney, Herb Carnegie—I think I'm a benefactor of those guys breaking down the barriers. They did all the hard work and I took advantage of the opportunity. Those guys were an inspiration to me, and I'd like to be an inspiration to other blacks that want to play the game.

I've heard that the press in the United States put in their stories that I'm the first black member of the Hockey Hall of Fame. But that was not in any newspaper here in Canada. There's a different mentality in Canada. I feel fortunate to have grown up in this kind of environment. Race isn't that big a deal. Either you're a good player or you're not, you're a good person or you're not. That's the way it should be.

I was fortunate to break into the NHL on a great team (the Edmonton Oilers, winners of five Stanley Cups). I played with a great bunch of guys and great players (Wayne Gretzky, Mark Messier, Paul Coffey, Jari Kurri, Kevin Lowe) and nobody wanted to be the weak link. It was great to hear people I played with call me a great big-game goalie. It's definitely a reputation you want.

It's going to be great to go into the Hall of Fame with another friend, Patty LaFontaine, a guy I played with on the Buffalo Sabres (1993–95). I'm still working on my acceptance speech. I've got two big speeches to make this year because the Oilers are going to retire my number (31). I'm not a big speechmaker. I normally answer questions short, sweet and straight to the point.

I'm going to try to let people know how much I enjoyed the game. A lot of people take hockey so seriously. They treat it like a business and don't enjoy it. I always enjoyed going to the rink. And I set goals for myself. My biggest goal was to be the best goalie I could be. You should always have goals and always try to reach them. Nobody can call you a quitter if you try your best. They can only call you a quitter if you don't try.

Grant Fuhr
Edmonton, Alberta, Canada, June 2003

Acknowledgements

Thank you to everyone who consented to be interviewed for this book. (Their names and the dates of the interviews appear in a separate section.) Thanks also to the indefatigable Nirva Milord and John Halligan of the National Hockey League; Wendy McCreary of the National Hockey League Alumni Association; Devin Smith of the National Hockey League Players' Association; Tyler Wolosewich, Craig Campbell and Philip Pritchard of the Hockey Hall of Fame; the entire research staff at the Fordham University library; hockey historians Stan Fischler, Tom Sarro and Ira Gitler; Jason Kay and Wayne Karl of *The Hockey News*; Craig Stanton of Ice Hockey In Harlem; Jason Vogel and John Rosasco of the New York Rangers; Mike Sundheim of the Carolina Hurricanes; Chris Botta and Jason Lagnese of the New York Islanders; Jeff Trammel of the St. Louis Blues; Zack Hill and captain Keith Primeau of the Philadelphia Flyers; Jack Carnefix of the East Coast Hockey League; Jo LaVerde of Nielsen Media Research; and for their inspiration and unwavering support, Irene Price, Fabian Price, Dr. Cyril Price, Dr. Winston Price, Oliver Price, Gordon Price, A. Victoria Hunter, Juliette Fairley, Nekesa Mumbi Moody, Gayle Williams, Yvette Blackman, Clarisel Gonzalez Lopez, Dr. Elizabeth Stone, Dennis Dalrymple, Teri Boggess, Jim Wolfe, Donald Bain and Dr. Richard Lapchick; and special thanks to Adrienne Weiss, Marijke Friesen, Richard Almonte and Mike O'Connor of Insomniac Press for believing in this project as much as I did.

Source Notes

Introduction
Salaries of 2002–2003 black NHL players: National Hockey League Players Association Web site (www.nhlpa.com). Note: The $19.5 million is the sum of the salaries of all fourteen blacks that played in the league in the 2002–03 season.

The Big Tree
1. J.A. Adande, "It's Canada's game again," *The Los Angeles Times*, Feb. 25, 2002.
2. Kevin Allen, "Iginla's scoring title first for him," *USA Today*, April 12, 2002.
3. Associated Press, "Capitals 4, Flames 1," *New York Post*, March 21, 2003.
4. Canadian Press, "Iginla agrees to 2-year, $13 million deal," Sept. 7, 2002.
5. CTV Sportsnet, "NHL brightest star reflects on his dream season," transcript of interview with broadcaster Rod Black, July 31, 2002.
6. James Deacon, "The real-life dreams of Jarome Iginla," *Maclean's*, Oct. 14, 2002.
7. Jason Diamos, "Iginla is being noticed for standout season," *The New York Times*, Feb. 2, 2002.
8. Eric Francis, "Stick around, Iggy," *Calgary Sun*, March 1, 2003.
9. Peter Hanlon and Sean O'Brien, editors, *Calgary Flames 1999–2000 Media Guide*.
10. Rich Hoffmann, "Iginla's Flame burning brightly," *Philadelphia Daily News*, March 8, 2002.
11. George Johnson, "Driving force in the gold rush: Iginla-Sakic-Gagne line powers Canada's 5–2 win," *Ottawa Citizen*, Feb. 25, 2002.
12. Allan Kreda, "Flames' Iginla works to pave the road," Bloomberg News, *Milwaukee Journal-Sentinel*, March 24, 2002.
13. Joe Lapointe, "Canada's 'big tree' has bright future," *The New York Times*, Jan. 5, 1996.
14. Lapointe, "Iginla's dream season heads into overtime," *The New York Times*, June 18, 2002.
15. Guy Lawson, "The Sports Issue," *Gentleman's Quarterly*, October 2002.
16. Dave Perkins, "Future is bright for Canadian hockey," *Toronto Star*, Feb. 25, 2002.
17. Robert Remington, "A trailblazing Flame," *National Post*, April 6, 2002.
18. Wayne Scanlan, "Celebration is 50 years in the making: Winning the hockey gold has restored pride in Canada," *Ottawa Citizen*, Feb. 25, 2002.
19. Steve Simmons, "What Makes Hockey Canada's Passion?" *Toronto Star*, Oct. 13, 2002.
20. Seth Wickersham, "Jarome Iginla," *ESPN The Magazine*, December 2001.
21. Kate Zernike, "A humble Iginla raises his profile," *The New York Times*, Feb. 25, 2002.

A Pioneer in Search of Fame
1. Associated Press, "4 Rangers injured in auto accident," *The New York Times*, Oct. 9, 1948.
2. Associated Press, "Rangers plan try-outs," *The New York Times*, Sept. 15, 1948.

3. William J. Briordy, "O'Connor to rejoin Ranger sextet in game with Hawks here tonight," *The New York Times*, Nov. 30, 1948.
4. Herb Carnegie with Robert Payne, *A Fly in a Pail of Milk: The Herb Carnegie Story* (Oakville, ON: Mosaic Press, 1997).
5. James Christie, "Colour bar shattered one Canadian's NHL dream," *Globe and Mail*, April 5, 1997.
6. Luke Cyphers, "The lost hero," New York *Daily News*, Feb. 25, 2001.
7. Dan Diamond, editor, *Total Hockey, Second Edition* (New York: Total Sports Publishing, 2000).
8. Diversus Productions, Montreal, "Too Colourful For The League," televised by Canadian Broadcasting Corporation, Oct. 7, 2000.
9. Steve Dryden, editor, *The Hockey News' Top 100 NHL Players of All Time* (Toronto: Transcontinental Sports Publications, 1998).
10. George Gross, "Holds no grudges," *Toronto Sun*, Jan. 8, 1973.
11. Hockey Hall of Fame archives, "Carnegie found doors sealed shut to talent," source and publication year unknown.
12. Roy Jurgens, "Hockey pioneers," *The Los Angeles Times*, Jan. 31, 2002.
13. Lois Kalchman, "Giant step toward NHL," *Toronto Star*, May 8, 2001.
14. *The New York Times*, "Rangers sign Russell," no byline, Oct. 11, 1948.
15. *The New York Times*, "O'Connor, Eddolls lost for 6 weeks," no byline, Oct. 10, 1948.
16. Rachel Robinson with Lee Daniels, *Jackie Robinson: An Intimate Portrait* (New York: Abrams, 1996).
17. Art Rust Jr. and Edna Rust, *Art Rust's Illustrated History of the Black Athlete* (New York: Doubleday, 1985).
18. Allan Ryan, "Black hockey player still waiting for recognition," *Toronto Star*, March 15, 2001.
19. Brandie Silva, "Push on for puck hero," *Toronto Sun*, Feb. 16, 2001.
20. *Toronto Star*, Letter to the editor from Allen Manly of Thornhill, May 5, 2001.
21. Mike Ulmer, "The last word," *Toronto Star*, March 16, 2001.
22. United Press International, "Rangers acquire Kaleta of Hawks," *The New York Times*, Oct. 12, 1948.
23. Dr. Garth Vaughan, "The Colored Hockey Championship of the Maritimes," www.birthplaceofhockey.com, Nov. 12, 2002.

Wrong Place, Wrong Time
1. Declan Bolger, Doug Hicks and Jesse Hicks, editors, *Washington Capitals 1999–2000 Media Guide*.
2. Diamond, *Total Hockey, Second Edition*.
3. Robert Fachet, "Marson traded to Kings for Clippingdale," *The Washington Post*, June 11, 1979.
4. Fachet, "Kelly hounds Capitals, 4–1," *The Washington Post*, Feb. 13, 1978.
5. Fachet, "Bedard stops penalty shot," *The Washington Post*, Jan. 22, 1978.
6. Fachet, "Late goal by Marson earns 2–2 tie," *The Washington Post*, Dec. 29, 1977.
7. Fachet, "Capitals trade Paradise, tie Wings," *The Washington Post*, Oct. 2, 1977.

8. Fachet, "Marson accepts less Capital money for longer lease on pro hockey life," *The Washington Post*, Aug. 30, 1977.
9. Fachet, "Marson opens his last drive for Caps berth," *The Washington Post*, Jan. 1, 1977.
10. Fachet, "McVie would isolate unhappy Caps' wives," *The Washington Post*, Jan. 19, 1976.
11. Parton Keese, "Don't point at me, point at my stats," *The New York Times*, Nov. 2, 1974.
12. Bill Libby, "Caps set precedent," *The Hockey News*, Dec. 12, 1975.
13. Libby, "A man apart," *The Hockey News*, Dec. 12, 1975.
14. Joan Ryan, "Marson's wife bitter as illusions fade," *The Washington Post*, Jan. 17, 1976.
15. Ron Weber, "Marson, Riley first blacks to play as regulars in NHL," *The Hockey News*, Jan. 21, 1977.
16. Russ White, "Capitals' Marson first black to make NHL in 15 seasons," *The Hockey News*, Oct. 25, 1974.

Unstoppable
1. Associated Press, Stan Maxwell obituary, *Newsday*, Sept. 10, 2001.
2. Bill Boyd, *Hockey Towns: Stories of Small Town Hockey in Canada* (Toronto: Seal Books, 1998).
3. Tony Cooper, "Shorthanded: Despite gains, black NHL players are rare," *San Francisco Chronicle*, Dec. 16, 1998.
4. John Davidson with John Steinbreder, *Hockey for Dummies* (Foster City, CA: IDG, 1997).
5. Diamond, *Total Hockey, Second Edition*.
6. Jason Diamos, "Team gets lesson in diversity," *The New York Times*, Dec. 1, 1999.
7. Diamos, "Berard's comeback attracts other teams," *The New York Times*, Sept. 25, 2001.
8. Mac Engel, "For O'Ree, a fight all the way," *The Washington Post*, March 2, 2003.
9. Cecil Harris, "More than a lesson," *The News & Observer*, Nov. 30, 1999.
10. Hockey Hall of Fame Web site, www.hhof.com. Referee Bill Chadwick is blind in one eye.
11. Heidi Holland, editor, *Boston Bruins 2000–2001 Media Guide*.
12. Roy Jurgens, "Hockey pioneers," *The Los Angeles Times*, Jan. 31, 2002.
13. Jean Lefebvre, "Pioneering NHLer to attend Jarome Iginla hockey camp," *Calgary Sun*, July 27, 2002.
14. *New York Amsterdam News*, "Boston has first Negro in hockey," no byline, Jan. 25, 1958.
15. Dan O'Neill, "NHL's first black player continues to diversify game," *St. Louis Post-Dispatch*, Feb. 11, 2001.
16. Willie O'Ree with Michael McKinley, *The Autobiography of Willie O'Ree: Hockey's Black Pioneer* (New York: Somerville House, 2000).
17. William C. Rhoden, "Hockey pioneer takes the sport to another level," *The New York Times*, April 28, 1999.

18. Anwar Richardson, "Black pioneers of hockey discuss the game," *The Tampa Tribune*, Jan. 21, 1999.
19. Sherry Ross, "The icebreaker; O'Ree gets NHL due 40 years after debut," New York *Daily News*, Feb. 15, 1998.
20. Joe Sexton, "Rough road for blacks in the NHL," *The New York Times*, Feb. 25, 1990.
21. United Press International, "Bruins set back Canadiens by 3–2," *The New York Times*, Jan. 2, 1961.
22. United Press International, "O'Ree makes debut," *The New York Times*, Jan. 19, 1958.

A Brand New Game
1. *1999 Canadian Global Almanac*.
2. Rachel Alexander, "Soul on ice in great white north," *The Washington Post*, April 16, 2001.
3. Kevin Allen, "Blues-Oilers features 7 black players," *USA Today*, Jan. 15, 2002.
4. Allen, "Youth-league taunts readied Grier for racial resistance," *USA Today*, Oct. 4, 1996.
5. Dan Barnes, "Simon says, 'I'm sorry,'" *Edmonton Sun*, Nov. 11, 1997.
6. Stephanie Batcho, "Immigration policy hurts Canada's multicultural image, critics say," Agence France-Presse, Sept. 28, 2002.
7. Ajay Bhardwaj, "We're from away: 18% of population born outside Canada," *Edmonton Sun*, Jan. 22, 2003.
8. *CIA World Factbook, Canada 2001*.
9. *CIA World Factbook, Canada 2000*.
10. Jonathan Curiel, "Blacks in NHL: Culture, economics are barriers," *San Francisco Chronicle*, Jan. 3, 1992.
11. Nicholas Davis, "Brothers on skates: Hockey's no longer a game for the visible majority," *Toronto Sun*, Nov. 5, 2001.
12. John Dellapina, "Goal, Glen," New York *Daily News*, March 12, 2003.
13. Diamond, *Total Hockey, Second Edition*.
14. Peter Diekmeyer, "Immigrants a boon to small businesses," *Montreal Gazette*, Oct. 21, 2002.
15. Michael Farber, "Soul on ice," *Sports Illustrated*, Oct. 4, 1999.
16. Frank Fitzpatrick, "Black NHLers still a rarity. Game simply too expensive for many U.S. kids," *Toronto Star*, Feb. 11, 1990.
17. Gary Graves, "Shift change: More and more black players making presence known in NHL," *USA Today*, Jan. 10, 2001.
18. Cecil Harris, "Anson Carter: National Hockey League superstar," www.blackathlete.com, August 1999.
19. Harris, "Canes deep-sixed; Bruins end Canes' season," *The News & Observer*, May 3, 1999.
20. Harris, "Crushing loss for Canes," *The News & Observer*, May 1, 1999.
21. Jim Kelley, "Hockey remains behind the times in race relations," *The Buffalo News*, Nov. 20, 1998.

22. Steve Knowles, editor, *Edmonton Oilers 1999–2000 Media Guide*.
23. Dr. Richard Lapchick, "2003 Racial and Gender Report Card," Institute for Diversity and Ethics in Sport.
24. Joe Lapointe, "Boston's gallery gods must be smiling," *The New York Times*, May 11, 1999.
25. Dave Luecking, "Big impact: Could Grier become hockey's Tiger Woods?" *St. Louis Post-Dispatch*, March 9, 1997.
26. Luecking, "Blues (Big) ninth-round pick is son of Patriots executive," *St. Louis Post-Dispatch*, June 27, 1993.
27. Jac MacDonald, "Oilers give reading a shot," *Edmonton Journal*, Oct. 3, 2002.
28. Eric Moskowitz, "No playoffs mean the puck stops for Cablevision," *New York Post*, April 1, 2003.
29. Steve Popper, "Out of Africa and into a Rangers sweater," *The New York Times*, Dec. 29, 1998.
30. Kem Poston, "All iced out," *King*, Spring 2002.
31. Stan Richardson, editor, *St. Louis Blues 2000–2001 Media Guide*.
32. Sherry Ross, "Ndur takes to ice. Nigerian hopes to give back," New York *Daily News*, Feb. 17, 1999.
33. Jeff Schultz, "Oilers a pocket of diversity in NHL," *Atlanta Journal-Constitution*, Feb. 5, 2002.
34. Kevin Stewart, "Black ice," *Savoy*, March 2002.
35. Chris Thompson, "History of blacks ignored: professor," *Windsor Star*, Feb. 12, 2003.
36. Elizabeth Thompson, "Canada's population is more diverse than it's ever been: stats," *Montreal Gazette*, Jan. 22, 2003.
37. George Vecsey, "Hockey's minority players moving past trailblazer stage," *The New York Times*, Aug. 23, 2001.
38. William N. Wallace, "To be young, black and gifted on ice," *The New York Times*, Feb. 7, 1995.
39. Tom Wheatley, "Race issue looms small in hockey," *St. Louis Post-Dispatch*, Feb. 20, 1999.

Somebody Always Wanted Me
1. Dave Anderson, "Agents' schemes and harmful effects," *The New York Times*, Nov. 19, 2000.
2. Anderson, "Csonka, Warfield and Kiick go to WFL," *The New York Times*, April 1, 1974.
3. Karen Davis, John Hahn, Michael Kuta and Kathi Reichert, editors, *Detroit Red Wings 1999–2000 Media Guide*.
4. Diamond, *Total Hockey, Second Edition*.
5. Paul LeBar, "Colour was no obstacle for Blues' McKegney," Associated Press, *Toronto Star*, Feb. 6, 1988.
6. Dave Luecking, "McKegney moves in on 300-goal mark for career," *St. Louis Post-Dispatch*, Feb. 16, 1990.
7. Craig Wolff, "Scoring touch returns for new Ranger," *The New York Times*, Dec. 25, 1986.

Masked Men
1. Chris Brumwell and Reid Mitchell, editors, *Vancouver Canucks 1999–2000*.
2. CBC Sports Online (www.cbc.ca), "Hurricanes lose Weekes for remainder," March 21, 2003.
3. Jack Curry, "From the shelf back to the ice," *The New York Times*, Feb. 18, 1991.
4. Diamond, *Total Hockey, Second Edition*.
5. Dryden, *The Hockey News' Top 100 NHL Players of All Time*.
6. Dave Fay, "He's the man," *The Washington Times*, May 9, 2002.
7. Mike Hanson, editor, *Florida Panthers 2000–2001 Media Guide*.
8. Paul Hunter, "Fuhr finds fans can be cruel," *Toronto Star*, Feb. 16, 1991.
9. Monica Joseph-McIntyre, "Kevin Weekes: From street hockey to the Stanley Cup playoffs," *Pride*, June 13, 2002.
10. Jason Lagnese, editor, *New York Islanders 2000–2001 Media Guide*.
11. Rick Minch, editor, *New Jersey Devils 1999–2000 Media Guide*.
12. Jerry Peters and Mike Sundheim, editors, *Carolina Hurricanes 2000–2001 Media Guide*.
13. *St. Louis Post-Dispatch*, "'Ugly year' nags at Oilers' Fuhr," no byline, Feb. 8, 1989.
14. Robert Tychkowski, "Fuhr's struggles with the flat stick continue," *Edmonton Sun*, July 12, 2002.
15. Kevin Weekes, *My Hockey Book* (Toronto: McMurrich School Press, 1982).

The N-Bomb
1. Associated Press, "Beezer resigns after racial slur," *New York Post*, March 11, 2003.
2. CBC Sports online, "Vanbiesbrouck banned by OHL," March 19, 2003.
3. Diamond, *Total Hockey, Second Edition*.
4. Lance Hornby, "Flyers' McCarthy claims racial slur. 'He spit in my face,' Domi says, denying charge," *Toronto Sun*, April 27, 1999.
5. John Kekis, "Black hockey player fights racist insults," Associated Press, *Chicago Sun-Times*, Feb. 16, 1992.
6. Michael Morrison, "Icing the stereotypes," www.infoplease.com, Oct. 22, 2002.
7. David Naylor, "Vanbiesbrouck resigns over racial slur," *The Globe and Mail*, March 10, 2003.
8. Dan O'Neill, "NHL's first Jamaican player puts only minor emphasis on blazing trail of integration," *St. Louis Post-Dispatch*, Feb. 18, 2001.
9. Sunaya Sapurji, "Racism rampant in OHL," *Toronto Star*, March 11, 2003.
10. Dave Sell, "Blacks and hockey: A tenuous relationship," *The Washington Post*, March 29, 1990.
11. Joe Sexton, "Racial slur alleged in Ranger victory," *The New York Times*, Feb. 4, 1990.

The Jackie Robinson of Amherst
1. Associated Press, "Graham dismissed as coach," *The New York Times*, Feb. 23, 1999.

2. Bolger, Hicks and Hicks, *Washington Capitals 1999–2000 Media Guide.*
3. Diamond, *Total Hockey, Second Edition.*
4. Robert Fachet, "Riley cuts tendon, out indefinitely," *The Washington Post*, Nov. 22, 1977.
5. Fachet, "Riley felt accepted by Caps," *The Washington Post*, April 2, 1977.
6. Fachet, "Capitals reward Riley with contract as a pro," *The Washington Post*, Jan. 20, 1977.
7. Bill Libby, "Caps set precedent," *The Hockey News*, Dec. 12, 1975.
8. Byron Rosch, "Caps contract lets Bill Riley forget welding," *The Washington Post*, Sept. 9, 1977.
9. Ron Weber, "Marson, Riley first blacks to play as regulars in NHL," *The Hockey News*, Jan. 21, 1977.

Hired Hands
1. Kevin Allen, "Fewer fights offshoot, not intent of rule," *USA Today*, Nov. 14, 2002.
2. Allen, "NHL games feature fewer fights," *USA Today*, Nov. 14, 2002.
3. Associated Press, "B.C. judge finds McSorley guilty," *The New York Times*, Oct. 7, 2000.
4. Mike Beaver, "Less is more, more or less," *The Village Voice*, Feb. 5–11, 2003.
5. Tony Cooper, "Panthers' Worrell downplays series of racial incidents," *San Francisco Chronicle*, Nov. 17, 1998.
6. Diamond, *Total Hockey, Second Edition.*
7. Diversus Productions, Montreal, "Too Colourful for the League," televised by Canadian Broadcasting Corporation, Oct. 7, 2000.
8. David Elfin, "Crack in the ice; NHL's hope for a sparkling future is melting," *The Washington Times*, April 9, 2003.
9. Hanson, *Florida Panthers 2000–2001 Media Guide.*
10. Steve Majewski, editor, *Philadelphia Flyers 2000–2001 Media Guide.*
11. Ray Murray, "Black players confront racism in hockey," *Montreal Gazette*, Sept. 27, 1995.
12. John Rosasco and Jason Vogel, editors, *New York Rangers 2000–2001 Media Guide.*
13. Sam Walker, "Top goon," *The Wall Street Journal*, March 7, 2003.

Tiger Hunting
1. Associated Press, "Graham dismissed as coach," *The New York Times*, Feb. 23, 1999.
2. Diamond, *Total Hockey, Second Edition.*
3. Kevin Paul Dupont, "That fighting spirit always draws a crowd," *The Boston Globe*, Nov. 1, 2002.
4. Bruce Eggler, "Brass, city still at odds," *The Times-Picayune*, March 19, 2003.
5. David Elfin, "Crack in the ice; NHL's hope for a sparkling future is melting," *The Washington Times*, April 9, 2003.
6. Deepti Hajela, "Ice Hockey In Harlem," Associated Press, Feb. 18, 2003.

7. Cecil Harris, "Ice Hockey In Harlem," www.blackathlete.com, August 1999.
8. Harris, "NHL awaits emergence of its Tiger Woods," *The News & Observer*, Oct. 3, 1999.
9. Pat Hickey, "NHL looking for hockey's Tiger Woods," *Montreal Gazette*, June 22, 2001.
10. Joanne Ireland, "Black pride bonds Oilers to New York's youth," *Edmonton Journal*, Dec. 20, 2001.
11. Larry Lage, "Hockey showing slow growth on TV," Associated Press, June 6, 2002.
12. Edward Moran, "Iginla, Grier might break more barriers in NHL," *Seattle Times*, March 9, 1997.
13. New Orleans *Times-Picayune* Web site (www.nola.com), Letter to the editor, March 19, 2003.
14. Josh Peter, "Brass players Laviolette, Downey overcame odds to play pro hockey," *The Times-Picayune*, Feb. 14, 1999.
15. Reed Business Information—United States, "Views from the top: NHL, NBA commissioners high on cable platform," Nov. 4, 2002.
16. Howard Richman, "Hockey has no black heroes," *Kansas City Star*, Oct. 19, 1996.
17. Dr. Garth Vaughan, "The Colored Hockey Championship of the Maritimes," www.birthplaceofhockey.com, Nov. 12, 2002.

Tomorrow's Game
1. Diamond, *Total Hockey, Second Edition*.

Interviews
Jack Abramson, New York, April 1, 2003.
Jean Beliveau, telephone, Sept. 24, 2002.
Donald Brashear, Philadelphia, April 20, 2002.
Sean Brown, telephone, March 30, 2003.
John Bucyk, telephone, Oct. 10, 2002.
Herb Carnegie, telephone, April 10, 2003; telephone, Sept. 30, 2002; telephone, Aug. 17, 2002.
Anson Carter, New York, March 21, 2003; MSG Network interview, March 13, 2003; New York, April 30, 2002; Greensboro, April 30, 1999; Boston, April 28, 1999.
Valma Carter, telephone, May 2, 2002.
Paul Coffey, Raleigh, Nov. 29, 1999.
Trudy Daley, telephone, July 15, 2002.
Art Dorrington, telephone, March 31, 2003.
Jonathan Dry, New York, April 1, 2003.
Mike Emrick, telephone, April 15, 2003; telephone, April 3, 2003.
Stan Fischler, telephone, March 10, 2003.
Emile Francis, telephone, April 6, 2003; telephone, March 8, 2003.
Ron Francis, Raleigh, June 9, 2002.

Grant Fuhr, telephone, June 24, 2003; telephone, April 7, 2003; Raleigh, Nov. 29, 1999.
Teresa Genaro, telephone, April 1, 2003.
Ira Gitler, telephone, March 20, 2003.
Jean-Luc Grand-Pierre, New York, Aug. 19, 2002.
Monique Gueits, New York, April 1, 2003.
William C. Hay, telephone, Sept. 30, 2002.
Elvis Iginla, telephone, July 19, 2002.
Jarome Iginla, Toronto, June 20, 2002; New York, June 18, 2002; NHL media conference call, April 9, 2002.
Paul Kitchen, telephone, March 26, 2003.
Richard Lapchick, telephone, April 29, 2003.
Edgar Laprade, telephone, March 8, 2003.
Georges Laraque, telephone, April 1, 2002.
Darren Lowe, telephone, July 15, 2003.
Frank Mahovlich, telephone, Sept. 24, 2002.
Mike Marson, Toronto, Nov. 2, 2002; telephone, Oct. 2, 2002; telephone, Oct. 3, 2002; telephone, Oct. 23, 2002.
Paul Maurice, telephone, April 14, 2003; New York, April 8, 2002.
Jamal Mayers, New York, Aug. 19, 2002.
Bryant McBride, New York, May 17, 2002; New York, June 1999.
Sandy McCarthy, New York, March 10, 2003; New York, May 3, 2002; New York, April 10, 2002.
Tony McKegney, telephone, Sept. 27, 2002; telephone, Sept. 29, 2002.
Eric Nesterenko, telephone, Oct. 2, 2002.
Ray Neufeld, telephone, March 31, 2003.
Willie O'Ree, telephone, March 14, 2003; Toronto, June 20, 2002; telephone, May 14, 2002; New York, April 30, 2002; Raleigh, Nov. 29, 1999.
Don Raleigh, telephone, March 8, 2003.
Paul Ranheim, Voorhees, April 19, 2002.
Bill Riley, telephone, Oct. 22, 2002.
Gladys Riley, telephone, Oct. 23, 2002.
Rachel Robinson, New York, Feb. 12, 1995; New York, Jan. 26, 1994.
Roy Rodney, telephone, April 30, 2003.
Jim Rutherford, telephone, Sept. 18, 2002; New York, April 8, 2002.
Tom Sarro, New York, March 21, 2003.
Glen Sather, MSG Network interview, March 13, 2003; telephone, Oct. 18, 2002.
John Saunders, telephone, Oct. 21, 2002.
Milt Schmidt, telephone, Oct. 10, 2002.
Susan Schuchard, telephone, June 25, 2002.
Jabari Scutchins, New York, April 1, 2003.
Red Storey, telephone, April 13, 2003.
Natasha Underwood, New York, April 1, 2003.
Carl Weekes, Toronto, June 22, 2002; telephone, June 16, 2002.
Vadney Weekes, Toronto, June 22, 2002.
Kevin Weekes, Raleigh, June 9, 2002; New York, April 8, 2002.

Breaking the Ice

Al Williams, telephone, March 11, 2003.
Peter Worrell, Raleigh, Feb. 24, 2000.
Steve Yzerman, Raleigh, June 9, 2002.

Index

ABC (American Broadcasting Corporation), 150, 182, 186-187
Aaron, Hank, 13
Abdul-Jabbar, Kareem, 115
Abramson, Jack, 185
Addesa, Mike, 154
Agincourt Collegiate High School, 203
Albert, Marv, 13
Ali, Muhammad, 13, 115, 163, 174
Allison, Jason, 99, 197
American Airlines, 187
American Football Conference, 102
American Hockey League, 125, 150, 175
Amherst Ramblers, 163
Amherst Royals, 195
Amodeo, Mike, 147
Amonte, Tony, 31
Art Ross Trophy, 18
Ashe, Arthur, 197
Atlanta Falcons, 192
Atlanta Knights, 155
Atlanta Thrashers, 104, 139, 197
Atlantic City Sea Gulls, 51-52

Babych, Dave, 118, 121
Baltimore Blades, 161
Banks, Darren, 177
Banks, Ernie, 75
Bassett, John, 18, 112
Beckford, Tyson, 105
Belanchuk, Larry, 159
Belhumeur, Michel, 66
Beliveau, Jean, 35
Belleville Bulls, 57, 189
Berard, Bryan, 21, 81
Bettis, Jerome, 107
Beukeboom, Jeff, 195
Binghamton Dusters, 71
Birmingham Bulls, 112, 154
Black Entertainment Television, 26
Blades, Erie, 178
Blake, Rob, 95, 174
Boschman, Laurie, 122
Boston Braves, 51

Boston Bruins, 9, 19, 37, 44, 74, 84-85, 89, 123, 148-150, 153, 176, 178, 180-181, 189
Boston Celtics, 39
Boston College, 100, 102
Boston Garden, 60, 85-86
Boston Globe, 189
Boston University, 102
Boucher, Frank, 39-40
Bourque, Ray, 154
Bower, Johnny, 205
Bowman, Scotty, 117
Branch, Dave, 147
Brashear, Donald, 92, 152, 175, 180
Brathwaite, Fred, 91, 144
Brodeur, Martin, 30, 140
Brooklyn Dodgers, 35, 41, 78
Brooks, Aaron, 139
Brown, Sean, 91, 148, 184, 188
Bryant, Paul "Bear", 113
Bucyk, John, 79
Buffalo Ankerites, 37, 46
Buffalo Sabres, 103-104, 113, 117, 132-133, 177, 205
Bure, Pavel, 101
Burns, Pat, 99, 176, 180

Cairns, Eric, 175
Calder Trophy, 21
Calgary Flames, 16, 18, 25, 112, 133, 143, 177, 179, 186, 204
Calloway, Cab, 37
Campanella, Roy, 42
Campanis, Al, 170
Canada Cup, 132, 134
Canadian Football League, 107
Cape Breton Oilers, 133
Carnegie, Audrey Redmon, 37
Carnegie, George, 46
Carnegie, Herb, 15, 34-38, 42, 45-49, 54-57, 116, 132, 148, 195, 205
Carnegie, Ossie, 34, 37, 46
Carnegie, Rane, 57
Carolina Hurricanes, 76, 99, 120, 128-129, 148, 207

Carter, Anson, 7-8, 10, 28, 59, 63, 91, 100, 126, 136, 149, 184, 187-188, 203
Carter, Valma, 97
Chadwick, Bill "The Big Whistle", 86
Charron, Guy, 167
Cheevers, Gerry, 63
Chelios, Chris, 95, 105, 120
Chicago Bears, 139
Chicago Blackhawks, 13, 36, 84, 114, 153, 155, 168, 193
Chicago Stadium, 86-87
Ciccarelli, Dino, 153
Cleaver, Eldridge, 70
Clifton, Nat "Sweetwater", 39
Clippingdale, Steve, 71
Cloutier, Dan, 139
Coffey, Paul, 100, 130, 147, 201, 205
Cole, Erik, 142
Colorado Avalanche, 21, 30, 95, 172, 174
Colored Hockey League, 78
Columbus Blue Jackets, 73, 105, 145, 169, 192
Colville, Neil, 43
Combs, Sean "P. Diddy", 95
Conacher, Charlie, 47
Conacher, Jim, 47
Cooper, Charles "Tarzan", 39
Craig, Berube, 152
Craig, Conroy, 29
Craig, Martin, 160
Crawford, Marc, 180
Cross, Cory, 95
Csonka, Larry, 112

Dafoe, Byron, 99, 197
Daley, Trevor, 147, 149, 155, 201
Daley Sr., Trevor, 149
Daley, Trudy, 149
Dallas Cowboys, 115
Dallas Stars, 28, 100, 148
Dartmouth Jubilees, 195
Dartmouth University, 201
Dayton Gems, 159, 164
Demers, Tony, 39
Detroit Lions, 102
Detroit Little Caesars, 97
Detroit Red Wings, 30, 36, 43, 64, 69, 84, 95, 142, 149, 169, 177
Detroit Tigers, 115
Doby, Larry, 42
Doig, Jason, 25, 92, 192
Domi, Tie, 151
Don Mills Flyers, 97
Dorrington, Art, 50, 103, 189, 191
Douglass, Kent, 80
Doyle, Jeff, 147
Dry, Jonathan, 187-188
Dryden, Ken, 205
Dunham, Mike, 101
Dvorak, Radek, 95

ESPN, 22, 150, 182, 186
ESPN The Magazine, 22
Eagleson, Alan, 113
East Coast Hockey League, 52, 155, 168, 190, 196, 207
Ebbets Field, 78
Edmonton Eskimos, 107
Edmonton Oil Kings, 119
Edmonton Oilers, 8-9, 17, 56, 90-91, 95, 130, 145, 167, 169, 184, 187, 204-205
Emrick, Mike, 140
Esposito, Phil, 60
Esposito, Tony, 205

Favre, Brett, 139
Ferguson, John, 121, 167-168
Fletcher, Steve, 176
Flin Flon Bombers, 119
Florida Panthers, 138-139, 145, 148, 152, 160, 174
Follis, Charles, 39
Foreman, George, 123
Forsberg, Peter, 174
Fort Wayne Komets, 145
Francis, Emile, 45, 81, 119-121
Francis, Ron, 110, 118-121, 147
Frazier, Joe, 13
Frazier, Walt, 115
Fredericton Capitals, 79
Fredericton Junior Capitals, 79
Fuhr, Betty, 133
Fuhr, Grant, 7, 14, 17, 33, 56, 91, 105, 130, 134, 204, 206

Future Aces Foundation, 53

Gage, Joaquin, 104, 145
Gagne, Simon, 26, 30
Garner, Tyrone, 145
Genaro, Teresa, 190
General Motors Place, 180
Gibson, Althea, 192
Gibson, Josh, 46
Gooding Jr., Cuba, 101
Goodman, T. R., 9, 95
Graham, Dirk, 155, 168
Grand-Pierre, Jean-Luc, 92, 105, 192
Gratton, Chris, 152
Gray, Pete, 49
Green Bay Packers, 139
Greensboro Generals, 155
Gregory, Jim, 55, 205
Gretzky, Wayne, 24-25, 130, 147, 186, 205
Grier, Bobby, 102
Grier, Mike, 14, 91, 102, 153, 178, 184, 188
Grier, Wendy, 102
Guelph Royals, 80
Guerin, Bill, 100

Halifax Eurekas, 195
Hall, Glenn, 205
Harris, Don, 149
Hart Trophy, 19
Hartford Whalers, 110, 119, 167
Hasek, Dominik, 132, 191
Harvard University, 102
Hay, William C., 54
Hayes, Bob, 115
Henry, Jim, 41
Herbert H. Carnegie Centennial Arena, 56
Hewitt, Foster, 47
Hextall, Dennis, 69
Hickey, Pat, 190
Hobey Baker Award, 103
Hockey Hall of Fame, 4, 8, 12, 14-16, 19, 34-36, 45, 53-54, 57-58, 74, 90-91, 110, 128, 130, 132, 143, 146, 158, 172, 184, 193, 204-205, 207
The Hockey News, 18, 24, 65, 84, 116, 207
Hockey Night In Canada, 85, 104
Hodge, Charlie, 86

Holik, Bobby, 101
Holland, Ken, 169
Horner, Red, 48
Hornets, Charlotte, 196
Horton, Willie, 115
Horvath, Bronco, 86
Houston Aeros, 155
Howe, Gordie, 112
Hull, Bobby, 63, 112

Ice Hockey In Harlem, 92, 95, 184-193, 195, 207
Iginla, Elvis, 22-23, 25, 29
Iginla, Jarome, 10, 14, 16-17, 32, 59, 76, 91, 114, 186
Imlach, George "Punch", 50, 82
Irbe, Arturs, 99, 139-140

Jackson, Bo, 24
Jackson, Busher, 47
Jackson, Reggie, 13
James, Valmore, 103, 177
Joe Louis Arena, 149
Johnson, Brent, 145
Johnson, Brian, 177-178
Johnson, Tom, 86
Johnstown Jets, 52
Joly, Greg, 64

Kaleta, Alex, 43
Kamloops Blazers, 24, 28
Kane, Tom, 194
Kariya, Paul, 26, 31, 174
Keenan, Mike, 202
Kelly, Bud, 195
Keon, Dave, 112
Khabibulin, Nikolai, 138
Khristich, Dmitri, 99
Kiick, Jim, 112
King, Colt, 150
King, Kris, 153
King Jr., Dr. Martin Luther, 70, 91, 147
Kitchener Canucks, 79
Kocur, Joey, 149
Kovalev, Alexei, 101
Kramden, Ralph, 60
Kromm, Bobby, 165

Kruppke, Gord, 154
Kryskow, Dave, 66
Kurri, Jari, 100, 130, 205

Lacy, Sam, 39
Lafleur, Guy, 13
LaFontaine, Patty, 205
Langway, Rod, 110
Lanier, Bob, 115
Laprade, Edgar, 40
Laraque, Georges, 90-91, 106, 135, 175, 184, 188
Laviolette, Ted, 197
Lee, Spike, 101, 111
Leetch, Brian, 14, 100
Lemay, Moe, 122
Lemieux, Mario, 26, 143, 186, 202
Lester B. Pearson Award, 18
Levinsky, Alex "Mine Boy", 48
Lewis, Lennox, 173
Lindros, Eric, 101
Lloyd, Earl, 39
Lloyd, John Henry "Pop", 52
London Knights, 177
Long Island Ducks, 178
Lord, Richard, 54
Los Angeles Blades, 78, 88
Los Angeles Kings, 61, 71, 88, 133, 150, 169, 197
Los Angeles Memorial Coliseum, 40
Los Angeles Sharks, 88, 161
Louis, Joe, 38, 149
Low, Ron, 169
Lowe, Art, 201
Lowe, Darren, 200-201
Lowe, Kevin, 95, 130, 205

MCI Center, 104
Maciocha, Danny, 107
Madden, John, 140
Madison Square Garden, 10, 13-14, 41, 51, 101, 149, 153, 155, 174
Mahovlich, Frank, 35
Maine Mariners, 153
Manitoba Junior Hockey League, 122
Mann, Jimmy, 167-168
Maple Leaf Gardens, 47, 73

Maravich, Pete, 114
Marchment, Bryan, 152
Marciano, Rocky, 63
Maritime Junior League, 168
Mariucci, John, 193
Marson, Jacqueline, 63
Marson, Mike, 14, 57-58, 62, 65, 69, 85, 104, 115, 132, 150, 160, 165, 205
Marson, Patricia, 69
Marson, Sidney, 63
Maurice, Paul, 139-140
Maxwell, Stan "Chook", 84
Mayers, Allan, 94
Mayers, Jamal, 91, 192, 203
McAmmond, Dean, 29
McBride, Bryant, 89, 197
McCarthy, Sandy, 92, 123, 148, 175
McCreary, Bill, 154
McCreary, Wendy, 207
McDonald, Steven, 179
McFadden, Jim, 43
McIntyre, Manny, 34, 37, 42
McKegney, Carol, 123
McKegney, Ian, 114
McKegney, Tony, 17, 33, 64, 91, 111, 114-115, 130, 132, 146, 149, 177, 193, 205
McLean, Doug, 169
McMorrow, Sean, 150
McNab, Max, 164
McNabb, Donovan, 139
McSorley, Marty, 180
McVie, Tom, 65, 69, 167
Meehan, Gerry, 165
Memphis Southmen, 112
Messier, Mark, 24, 100, 130, 205
Miami Dolphins, 102, 112
Michigan Stags, 161
Michigan State University, 98
Millen, Corey, 29
Milwaukee Braves, 83
Minnesota North Stars, 117, 153, 193
Minnesota Wild, 143
Moe, Bill, 43
Moncton Alpines, 133
Moncton Gagnon Beavers, 168
Montreal Canadiens, 13, 19, 36, 39, 44, 50, 79, 84, 105, 167, 176

Montreal Forum, 73, 84
Montreal Royals, 41
Moog, Andy, 138
Moore, Sylvia, 12
Murray, Rem, 95

NBC, 26, 182
NCAA, 103, 137
NHL All-Star Game, 87, 178
NHL League Pass, 196
NHL Players Association, 113, 198
Nagin, Ray, 196
Nash, Rick, 73
Nashville Predators, 95
National Basketball Association, 24, 39
National Football League, 24, 39
National Hockey Association, 56, 92
National Hockey League, 8-9, 13, 16, 44, 46, 58, 61, 76, 85, 90, 132, 144, 146, 158, 164-165, 172, 175, 207
National Hockey League Alumni Association, 207
Ndur, Rumun, 104
Nedved, Petr, 101
Negro Leagues, 39, 41-42, 46, 52
Nesterenko, Eric, 86
Neufeld, Ray, 110, 118, 130
New England Patriots, 102
New Haven Ramblers, 39-40
New Jersey Devils, 128, 139, 181, 201
New Orleans Brass, 196
New Orleans Saints, 139, 196
New York Giants, 78
New York Islanders, 64, 136, 154, 207
New York Knicks, 39
New York Mets, 26
New York Raiders, 161
New York Rangers, 8-9, 13, 28, 37-38, 43, 48, 79, 84, 95, 103-104, 117, 136, 151, 153, 169, 179, 187, 190, 193, 207
New York Rovers, 39-40, 51
New York Times, 103, 132, 190
Newman, Paul, 138
Nicholls, Bernie, 201
Niedermayer, Scott, 181
Nieuwendyk, Joe, 29
North York Centennial Arena, 56

North York Rangers, 201
Northeastern University, 102

Olympic Games, 25
Ontario Hockey Association Junior League, 81
Ontario Hockey League, 81, 147
Ontario Junior Hockey League, 201
Ontario Senior Hockey Association, 42, 50
Ontario Senior Hockey League, 201
Ontario University Athletics East Division, 200, 202
O'Ree, Willie, 14, 19, 36, 44, 61, 74-75, 89, 91, 106, 115-116, 132, 148, 189-190, 197, 205
O'Reilly, Terry, 177-178
Orr, Bobby, 60, 113, 147
Osgood, Chris, 145
Oshawa Generals, 150
Owen Sound Mercuries, 50

Pacific Coast League, 89
Paige, Satchel, 42
Parcells, Bill, 102
Paris Jr., John, 155
Parsons, George, 47
Patrick, Craig, 169
Patrick, Lynn, 40, 84
Patrick, Muzz, 40-41
Pearson, Lester, 202
Peca, Michael, 136, 149
Pete Stemkowski, 13
Philadelphia Eagles, 139
Philadelphia Flyers, 26, 106, 112, 151-152, 163, 181, 207
Philadelphia Rambler, 52
Pisa, Ales, 95
Pittsburgh Penguins, 64, 169, 200-201
Pittsburgh Pirates, 133
Pittsburgh Steelers, 107
Pleau, Larry, 93
Poitier, Sidney, 64
Pop Warner League, 102
Potvin, Felix, 139
Presley, Elvis, 23
Primeau, Joe, 47
Proudfoot, Jim, 54

Quebec Aces, 50, 56, 82, 84
Quebec Frontenacs, 79
Quebec Junior League, 79
Quebec Major Junior Hockey League, 175
Quebec Nordiques, 9, 98, 146, 150, 167
Quebec Provincial League, 39-40, 45
Quebec Senior League, 45, 50, 55, 82
Queen Latifah, 101
Quinn, Dan, 144
Quinn, Pat, 28

Ray, Rob, 175
Rayner, Chuck, 43
Reddick, Smokey, 145
Rensselaer Polytechnic Institute, 154
Rhames, Ving, 174
Richard, Maurice "Rocket", 19
Richer, Stephane, 140
Richter, Mike, 31
Rickey, Branch, 35-36
Riley, Bill, 65, 104, 115, 132-133, 158-161, 164, 166, 181, 190
Riley, Gladys, 161-163
Riley, James, 161
Roberts, Jimmy, 117
Robinson, Jackie, 7, 14, 35-36, 44, 46, 51, 74, 78, 85, 106, 116, 159, 162, 170
Rochester Americans, 150
Rocket Richard Trophy, 18
Rodney, Roy, 196
Roy, Patrick, 21
Royal Military College, 150
Rutherford, Jim, 139
Ryerson College, 150, 202

Saddledome Arena, 25
St. Albert Midget Raiders, 28
St. Catharines Orioles, 12
St. Jean Lynx, 108
St. Louis Blues, 91, 102, 105, 116, 133, 144, 146, 150, 207
Sakic, Joe, 26, 30, 174
Salt Lake Golden Eagles, 177
Salvador, Bryce, 91
Samsonov, Sergei, 99
Sanders, Deion, 24

San Diego Chargers, 89
San Diego Gulls, 126
San Diego Hawks, 89
San Jose Sharks, 152
Sarnia Black Hawks, 115
Sather, Glen, 96, 130, 179
Sault Ste. Marie Greyhounds, 147
Saunders, Bernie, 130, 150, 186
Saunders, John, 150, 186
Savvis Center, 91, 94
Sawchuk, Terry, 205
Schmidt, Milt, 64, 84
Schoenfeld, Jim 167
Schuchard, Rick, 23
Schuchard, Susan, 21, 25, 29, 32
Schultz, Dave, 163
Scutchins, Jabari, 188
Seattle Seahawks, 194
Selanne, Teemu, 174
Selassie, Haile, 38
Selke Sr., Frank, 195
Shanahan, Brendan, 26, 30
Sharrers, Jay, 197
Shavers, Earnie, 174
Shawinigan Falls Cataracts, 39
Shea Stadium, 26
Sheffield, Howard, 201
Shelley, Jody, 175
Sheppard, Ray, 99
Sherbrooke Canadiens, 176
Sherbrooke Randies, 39
Simon, Chris, 103, 152
Sinden, Harry, 99
Sirois, Bob,167
Smail, Doug, 122
Smith, Gary, 201
Smith, Wendell, 39
Smythe, Conn, 36, 47-49, 202
Southeastern Conference, 113
Stanley Cup, 9, 20, 25, 30-32, 48, 85, 99, 101, 120-121, 128-132, 135, 139, 142-143, 145, 167, 176, 187, 202
Stanley Cup Finals, 31, 121, 129, 142
Stanowski, Wally, 43
Stewart, Anthony, 201
Stewart, Kordell, 139
Stock, P. J., 175

Storey, Red, 38
Strode, Woody, 40
Sudbury Wolves, 63
Sutter, Brian, 124
Suter, Gary, 31
Syracuse University, 194

Talbot, Jean-Guy, 86
Tampa Bay Lightning, 138-139, 179
Team Canada, 10, 25-28, 32, 98, 101, 201
Team USA, 31
Tellquist, Mikael, 101
The Notorious B.I.G., 10
Theodore, Jose, 20-21
Titanic, Paul, 202
Thomson, Jim, 47
Toronto Junior Rangers, 47
Toronto Maple Leafs, 9, 16, 21, 36, 47-48, 81, 84, 104, 112, 118, 133, 151, 178
Toronto Northmen, 112
Toronto St. Pats, 47
Toronto Star, 48
Toronto Sun, 43
Townshend, Graeme, 153
Tretiak, Vladislav, 56
Trottier, Bryan, 60
Tucker, Darcy, 152

UCLA, 35
USA Hockey Diversity Task Force, 20, 75, 187, 191, 197
Underwood, Natasha, 195
United States International University, 201
University of Alabama, 113
University of Alberta, 22
University of Maryland, 70
University of Minnesota, 193
University of Montreal, 105
University of Toronto, 4, 200-201

Vanbiesbrouck, John, 145, 147-148
Vancouver Canuck, 138
Vasicek, Josef, 141
Verdejo, Marc, 187
Vezina Trophy, 129, 132
Vick, Michael, 192
Victoria Cougars, 133

Vilgrain, Claude, 106

Wallin, Niclas, 142
Walter Brown Award, 103
Walter, Ryan, 120
Warfield, Paul, 112
Washington Capitals, 9, 25, 58, 61-62, 71, 88, 98, 101, 104, 110, 139, 150, 152, 158, 160, 178, 184
Washington Lions, 52
Washington, Kenny, 40
Washington Post, 66, 69
Watson, Phil, 40, 79
Watt, Tom, 202
Weekes, Carl, 135-136
Weekes, Kevin, 63, 76, 92, 98, 126, 128-129, 135, 148, 203
Weekes, Vadney, 136
Weight, Doug, 103
Wesley, Glen, 141
West Coast Junior League, 119
Western Hockey League, 24
Western Michigan University, 93
Wildey, Ed, 47
Wilk, Dave, 190
William Jennings Trophy, 132
Williams, Al, 161, 166
Williams, Gary, 72
Williams, Tiger, 163
Williams, Venus, 195
Wilson, Earl, 115
Winnipeg Jets, 118, 121, 145, 160, 167, 177
Woods, Tiger, 186, 191-192, 194-195, 197
World Football League, 112
World Hockey Association, 63, 112
World Junior Championships, 98
Worrell, Peter, 92, 152, 172-173

Yankees, 10
Young, Whitney M., 160
Yzerman, Steve, 26, 30

Zeidel, Larry, 45